OKLAHOMBRES

Late photograph of E. D. Nix.

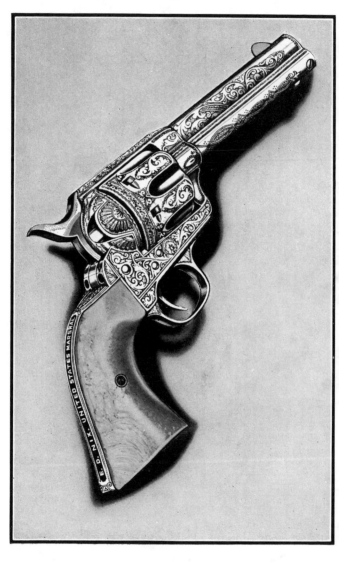

A cherished present—one of Colt's finest. Its gold and silver mounting speaks to me of the pioneer days.

OKLAHOMBRES

Particularly the Wilder Ones

By

EVETT DUMAS NIX

*Former United States Marshal in Old Oklahoma
Territory and the Cherokee Strip*

As told to

GORDON HINES

Introduction to the Bison Book Edition by
Gary L. Roberts

University of Nebraska Press
Lincoln and London

Introduction to the Bison Book Edition copyright © 1993 by the University of Nebraska Press
Manufactured in the United States of America

First Bison Book printing: 1993
Most recent printing indicated by the last digit below:
10   9   8   7   6   5   4   3   2   1

Library of Congress Cataloging-in-Publication Data
Nix, Evett Dumas, b. 1861.
Oklahombres: particularly the wilder ones / by Evett Dumas Nix as
told to Gordon Hines; introduction to the Bison book edition by Gary L.
Roberts.
p.   cm.
"Bison."
Originally published: St. Louis: s.n., 1929.
ISBN 0-8032-8366-0
1. Outlaws—Oklahoma—History.   2. Crime—Oklahoma—History.   I. Hines, Gordon.   II. Title.
HV6452.O5N59   1993
364.9766—dc20
92-37966   CIP

Reprinted from the original 1929 edition published by Eden Publishing House, St. Louis

∞

INTRODUCTION TO THE BISON BOOK EDITION
By Gary L. Roberts

When Oklahoma Territory was created in 1889, the new political entity inherited a legacy of violence. For many years, outlaws and others who lived on the fringe of the law had used the old Indian Territory as a refuge. The reasons were simple enough: the Indian nations, ostensibly sovereign in the region, were not permitted to enforce their laws against Anglo-American bandits. The combination of limited enforcement and unsettled land that provided many places to hide created a law enforcement vacuum only partially relieved by federal action.

From 1875 until the 1890s, the only legitimate authority in the region was Isaac Charles Parker, "the hanging judge" at Fort Smith, Arkansas, who administered justice in the region as the absolute authority in the war against the worst infestation of outlaws in the country. The United States marshal assigned to Parker's court had the largest force of deputies in the country at his disposal, and they generally had a free hand in their methods. Even so, their effectiveness was limited, and the criminal activities of some of them tainted the whole force. Despite a court docket that was phenomenal in its volume and a reputation for severity, lawlessness remained rampant in the Nations. Violence became systemic, with the non-criminal population of the region often aiding and abetting the outlaws. Judge Parker's efforts won him as much criticism as praise.

The opening of Oklahoma to white settlement in 1889 did not end Judge Parker's reign at Fort Smith immediately, but the introduction of a huge new population complicated the task of maintaining order in the region. The land rush itself generated an incredible tangle of conflicting land claims which, in turn, spawned both litigation and violence. Without common social norms, vigilantism, factional disputes, and public distrust compounded Oklahoma's pervasive lawlessness.

Violence occurred in Oklahoma because prevailing conditions undermined or preempted the normal forces that moderated social intercourse elsewhere, even elsewhere on the frontier. Violence prevailed there because the authority structure lacked credibility. In the first place, law enforcement was insufficient for the situation. In the second place, the peculiar admixture of natives, cowboys who predated the land rush, "sooners," "boomers," farmers, and foreigners in the region precluded shared social norms. In the third place, inefficiency and corruption on the part of deputy marshals resulted in a loss of public support.

In ways that are now somewhat difficult to comprehend, notions of legality and illegality were malleable at best to Oklahomans of that era, as they were to inhabitants of other parts of the American West in the nineteenth century. The view was never stronger that men had to look out for themselves. The opening of Oklahoma to settlement dislodged a class of men, mostly cowboys who had worked the Cherokee Strip before the land was opened to white settlement. These men saw their way of life threatened by the influx of new settlers and the social changes they brought with them. The majority of them were hardy, self-reliant sorts, men who were used to hardship, skilled with firearms, recklessly indifferent to danger—men who saw their problems in personal terms and resolved them accordingly, even if that meant violence.

From the outset, the new territory's population was divided into multiple factions based upon association, economic interests, and kinship, and the results were hostility, personal feuds, vigilantism, and vendettas. Some of the outlaws who roamed the territory were unmitigated scoundrels like Zip Wyatt, Red Buck Waightmann, and Dock Bishop. They gained little sympathy from the public and were not mourned when they died on the gallows or in a hail of bullets. But a surprising number of outlaws—including the Daltons, the Doolin gang, Henry Starr, and the Jennings gang—developed and sustained a broad base of support among the respectable people of the territory. They accomplished this in part by concentrating their depredations on institutions such as banks and railroads that ordinary folk saw as predatory toward them.[1]

In fact, the parallels to the legend of Jesse James went beyond "robbing from the rich and giving to the poor." The Indian Territory shared with Missouri a bitter legacy from the War between the States that directly contributed to the lawlessness. In an environment already rife with suspicion and bitterness toward authority, public support for outlaws also derived from the perception that they were men who defended themselves against wrongs inflicted upon them and took revenge because the corrupt authority structure would not set things right. At the same time, nineteenth-century Americans admired the "masculine" qualities of daring, toughness, shrewdness, generosity, self-reliance, honor, and freedom. The outlaw gangs seemed to model those qualities. Even among people who deplored their crimes, admiration for their peculiar code was hard to hide.[2]

Oklahombres is a book about the war against Oklahoma's bandits. It is not a definitive account of law enforcement during the territorial days, nor even a completely accurate one, but it does offer important insights into those times from the point of view of one who was intimately involved in the story. Evett Dumas Nix was a Kentuckian, born on September 19, 1861, in the first months of the Civil War. As a youth, he entered the grocery business in his home state and did well. In 1889, however, he caught the "westering fever" and joined the rush to Oklahoma. In the boomtown of Guthrie, he opened a general store with a partner named Ed Baldwin. Less than a year later, he bought out his partner and soon thereafter opened a wholesale grocery business in partnership with Oscar D. Halsell.[3]

The partnership with Halsell was auspicious. Both men were ambitious and anxious to expand their operations, but O. D. Halsell was of a different cut than his partner. Though near the same age, Halsell was a veteran of the "hell's fringe" environment. He was a Texas rancher who had been attracted to the Cherokee Strip as early as 1882. In his early days, he had been a "rounder." He was mixed up in a gunfight at Hunnewell, Kansas, in 1883, which left the town marshall wounded and a deputy dead. Although he fled into the Nations as a fugitive, Halsell eventually resolved his dispute with Kansas justice. But he knew and sympathized with the cowboy's view of things, and his ranch had been home to more than a few hardcases, including Bill Doolin, Richard "Little Dick" West, and William F. "Little Bill" Raidler, all of whom would take their places in the annals of Oklahoma outlawry.[4]

Halsell would doubtlessly influence Nix's view of life on the frontier, and he would be influential in securing his partner's appointment as United States marshal for Oklahoma Territory. In 1891, Nix proved his administrative abilities as receiver for the failed Commercial Bank of Guthrie, and when President Grover Cleveland was elected in 1892, Nix got his chance to become a part of Oklahoma legend. As one of twenty-three applicants for the post of U.S. marshal—and a reluctant one at first— he seemed a long shot. Nix was not a gunfighter, nor did he have any experience as a peace officer. It was Halsell who persuaded him to seek the post, and on July 1, 1893, he took office, having beaten out some tough opponents, including the highly regarded and experienced Henry Andrew "Heck" Thomas.[5]

What Nix brought to the task was organizational skill, and under his direction 150 deputy marshals were put into the field with a firm determination to end the reign of the outlaws in Oklahoma. Nix set high standards, telling the *Guthrie Daily News* that he would have "none but honest men around me." In a candid interview, he told the press that he would insist on men who were courteous, of good character, and good standing in the community. "The time has gone for swashbucklers who fence themselves round with revolvers and cartridges," he told the *News*. "A revolver will be for business and not for show."[6]

His opposition accused him of "searching the ranks of democracy with a microscope to find this brand of Sunday school moralists from which to make sleuthhound saviours of banks and express trains."[7] But Nix soon proved his critics wrong. His deputies included some of the best lawmen in the West, including men like William Mathew "Uncle Billy" Tilghman, Chris Madsen, Frank Canton, Bud Ledbetter, James Masterson, and John Hixon. Even Heck Thomas, his erstwhile opponent, who told

Nix that success would depend more on "the striking force" he put into the field than upon "the character of the men you chosen or the way they wear their weapons," signed on as one of the first appointees.[8]

How Nix and his deputies fared is the main subject *Oklahombres,* which was ghostwritten by Gordon Hines, an associate of Nix's. How much of the detail came from Nix and how much from Hines is hard to discern, but it is reasonable to assume that the main themes and points of view, if not the words and the details, are Nix's. Still, the book is not properly a book of reminiscences, not only because it was ghostwritten, but more importantly because much of the book deals with events to which Nix was not an eyewitness. The stories of the Daltons and Bill Doolin and Red Buck and Henry Starr and Al Jennings that constitute the bulk of the book and the parts of greatest interest to most readers are mostly second hand.

For this reason, Burton Rascoe, in his *Belle Starr: "The Bandit Queen,"* belittled the book. In *Burs under the Saddle,* Ramon F. Adams provided a list of factual errors that undoubtedly could be supplemented in the light of more recent research. The errors in question are largely attributable to either memory loss (he did not begin the book until many years later) or to the simple fact that he was not an eyewitness to the events which he described. For instance, Nix has Charlie Bryant kill a telegraph operator in the Red Rock holdup that occurred more than a year after Ed Short had captured and killed Bryant. His account of the gunfight with the Doolin gang at Ingalls includes all of the romantic claptrap about the Rose of Cimarron. His account of Cattle Annie and Little Breeches is confused; he repeats the legend that Little Bill Raidler and Bitter Creek Newcomb went to the World's Columbian Exposition in Chicago after the Woodward robbery in 1894, even though the exposition had closed months earlier; his account of the death of Bill Dalton is garbled; and his accounting of details is sometimes inaccurate.[9]

No doubt, some of the misinformation probably came from other published works that he had read since his days in Oklahoma (a problem that Rascoe pointed out was common in the reminiscences of many old timers), and he might be forgiven for getting names wrong after decades had passed. And, even now, it is difficult to say how much of the detail was provided by Nix and how much by Hines who (arguably) should have checked names and dates more closely. Moreover, as the research of Glenn Shirley has shown, a close review of Nix's errors suggests that Hines relied upon earlier published works such as Fred Sutton's notoriously inaccurate *Hands Up!* and Al Jennings' *Beating Back* to fill in the gaps.[10]

In a few places, Nix or Hines embellished and fictionalized the known facts. For example, the book places Bill Doolin at the Dover train robbery of April 3, 1895, and created a scene in which Doolin flies into a rage and threatens to kill Red Buck Waightmann for murdering an old man needlessly. The robbery occurred. The murder occurred. But Doolin was involved in neither, and who killed the old man is still unclear.[11]

Why such liberties were taken with known facts is not completely clear. Perhaps it was the product of fading memory. Perhaps it was to give the story more excitement. What is clear is that Nix was not on hand when most of the events described in the books occurred. He was the marshal. His responsibility was to direct the efforts of his deputies. They did the day-to-day work of carrying out his orders and chasing criminals. It is not surprising, then, that he, or Hines, or both, relied upon second-hand memory and the writings of others to construct *Oklahombres*. Charitably, then, some mistakes were inevitable.

Yet, even with these problems, Adams wrote that "the book is an interesting account of life in Oklahoma during the trying days of its first settlement."[12] And Paul I. Wellman, in his classic *A Dynasty of Western Outlaws,* described it as "an immensely valuable account of the campaigns of the great marshals of the Territory, as seen through the eyes of Nix," and recommended it as a "spirited account of the years covered."[13]

The verdict of Adams and Wellman is a just one. Recollections are not about historical detail, anyway, but about remembering, and there is more to remembering than the facts. Nix's feelings, his values, his reflections about the times and the men—good and bad—who rode the territory, reveal much about the principles that drove him. The book includes vivid word portraits of peace officers like Tilghman and Thomas, outlaws like Doolin and Jennings and Starr, famous frontiersmen and obscure ones. A few of his attitudes may be troubling to modern readers. For example, he is patronizing and condescending toward American Indians. He is not deliberately mean-spirited. In fact, he probably thought of himself as enlightened. He simply reflected a well-meaning but paternalistic way of thinking that was typical of many of his generation.

Ultimately, the importance of Nix's book may lie primarily in the insights it provides into the myth-making process. What has been overlooked in the study of the Western myth is its contemporaneity with the men and events themselves. The myth was a dimension of reality in the 1890s. The legend not only affected men like the Daltons and Bill Doolin, both in terms of actions and in terms of creed, but also it influenced the response of men like Nix. The outlaws of Oklahoma and their more law-abiding contemporaries temporized and justified and rationalized their own behavior with precisely the same homilies that the legend attributed to Jesse James.

To some degree, the Oklahoma outlaws, the press, and even men like Nix, allowed the myth to drive the reality. That does not mean that the outlaws were good men or that they were actually justified in their criminal behavior, but it does mean than men on both sides of the law saw them as something more than common criminals because of the attitudes they held. Significantly, then, when modern writers and scholars decry the romanticization of criminality on the old frontier, they may in fact distort the record if they do not take into account how the criminals perceived their actions. Far from an after-the-fact invention of blood-and-thunder writers and movie makers, the myth of frontier violence was an integral part of history itself. The legends were contemporary explanations, rationalizations, and justifications that so romanticized violence that they actually contributed to a more violent reality. Some of the outlaws and the lawmen, not to mention a gullible public, actually believed their own myth.

This is no minor point. The legend was a part of the reality before the Daltons died at Coffeyville, before Bill Tilghman arrested Bill Doolin, before Al Jennings or Henry Starr ever robbed a bank. The legend was a motivating force in the patterns of behavior of the times. In human affairs, it is well to remember that what people believe to be true is always more powerful than the objective reality because people act on what they believe. That so many cowboys thought of themselves as a unique breed, that so many local citizens distrusted federal deputies, that so many farmers and ranchers befriended the outlaws, that so many editors and peace officers openly admired the daring and what they called the "manhood" of the bandits, provide keys to why the myth has been so hard to bring to bay.

Nix, for example, decried the glorification of the Oklahoma outlaws, but near the end of *Oklahombres,* he (or Hines) wrote:

> As for the old time Oklahoma outlaw, I am reluctant to compare him with the highjacker and gunman of today. As one who fought him to extinction, I must admit that I admire his sportsmanship when I think of the cowardly tin-horn holdup man of today. I don't believe Bill Doolin ever shot a victim in the back and I know very well he didn't make a practice of robbing needy individuals of their petty all. He and his gang went after organized capital—the railroads, banks and express companies. If he took a horse or forced a lonely rancher to feed his men, it was because of dire necessity and he always tried to compensate the person who was called upon for help.
>
> These men regarded the banks and railroads as being mostly responsible for the breaking up of their ranges. They felt that they had been robbed of their own little world and that they had a right to fight back. And when they fought they stood up to it and took defeat like the cast-iron breed they were (pp. 270–71).

The "decisive allure" that historian Richard White believes early settlers found "in strong men who defended themselves, righted their own wrongs, and took vengeance on their enemies despite the corruption of the existing order," explains the almost unabashed praise for the attributes, if not the acts, of a certain group of outlaws, even among men like Nix who were their adversaries. What they admired were "certain culturally defined masculine virtues the outlaws embodied," to borrow White's conclusion.[14] That same allure sustained the myth into the twentieth century and for largely the same reasons. Ask any man who grew up on Westerns. So, ultimately, the legend and the reality can hardly be separated without destroying the truth, and those who seek only "the facts" are victims of the myth as surely as those who accept its tenets uncritically.

E. D. Nix proved to be a good United States marshal. From 1893 until 1896, his deputies made sixty thousand arrests on federal charges. He also forced his officers to maintain high standards. False arrests and padded expenses meant discharge, and the deputies knew it. But, in January 1896, an investigation into Nix's management of his office raised questions about his conduct. The charges were politically motivated, but Nix resigned and returned to the life of a businessman. His successor retained many of Nix's deputies to continue the fight.[15]

Eventually, in 1898, Nix moved to Joplin, Missouri, where he continued his work as a wholesale grocer. Later, he moved to St. Louis, Missouri. He opened an investment firm that specialized in oil, land, and mining properties and became very successful. In 1913 he returned to Oklahoma to visit his old friend and former deputy, Bill Tilghman. Tilghman and other lawmen were incensed at the portrayal of federal officers in a movie portraying the career of Al Jennings. Nix underwrote the filming of Bill Tilghman's *The Passing of the Oklahoma Outlaws,* serving as president of the Eagle Film Company, with Tilghman as vice-president and Chris Madsen as secretary. After the film was released in 1915, Tilghman and others, including Arkansas Tom Jones, an old-time outlaw who later worked as an accountant for Nix, toured with the film. Although never a huge financial success, the film seemed to please Tilghman and Nix. They saw themselves setting the record straight.[16]

When *Oklahombres* was published in 1929, Bill Tilghman was dead, having been shot down by a drunken Prohibition agent at Cromwell, Oklahoma, on November 21, 1924. Nix wrote his book for men like Tilghman to provide a clearer understanding "not of the calibre of guns, but of the calibre of some of the men who used them, as a duty of citizenship, in the building of the glorious Southwest (p. xxx)." Considering what Nix and Tilghman and Madsen and Thomas and the rest had accomplished, Nix may fairly be excused for trying to affect how they would be remembered.

Nix outlived most of his contemporaries, dying on February 5, 1946, at St. Louis, Missouri. Still, despite a long and noteworthy life as a businessman and family man, he is remembered today largely for his role in bringing the law to Oklahoma. His book provides not only a vivid portrait of a hard time when lawlessness prevailed in Oklahoma, but also a glimpse into the values and attitudes of his generation. It is a worthy contribution to an understanding of both the myth and the reality of the violent West.

NOTES

1. Glenn Shirley's *The Law West of Fort Smith* (Lincoln: University of Nebraska Press, 1968); and *West of Hell's Fringe: Crime, Criminals, and the Federal Peace Officer in Oklahoma Territory, 1889–1907* (Norman: University of Oklahoma Press, 1978), provide the broad background for the study of Oklahoma outlawry. See also Paul I. Wellman, *A Dynasty of Western Outlaws* (reprint; Lincoln: University of Nebraska Press, 1986), p. 361. For the interpretive frame of American violence suggested here, consult Richard Maxwell Brown, *Strain of Violence: Historical Studies of American Violence and Vigilantism* (New York: Oxford University Press, 1975), and *No Duty to Retreat* (New York: Oxford University Press, 1991); Roger D. McGrath, *Gunfighters, Highwaymen, and Vigilantes: Violence on the Frontier* (Berkeley: University of California Press, 1984); Richard White, "Outlaw Gangs of the Middle Border: American Social Bandits," *Western Historical Quarterly,* 12 (1981): 387–408; Gary L. Roberts, *Death Comes for the Chief Justice: The Slough-Rynerson Quarrel and Political Violence in New Mexico* (Niwot: University Press of Colorado, 1990), pp. 127–57; Robert R. Dykstra, *The Cattle Towns* (New York: Alfred A. Knopf, 1968), 112–48. Also very useful in establishing the milieu is Michael Fellman, *Inside War: The Guerilla Conflict in Missouri during the American Civil War* (New York: Oxford University Press, 1989), and Richard Slotkin, *The Fatal Environment: The Myth of the Frontier in the Age of Industrialization, 1800–1890* (New York: Atheneum, 1985).

2. White, "Outlaw Gangs," pp. 390–402.

3. Shirley, *West of Hell's Fringe,* pp. 134–35.

4. For information on Halsell, see *Ibid., passim;* Harry H. Halsell, *Cowboys and Cattleland* (Nashville, Tenn.: Parthenon Press, n. d.); and two articles by Gary L. Roberts, "Hamilton Rayner and the Shootout at Pat Hanly's Saloon," *Real West,* 28 (October 1985): 19–26; and "Highjinks at Hunnewell," *True West,* 39 (July 1992): 14–20.

5. Shirley, *West of Hell's Fringe,* pp. 135–36.

6. *Guthrie (Oklahoma) Daily News,* June 6, 1893, quoted in *Ibid.,* p. 136.

7. *Oklahoma State Capital,* June 7, 1893, quoted in *Ibid.,* p. 136.

8. *Ibid.,* p. 137.

9. Burton Rascoe, *Belle Starr: "The Bandit Queen"* (New York: Random House, 1941); and Ramon F. Adams, *Burs under the Saddle: A Second Look at Books and Histories of the West* (Norman: University of Oklahoma Press, 1964), pp. 381–83.

10. Shirley, *West of Hell's Fringe,* pp. 456–57, 461. See Alphonso J. Jennings and Will Irwin, *Beating Back* (New York: D. Appleton, 1914); and Fred Ellsworth Sutton and A. B. McDonald, *Hands Up! Stories of the Six-Gun Fighters of the Old Wild West* (Indianapolis: Bobbs, Merrill Co., 1927).

11. Shirley, *West of Hell's Fringe,* p. 457.

12. Adams, *Burs,* p. 383.

13. Wellman, *Dynasty,* p. 361.

14. White, "Outlaw Gangs," p. 403.

15. Shirley, *West of Hell's Fringe,* pp. 338–41.

16. Glenn Shirley, *Guardian of the Law: The Life and Times of William Matthew Tilghman* (Austin: Eakin Press, 1988), pp. 392–421.

FOREWORD

"Kentucky—the State, suh, where the hosses run so fast that lightning can't keep pace with them, and where the women are so beautiful, suh, that bachelorhood is unknown—."

Kentucky—the sheer brilliance of whose traditional background cannot be compared; whose earliest days demanded all that was brave and strong and true of the pioneers who conquered its wilderness; whose very perplexing and hazardous early difficulties developed in her people a foundation of depth and character that lives in her cultured and worthy issue of today.

Why this blurb for Kentucky when our story concerns Oklahoma? Kentucky bred and developed the character with whom our story is concerned. It was the inherent pioneering spirit of the early Kentuckians that led young Nix to young Oklahoma —the adventurous promise of the new country calling to the adventurous youth in the man.

For your sake, friend reader, it is a good thing that books have Forewords. Otherwise, although Nix tells this story in the first person, you might know little of him, personally, at the end. His unreasonable modesty invariably leads him away from self to the deeds of the men whose affairs he directed. In writing this story of his experiences I, as his collaborator, have been distressed over the reluctance of the man to provide me with material that would give him a proper place in the estimate of the reader. A commendable quality, but hardly a usual one in men who have been induced to write their personal experiences.

So I must help you to know this man Nix before he sets out upon the story.

During my several years of contact with all sorts of humanity, it has never been my good fortune to meet another man who represented so compositely, so entirely, all of the best elements of Kentucky's traditions.

This man Nix is a true Kentucky gentleman; and one of the most paradoxical characters I have ever known.

How could a man of his soft, gentle nature be expected to deal effectively with the hardest, most determined set of outlaws our country has ever known?

Sentimental to the point of tears when minor things touch his heart ever so lightly; demonstrative in his friendly affections; liberal to an excessive degree; deeply in love with his family—including all his in-laws!—it would seem that a man of such tenderness would be unfit to cope with fearless, unscrupulous outlaws; yet they learned, to their sorrow, that he could be as hard as nails when circumstances required that he should be. And though United States Marshal Nix realized that the outlaws he sought would murder him and his men without the slightest compunction, I don't believe the man ever had one bitter thought toward the men his organization was hounding to death. To him they were not criminals, to be slaughtered with vengeance, but an impersonal group that constituted a social and economic problem that had to be solved for the common good.

Marshal Nix's brave assistants—Bill Tilghman, Chris Madsen, Heck Thomas, Frank Canton, John Hixon and a number of others were given national acclaim—and justly so—for their splendid accomplishments. But no one except his great group of friends seems to know what a tremendously important part Marshal Nix played in this Oklahoma drama.

The man's modesty again. Not that the others were publicity seekers. They were as fine and manly a group of fellows as ever got together but they were human enough to accept a part of the credit that should have been theirs. Ed Nix has always dodged reporters and all forms of newspaper notoriety. To this day, the man has never given a photograph to the newspapers, even though a considerable number of achievements have made him good "copy".

I don't believe we (myself and his friends) ever would have succeeded in getting this story from him if it were not that he is slightly resentful toward much of the slush that has been written about Oklahoma's outlaws.

To me, the strangest thing of all—almost a wonder of wonders—is how a man of the calibre and character of E. D. Nix ever came to be appointed to such an important office, considering the bungling manner in which public appointments are so often made. He was a quiet, unassuming business man with none of the bombast of the early day politicians, with no political aspirations, who only wished to rear his family and conduct his business in peace. His community drafted him into service and pulled the necessary wires to get the appointment, not because they wanted to give him a political sinecure, but because their homes and their lives were at stake and E. D. Nix seemed to be the man who could make this part of Oklahoma Territory safe for respectable people.

He *was* the man and he *did* the job.

I might mention that his organization captured or killed more criminals and collected more rewards than ever did that of any other pioneer officer.

Although Nix played an important part in the opening of this new country and in the establishing of law and order that made the peaceful development of its natural resources possible, he has shared but little in the tremendous profits that have been made from the exploitation of Oklahoma's oil and mineral wealth. When he accepted his appointment as United States Marshal and the heavy responsibilities placed upon his shoulders, he did it solely determined to apply himself to the solution of Oklahoma's outlaw difficulties and to return to civil life and the peaceful pursuit of his own business as soon as the task had been accomplished. This same restlessness that brought him to Oklahoma led him later to Joplin, Missouri, when Joplin was in the period of its great mining boom. He founded there a wholesale grocery business that is still prosperous, but neither did he stay rooted there. His desire for more of an out-door life led him to St. Louis where he engaged in the investment business, making land, mining and oil a specialty, which undertaking took him into the South and Southwest. I wish the reader might have the privilege of knowing this man personally (many hundreds of you do know him for he is the type of man that makes friends and keeps them). When seated in a friendly group he can relate a personal narrative rich in romance of business and industry —replete with the names of famous characters and friends. There is nothing of the swashbuckler about him, although he will tell you many true tales of men who loved to play up to the romantic impression that existed in the minds of many people regarding Western men. I am inclined to believe that the swashbuckler of the early West would have accomplished little in the development of the country if it had not been for the quiet, substantial men who remained in the background and did their work most effectively. E. D. Nix manages to be quite modern in his thought without forsaking for a moment the characteristics and charming manners of the aristocracy of a generation ago.

But in his story you will find very few pronouns of the first person. He will tell you about the sterling character, the keen judgment and the supreme bravery of the men who worked under him, he will relate their deeds with all the pride of a doting *pater*, but he'll say mighty little of E. D. Nix. If one of his living ex-deputies were to attempt a book, you would probably get a truer picture of Nix's part in Oklahoma's outlaw war.

I don't believe a man ever was more deeply loved by his subordinates. I have seen hard, crusty old timers who have probably not kissed their own wives since the wedding day, greet their old Marshal with a whoop and an enthusiastic bear-hug that embarrassed them when the warmth of the greeting had slightly subsided.

Knowing him, he'd be the first man you'd ask for a favor, and you'd gladly give him your shirt if he needed it.

That's the kind of man and friend he is.

Gordon Hines.

INTRODUCTION

I happened to be in St. Louis on legal business just at the time this volume was being made ready for the press and, naturally enough, I called on my good friend, Col. E. D. Nix, to pay my respects and he informed me of the fact. Being much interested, Col. Nix gave me a typoscript copy of the story which I read with deep interest and pleasure.

I had served as one of the United States and Territorial Judges during the period of Col. Nix's service as United States Marshal and many of the circumstances related by him were matters of official record in my court. With others I was familiar as things of common knowledge, and for these and other reasons I am glad to be able to say a few commendatory words for Col. Nix and his story by way of this introduction. Space will not admit of further enlargement on many historical and other matters concerning early Oklahoma, which might be appropriate and of interest to the reader.

The entire area now comprising the State of Oklahoma, for many years prior to the opening of any part of it to settlement, had been the home of many tribes of Indians located largely in widely separated Indian villages with far-reaching stretches of open country between, almost entirely unprotected by legal authority, thus becoming the haven of outlaws and fugitives from justice, with its mountain fastnesses for hiding places and its rolling prairies as their parade grounds.

With the opening of Oklahoma Territory to settlement on April 22, 1889, all this was changed. The last great frontier was being settled by farmers and townspeople. The cattle kings were losing the paradise of their flocks and herds and the outlaws and fugitives were menaced by the long arm of the law. The outlaws reinforced themselves in their most secluded places and were joined by a few disgruntled cowboys who had been forced out of employment and who had listened to the lurid tales of easy money and fell. A few others formed bands of their own, becoming some of the most dangerous of their kind.

This is a very fair and brief appraisal of the conditions when Col. Nix was appointed United States Marshal with the incoming administration of President Grover Cleveland, bringing on with little delay the historic war of extermination, so graphically told by Col. Nix in his story, along with other triumphs in the establishment of law and order equally notable and effective, if not of such a sensational character.

It is not too much to add that, this achievement of Col. Nix and his brave corps of loyal and faithful deputies, to whom his great heart and generous spirit has always accorded deathless praise, in the extermination of this class of lawlessness and crime, stands without a parallel in the history of the West.

It would be unpardonable in me to omit reference to other immediate official associates of Col. Nix in the prosecution of this strenuous work, who were as closely allied with him as myself. They were each and all men of high character, noble purposes and distinguished ability.

I refer first to the Hon. Frank Dale, Chief Justice of the Territorial Supreme Court, and the Hon. A. G. C. Bierer, Associate Justice. Both are still living in Guthrie, which has been their home since the first day of the opening of the country, still maintaining with their fullness of years the love and respect of all who know them.

Hon. John H. Burford and Hon. John L. McAtee, also Associate Justices, have both passed on to the greater life beyond, leaving behind memories of busy and useful lives and records of distinguished service.

Hon. Caleb R. Brooks, an eminent lawyer and a man of fine character and impulses, has also joined the great majority, leaving as a heritage to his family, his friends and the people of Oklahoma a distinct and creditable record as United States District Attorney.

General Roy V. Hoffman, Roy as we all called him in those days, was a young man of lordly gifts, fine attainments and tireless energy. He made a record, par-excellent, as an Assistant United States Attorney, and after the expiration of his term of service took an interest in the military affairs and organization of the Territory and State, becoming one of the most prominent figures. Still later when the World War forced the United States into its maelstrom, he was among the first to go to the front, emerging at its close as a Brigadier-General. He now lives in Oklahoma City and is an outstanding figure of the State and Nation.

Hon. Thomas F. McMechan, an Assistant United States Attorney, also made a distinguished record in that office of which any young man in the land should feel justly proud. After the advent of Statehood, he became a State Senator, where he again made a most creditable record. For some years past he has been identified with one of the great insurance companies of the country, giving continued evidence of honest and faithful service.

We now come to the title of the book—"Oklahombres," which appears to me a happy one. "Oklahombres," is a coined word, intended to be used in either the singular or plural. It is ingenious, direct and impressive. Oklahoma, meaning the land or home of the red man or red people, and hombre, meaning in Spanish, man or mankind. "Okla," meaning doubtless land or home, affixed by hombre, constitutes the title word as stated. The Spanish language employs the word hombre in a highly dignified sense, more generally than we attribute to the word man. Oklahombre or Oklahombres should become a permanent word in the Oklahoma vernacular, and be recognized as a tribute to the energy and progressiveness of the people of the State.

The story told by Col. Nix in "Oklahombres" is not designed as a literary classic, but as a plain, simple, truthful and fascinating recital of early Oklahoma history, covering one of the most important and notable epochs in the settlement and development of the western hemisphere. Col. Nix has never attempted to glorify the gory work of exterminating more than three score of notorious outlaws and the arrest of more than fifty thousand of lesser criminals during his term of office. To my certain knowledge, this is the first time the gruesome details of this carnage of criminal expiation has ever been told by Col. Nix, and he does so now with charity and forgiveness in his heart for the misguided victims.

Col. Nix is not unmindful in grateful acknowledgement to the good people of Oklahoma, who did their full share in upholding his hands in this supreme work of establishing law and order during this lurid and memorable period in the early history of what is now the great commonwealth of Oklahoma. Though space has not permitted the elaboration of this contribution that it deserves, he is none the less sensible of its value.

Personally, I desire to express with profound feeling that I deem it an honor and a privilege to be permitted to bear testimony in the manner and form presented in this Introduction. I wish each and every reader of Col. Nix's book to accept my statements as written by one who speaks with authority, for I know whereof I speak, and do so without qualification or reservation. There are, in fact, many other points of interest to which I would like to refer, if space permitted, with the same candor and purpose.

I trust, also, that all those readers who may be in a position to do so, will contribute their influence to the success of this volume—the success it so richly deserves. I especially commend it to the youth of the land and pray that it will impress upon them that glory and prosperity does not attend direspect for the law, but that humiliation, ostracism, degradation and tragic ends bring certain retribution for transgression and unrighteousness.

In concluding I am sure I speak the sentiments of one and all closely associated with Col. Nix in those strenuous days, in wishing that he shall live long and prosper and that each year that circles round his chastened brow shall leave in its track a new ring of glory.

Henry W. Scott.

New York City
1929

PREFACE

Friends have forewarned me that the introductory announcement to a book is the most serious part of the entire business of writing and that success is gained or lost in the phrasing of it. I now find myself with this serious business on my hands and the publisher 'phoning me for the release of final proofs.

The emergency finds me somewhat unequal to the task. I had not realized in the beginning how closely I was to live this past year with men and events of long ago. Father Time has borne me onward with his never ending tide, while I still feel age a stranger.

Bill Tilghman, my old deputy, killed by a drunken hoodlum. Oscar Halsell, my friend and lasting partner, gone.

Bill Tilghman, Heck Thomas, Chris Madsen, Bud Ledbetter, Frank Canton, John Hixon, and many other deputies stand out before me as sentinels of law and order. Old streets, old adventures, Bitter Creek, Tulsa Jack, the worst of the Doolins and the best of the Daltons—living or dead, their faces have been the ones I have gazed into this past year while sharing again their laughter and hazards. This task, undertaken at the start as a final duty, has proved a pleasure.

It is good to have known such friends, and to have held the respect of such enemies. It has been a pleasure of my later years to meet as friends some of those few still living who were once such dangerous adversaries.

Will the reader please bear with me if I claim the privilege of my years. Instead of the piece of business strategy I am told it would be—may I make this prefatory presentation a sentimental dedication to those shadows that have given me another year of comradeship.

To the men and women of the "Old Territorial Days" this book is inscribed by their humble servant, resting in reminiscent reflection. To record in print the heroic period of early Oklahoma has long been my ambition—one perhaps too long delayed in its fulfillment. Where my own memory has been found incomplete, I have had to piece by searching here and there for those still living who could help. To all of them my grateful greeting. These visits have enlivened my spirit and stimulated me with a newness of life. No man who knew the Southwest of the Old Territorial Days can revisit the great States of Oklahoma and Texas today without the same quickened pulse with which he first encountered them; for in them lie great fields of opportunity, great futures just begun.

To record the first beginning—or the days of the saddle and gun that preceded the real beginning—is the chief function of this book. Its fulfillment has been delayed until many are dead who might have found more pleasure in it than the reader. To the young reader I should explain that I have always felt that publicity and personal glorification had no place in an officer's duty. Never before have I recounted many of the things recorded in this book of the early Southwest. I do so now that a present and a future generation may have a clearer appreciation and understanding, not of the calibre of guns, but of the calibre of some of the men who used them, as a duty of citizenship, in the building of the glorious Southwest.

My book, while written for Today, is dedicated to Yesterday and a few brave men and women who still linger in the shadows of the eventide.

To these last survivors is my final message—*Adios!*

                                        E. D. Nix.
St. Louis, Mo.

TABLE OF CONTENTS

CHAPTER I
KENTUCKY DAYS

Kentucky days! We all refer to our native states with loyalty, love and pride. Love of home and country is an exultation of human emotions surpassing all other earthly affection. With these reflections I will forego any extended reference to my "Kentucky Days" beyond a circumstance happening in my childhood that seems after this lapse of years, to have been a premonitory vision of that part of my life in the territory of Oklahoma which is the subject of this volume.

One of the outstanding recollections of my Kentucky boyhood concerns a public hanging. A man named Pud Diggs had led a marauding band of guerrillas during the Civil War, and his band's depredations had continued for several months after the close of the war.

Our community had suffered from their escapades in many ways and our people had rejoiced when Pud Diggs was apprehended. There had been a speedy trial and the indignant Kentuckians had decided that Mr. Diggs must die. My uncle, Joel Ferguson, was sheriff and my father was a deputy under him. It fell to the lot of Uncle Joel to carry out the court's order.

A special scaffold was constructed in an open field near the town of Murray, the county seat, and Calloway County folks gathered to witness the county's first legal hanging. Men, women and children—white and black—had gathered from many

1

miles around and the public square at Murray was in a turmoil with excitement and curiosity over the gruesome event. There was also an element of thrilling suspense in the fact that it had been rumored that members of Diggs' band were going to rescue him from the scaffold. The people were tense, and every stranger was eyed with suspicion and carefully watched by grim-jawed citizens. I remember being rather surprised that so many fine ladies of the countryside had gathered for the affair. I had anticipated the event for a number of days and had looked forward with boyish enthusiasm to being allowed to attend the spectacle, and because my father was associate officer, I felt that this was to be a he-man affair. My mother had declared that she would not go and some of the neighbors had chided her about being chicken-hearted, but she insisted that she would be horrified.

When the day came, however, the family drove to town and Mother led me by the hand to the edge of the crowd that surrounded the gallows. I sized up the platform and its gibbet, thinking of the fun we boys could have with the thing if the sheriff would just turn it over to us.

Poor old Pud Diggs was led out, shackled, and a little procession mounted the structure. I could feel my mother's hand trembling in mine and I looked into her face. It was chalky white. She turned away. "Son, let's go," she said with a queer tremolo. I was sorry I was not with my father. This was no place for a woman and I was interested in the proceedings. I heard a darky back in the fringe of timber wailing, "O, Lawd—Jesus, O-o-o, O-o-o—." My Uncle Joel's hand touched the trap. It seemed the entire crowd heaved an intense sigh in unison, then everything was quiet—deafeningly still.

"Anything you want to say?" my uncle asked the man who was about to die.

"Yeah, plenty—" and Pud Diggs launched into what was probably meant as a long harangue to play for time, hoping his rescuers would arrive.

A shot rang out. Women screamed. Men ran toward a tree from which the shot had come. That is, they *were* running toward the tree until some mysterious thing caused them to turn about and run wildly in other directions.

Then another cry, "Look the sheriff's sprung the trap!" I looked toward the gallows and saw Pud Diggs go hurling through the hole in the raised platform and saw the rope tighten when his weight struck it. There was a sickening snap as his neck broke and his body hung there trembling.

About that time something hot struck me behind the ear and then again with a burning jab in the nether region of my anatomy. Mother had already left, apparently in a great hurry, and she was calling frantically to me over her shoulder. By this time the crowd had gone wild and was scattering in every direction. A nigger on a flea-bitten mule dashed past me and yelled, "Run fo' yo' life, white boy! it's ho'nets!" By this time I found my stride and tried to catch my mother. I made a mighty leap to clear a ditch and my barefoot slipped on its wet bank. The crowd and the hornets passed on. I have never heard of a more wide-spread epidemic of hornet sting than Murray, Kentucky, suffered that day.

It seems that a man named Ryan who had an unusual sense of humor had sneaked himself and his trusty pistol in a tree not far from the gallows. He knew that some fear existed regarding a possible attempt to rescue the prisoner and he determined to have his little joke. At the crucial moment, just as the trap was about to be sprung, he raised to fire his gun and his hold slipped. As the gun discharged, he fell through the thick branches, knocking a hornet's nest to the ground.

So mad was the rush of the crowd that several people were slightly hurt. Next day Murray resumed the peaceful routine of county-seat life, al-thought a few of the village's leading lights, whose stings were most inconveniently located, did not appear in public for a few days.

* * *

Our part of Kentucky had gone through some strenuous Civil War experiences, although I was too young to have more than a hazy recollection of the hazards that surrounded my own family. I was born September 19th, 1861. My father and mother were deeply religious, and war was abominable to them. When it came, however, Father did his part like a sincere patriot, earning a lieutenant's commission at the age of twenty-two.

On one occasion our home was raided by a group of fifteen Union soldiers. My grandfather had driven all of our best stock back some distance into the deep woods where they were being held to pro-tect them from marauding soldiers and guerrillas. Considerable stores of food and food stuffs were also concealed at this isolated spot and Grandfather spent considerable time standing guard over this hidden property. He was here at the time of the raid of which I write. My Uncle Joe, then a boy of fourteen, tried to resist the soldiers and they bound him, abusing him severely. The boy's resistance was so hostile that the leader of the band suggested hanging him. My grandmother and two of my aunts became hysterical, and one or two of them fainted. When the soldiers had ransacked the house and the premises they departed, taking their young prisoner with them. Old black Aunt Mary fought them like a tigress and one of them jabbed a bayonet into her breast, inflicting an ugly wound. A few hours later my grandfather returned home and he started out alone in pursuit of the soldiers, vowing vengeance if they had harmed the boy. He'd gone but a mile or two, however, when he met the tired, frightened youth trudging homeward.

On another occasion near the close of the war, while Father was at home recovering from a wound received in action, our place was attacked by a small band of guerrillas led by a man named Hixson. Father stood them off with a shotgun. The marauders fired a number of shots at the home and shattered a window or two but did no serious damage. The bullet holes in the house became a source of family pride among the younger members of the family. Years afterward when my brother and I wanted to impress a visitor particularly we would show him the bullet holes and tell most exciting stories about the battle. Father had recognized a young man named Alex Morris in the gang. A number of years before young Morris had lived with a relative a few miles from our home and Father had

known him slightly. So when the band returned about a week later led by Alex Morris, Father courteously invited them into the house and he would have treated them like gentlemen if they had not determined to commandeer his favorite saddle horse, his saddle, bridle and a fine pair of boots. Father went wild with anger and sprang at Morris, shaking his fist in his face.

"You'll take them over my dead body!"

Mother ran out of the house screaming and, hearing the commotion, my grandfather, Father's older brother and Uncle Billy Skinner, a neighbor, rushed to the house from an adjoining field. When they entered they were sensible enough to see that the guerrilla band had the advantage. In spite of their number, Father would have waded into them unarmed if Grandfather and the others hadn't overpowered him. They threw him on a bed and sat on him while the guerrillas made away with their booty.

Morris was never heard of again in our County. Years later Father located some property of Morris' in the possession of an uncle of Morris', and was successful in securing full payment of his stolen property.

My grandfathers, William Holland and R. F. Nix, had come from South Carolina to Kentucky as young men and had become prominent as farmers and business men. They operated large plantations and mercantile stores and delt extensively in tobacco. They were partners in several business ventures. Both owned slaves and, following the war, most of their ex-slaves chose to remain with them for many years. Grandfather Nix served as sheriff of Calloway County, as did two of my mother's brothers, R. B. and W. L. Holland. Our family never seemed to have political aspirations, yet every generation has done its bit in public service.

My parents were the old-fashioned sort that believed in teaching children to work. My father was associated with my two grandfathers and, at seven, I was put to work sorting tobacco and doing odd jobs in the tobacco rehandling houses. At this time we were living in the country, and our school term was very short. For three months each winter we children trudged over the long woods road to a log house that was our institution of learning. When I was fourteen, our family moved to Murray in order that we children might have the advantage of a five months' school term.

At Murray Father started a wagon and buggy factory and, when I was not attending school, I did a man's work at the factory. Working before the forges, swinging a twenty-five pound sledge for several hours a day, gave me a physical development that has probably been responsible for the excellent health and strength I have enjoyed all my life. I have read many biographies in which men have complained of their childhood difficulties and of parental strictures upon their boyhood freedom. I don't suppose a more affectionate or considerate family than ours ever lived and, while my brother and I and our five sisters were taught industry, we heartily enjoyed our home life and we are all grateful to our loving parents for their sacrifices and labors in our behalf.

When at seventeen I had finished common school,

my grandfather Nix backed me in a grocery, hard-
ware and furniture business at Coldwater, Kentucky.
In spite of my youth the business was successful and
in 1880 I sold it at a good profit.

By this time our part of the country had become
rather thickly settled, and the pioneering urge that
seemed inherent in me made me restless to go farther
west.   Circumstances, however, led me into a new
work that held my interest for a few years.   Influenced by a friend in the wholesale confectionery and
fancy grocery business, I went to Paducah, Kentucky, and took a position with his company as a
traveling salesman.   Two years later I had joined
the staff of J. K. Bondurant and Company, wholesale grocers, as traveling salesman.   With a shining
red-wheeled buggy and a spanking pair of trotters I
cut quite a swath over the territory.   Shortly afterward began the romance that has continued to this
day.   On July 15th, 1885, I was married to Ellen
Felts.   We had gone to school together and our parents had been raised together.   She, too, was of
pioneer stock and her influence seemed to fan the
westward urge, for we immediately began saving for
the start we wanted in the new country.

In the fall of 1889 we made our decision and
burned our bridges behind us, in spite of the protests
of loved ones who would have us stay.   We have
never regretted the move.   Our experience repre-
sents the most interesting period of our lives, and
we are happy in having had a small part in making
the way clear for the Great Commonwealth of Oklahoma.

CHAPTER II

I AM AN EIGHTY-NINER

"Eight-niner," or "89'er," as the term is abbreviated, means a person who settled in the territory of Oklahoma at any time on or after noon the 22nd day of April, in the year 1889. Those who entered the territory prior to 12 o'clock noon of said day became known as "Sooners" and this term is as permanently fixed in Oklahoma history as the name of the state itself. I made up my mind to go to this enchanting land in October, 1889, following the opening in April.

Trains traveled slowly in those days and, to many destinations, very indirectly. To get to Oklahoma from Kentucky in 1889 it was necessary to go northwest through St. Louis and Kansas City, thence south on the Santa Fe to the new country.

Charles Meacham, a young friend who had been in the furniture business at Fulton, Kentucky, joined me on the great adventure.

I had left my weeping wife and a number of weeping relatives on a little station platform back home and we were on our way. Although I was twenty-eight years old and had a few of the rough edges knocked off in my travels as a salesman, it seemed to my inexperienced mind that I was entering a new world and I was very impatient to explore its wonders. Rumor and many published stories had given Oklahoma a glamour in my thought and I wondered if the new territory would come up to my expectations. We went through St. Louis at night and our change was made quickly at the Kansas City station, so we saw practically nothing of these two cities. After we left Kansas City I began to sense something of the vastness of the western prairies,

and I remember that the magnitude of the great unsettled space gave me a sense of freedom that I had never known before. The healthy green of the lush, waving grass was proof enough of the richness of the soil, and occasionally we would cross clear, cool streams fringed with trees and undergrowth that had been lightly touched by an early fall frost, which had transformed their foliage into a vivid array of charming colors. Here and there would be a wheat field planted by an energetic settler who had already tried his plow in virgin soil. I remember passing a crude dugout home built on a cool creek bank. A large family of children scampered about.

A buxom housewife threw a pan of dishwater into the yard and stopped to wave at the speeding train. A half mile away the husband was breaking ground with a yoked team of roan steers, his trusty rifle swung to the plow handles. This little scene seemed to me to symbolize the bravery, the determination, the industry and the happiness of the true and typical pioneer family.

At Arkansas City, Kansas, near the line of what was then the Cherokee Strip, it was necessary to stop over for a night. As Charlie and I alighted from the train we stopped short, almost tremblingly, before a group of fierce looking Indians. They  seemed to be making an attack upon us in close formation but as they brushed on by, ignoring us, we realized that they were only making a rush to find comfortable seats on the palefaces' kivvered cars. Our very vague impressions of Indians had been gained through the wild, romantic literature of that day, and these native Americans had seemed savage to us. Later we were to learn a great deal more of the Indian and come to regard some of the tribal leaders affectionately. We caught a cab that hauled us up the steep hill of Arkansas City's Fifth Avenue to the main part of the city. We were taken to the Fifth Avenue Hotel and, as we drove up to the entrance, its five-floor height seemed to me to brush the moonlit clouds. I was quite sure that the Fifth Avenue Hotel of New York City could be no more gorgeous than this. We trod its carpeted halls gingerly.

During the evening Charlie and I walked down Summit Street, the main stem of the ambitious village. The bustling young frontier town had done itself proud in the erection of two and three-story  buildings, and we were very much impressed with the metropolitan atmosphere of the place. Our part of Kentucky had not developed its towns quite so elaborately. Charlie and I felt that we must watch

our p's and q's if we were to avoid the pitfalls of a
great city. Walking down Summit Street we passed
saloons and gambling halls at almost every other
door on the west side. It seemed that all of the women's stores were arranged up and down the east
side and that the rougher element held full sway on
their side of the street. The town seemed peaceful
enough, although there were enough tough looking
characters on the street to make us conscious of the
troublesome potentialities of the place. We passed
numerous stairways with bell attachments on the
screen doors at the sidewalk and with dim red lights
in the halls at the top of the stairs. Passing them

one could hear muic and ribald singing. There was
something primitive about the place and, while we
felt slightly intimidated in this new wild atmosphere,
we bolstered up our courage and determined to be
equal to any situation that might arise.

Morning came and we made our way to the rail-
way station, anxious to be on our way into Oklahoma. A train stood waiting and as we swung up
the steps of a coach an armed guard stepped aside
for us to pass. We found a seat and stacked our
luggage, then strolled outside. There seemed to be
a great many heavily armed men about the train.

I inquired and learned that the express and railroad
companies were compelled to maintain strong forces
to protect passengers and shipment from outlaw
bands that were beginning to seriously obstruct the
march of civilization. It was also the custom to
search all persons going into the Indian country for
intoxicants as it was a violation of the federal law to
carry liquor into the reservations.

Santa Fe Depot, Guthrie, April 23, 1889. Only wood building outside land office.

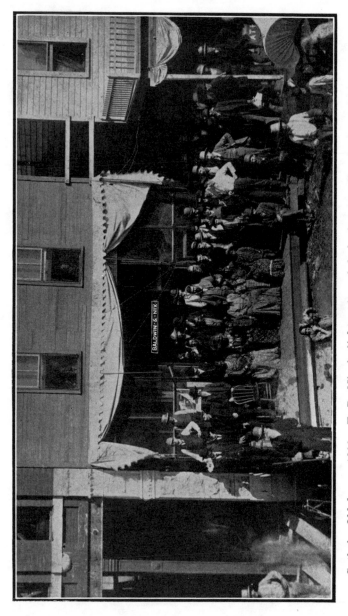

Guthrie, Oklahoma, 1890. E. D. Nix in light suit and derby hat standing in door of his store.

Something in the general atmosphere seemed to challenge primitive instincts in me as the train carried us across the line of Kansas into the Cherokee Strip. Many of our fellow passengers were new to the country and I could sense a tenseness and a nervous excitement even among the train's crew. There was no indication that anything would happen, still anything might happen. We had all heard bloody tales and our imaginations were stimulated.

Below the Kansas line the open prairies seemed even more vast—almost infinite, with tall, lush grass rippling as the eternal strong wind of the Indian country swept across it. Somehow I felt that man was indeed an infinitesimally small and weak creature as compared with the magnitude and strength of nature.

Here was a country of wide unconquered spaces that would richly reward every honest worker who applied his hand and his thought to his problem. I was eager to join the good men who had already conceived its potentialities and who, fully cognizant of the hazards and of the many obstructions that would be placed in their way, had thrown caution to the winds and determined to wrest their fortunes from the resources that lay here undeveloped. I was conscious of a burning desire to become a part of all this. I hoped that my fate would assign me to important tasks, the accomplishment of which would make me feel that I had contributed my bit to the civilization that was to come. I little realized the role that fate was to assign me in the opening of the Cherokee Strip, across which the train was speeding, as my mind dwelt upon my future hopes and plans.

As I sat staring dreamily out of the car window I was attracted by a conversation going on behind me that gave me an insight as to the feeling of the cow men whose ranges were being cut into farms down below the Strip in Oklahoma Territory and who realized that it would not be long until the settlers would infest the whole country—to their minds—a pestilence. Some of the early cow men realized that this new development was inevitable and that it was necessary to the growth of the country and they had prepared to adapt themselves to the changing conditions. Others were resentful, as were the two fellows who sat behind me in the train.

"I believe God Almighty made this-here for a cow country an' it's a damn shame to see th' way they're lettin' it be cut up in measly farms," one of them was saying.

"Yeah—measly garden patches fer some lazy louts t' starve their wimmen an' brats on—either that er work 'em t' death. I al'ays said th' wimmin ort t' favor a cow country. Th' men do all th' work. This-here country is cow-range. Them brainless kites in Washin'ton cain't change it by mere sayin' so er by passin' fool laws."

"Now yo're talkin'. Well all I say is they better not build no fences across my range. They'll likely ketch lead poisonin'."

These were men who felt, conscientiously, that they were being imposed upon by a misunderstanding government. There were many hundreds like them. Some of the best range country in Texas had been settled and the Texas country's cow men had drifted north with their cattle, ranging over the Panhandle and into the Indian Territory, leasing hundreds of sections of grazing lands from the Indians for practically nothing. They were nearer the cattle markets, the Indians were not molesting them seriously and the cattle business was thriving.

Their ranges were ridden by a heterogeneous lot of care-free spirits assembled from many parts of the world, from widely diversified strata of society and from varied previous conditions of servitude. Some of them came to the new country because their new associates would not be too curious about their past lives or their former names; some came running away from secret sorrows to become melancholy, silent brooders among their livelier friends; some came for the sheer love of wild nature; some were already there because they had grown up with it and were a natural part of it. Their environment developed them as individuals in an unorganized social group. For lack of social organization, they, as individuals, solved their problems quickly and without compunction, often with flaming six-guns spitting death most carelessly.

They worked hard, they fought bitterly, they played intensely. Many of them developed the wild spirit of the ingenius vagabond, fastening to nothing that would anchor their interests and limit their meanderings. They were drifters, and they liked it.

These were a lot of wild, spoiled boys. Few of them had the inherent qualities that make outlaws and criminals but many of them became outlaws and criminals when civilization tried to force them to adapt themselves to a routine of existence that they detested with all the energy they possessed.

Plow virgin land?—or any kind of land!—milk cows?—fool with a mess of chickens? *To hell with all that!*

And when civilization forced them too far, they rebelled; they became outlaws and felt perfectly justified.

Rumor had it that a number of new bands were being formed at the time I arrived in Oklahoma. The business men and the settlers were considerably aroused over the depredations that were, in themselves, dire threats against the peace and welfare of the territory. All the business between the principal towns and the outlying trading posts necessitated overland travel. Sometimes salesmen or other business representatives found it necessary to handle considerable sums of money and to carry it, poorly protected, through wild stretches of country where anything might happen without the slightest chance of the culprits' meeting with opposition that would discourage their predatory tendencies.

For many months Oklahoma outlaws moved in safety in any part of the territory, due to the lack of effective legal machinery.

Citizens were just becoming conscious of the fact that they had a serious outlaw problem.

CHAPTER III
GUTHRIE HAS GROWING BOOM

Within a few hours our heavily guarded train had crossed the Cherokee Strip and entered Oklahoma Territory.

When we alighted from the train at Guthrie both Charlie and I stood gaping at the sight that lay before us. There was a broad street cut deep with ruts by heavily loaded wagons, its two sides lined with the most nondescript group of buildings that ever I beheld. Here would be a shack of bright new pine; there a habitation of jack-oak logs—and anybody knows that knotty, scrawny jack-oak logs would make an eccentric house—there were tents by the dozens, some with torn, dirty canvas flapping, affording little shelter for the tired women and children who huddled beneath them. The fall air was crisp and wisps of gray smoke rose here and there to be playfully tossed and wafted away into space by the north breeze. A group of cowpunchers rode down the street, grinning in derision at a wagoner who asked them to lend their shoulders to lift a wheel from a crooked rut that threatened to twist off its spokes. He could rot there for all they cared. Then a pretty girl lifted a flap of the canvas cover and, before a gnat could wink, several punchers were groaning and straining at the stalled wheel, while the driver cursed his oxen and flayed them with a blacksnake whip. The wagon moved on, the punchers looking after it, eyes riveted to the flap that did not lift again. They looked at each other sheepishly, cursed a little and mounted their horses.

An Indian brave, driving a team of spotted ponies hitched to a light spring wagon, with a squaw and two papooses crouched in the bed of the wagon behind the seat, whipped his team to a wild run and the wagon careened past the depot, the buck giving forth challenging war whoops and the squaw screaming shrilly. Civilization did that. The white man's fire water.

A shot rang out in the street and someone said that Cap Red Shirt was on a tear and was taking his revenge against a plate glass mirror up at Reeves Brothers' saloon and gambling hall. It seems the mirror had given Cap the first glance of his dirty face he had had in many moons and Cap believed the mirror had insulted his manly beauty.

Two painted women brushed past Charlie and me and Charlie's face turned red as a firecracker. I suppose mine did too. Charlie was too flustered to notice.

We took up our baggage and walked toward the hotel, picking our way carefully through the slick red clay mud that seemed everywhere. As we passed a saloon we saw three roisterers holding a nervous pony for a drunken cowbody, urging him to get on quick. The pony was wild-eyed, and we suspected a joke of some kind. The puncher finally hit the saddle, but before he could find the stirrups the bronch bawled and whirled like a cyclone, jumping straight up and down in one spot, giving a spiral twist to each jump. One jump—two—three—four—and the puncher took flight, landing on the roof of a wooden awning at least four feet above the pony's back. I have always felt that pony should have had a medal. The bronch bucked another time or two in the same spot before it seemed to realize that its burden was gone, then it lit out down the street, pitching, bawling, but at the same time making more speed than I ever saw a bucking horse make.

The three jokers watched the inebriated puncher as he tried to make up his mind just where he was. His buddies were grinning and winking at each other.

"Ef th' hoky-poky holds out that hoss'll be passin' Oklahoma City in about eighteen minutes!" They all laughed uproariously as the drunk half scrambled, half fell from the awning. As we drew near the hotel we came upon an old drunken Indian who lay asleep on a muddy path, surrounded by more than a

dozen mongrel dogs of all colors and mixtures of breeds. The dogs huddled closely about the old Indian and most of them were sleeping as peacefully as was their master. One or two of the curs growled sleepily as we passed by.

When we reached the hotel we were greeted by an example of the splendid friendly spirit that did so much toward making the right sort of strangers feel at home in their new surroundings. We were greeted most cordially by a small group of citizens, among whom was Cassius M. Barnes who was then in charge of the government land office and who was later to become governor of the Oklahoma Territory and Dennis Flynn who proved to be one of Oklahoma's most popular postmasters and congressman.

Flynn was operating the community post office in a tent a few doors from the hotel, and we became close friends. Ed Kelly, town marshal, was also a man whose genial personality appealed to me, and we developed a friendship that has lasted through these many years. We were introduced to numerous others who were to have a prominent part in the development of the new country. The better element of citizens was always very cordial to the strangers, if the strangers seemed of the sort that would be desirable as neighbors and citizens. The cordiality of our reception at once made us feel that we were among friends.

At this time Guthrie boasted a population of about seven thousand. The people were beginning to get settled in a fairly comfortable way, and stores of all sorts had to be established to supply the needs of the community and of the broad territory about

it. There were ten saloons and gambling halls, and
a good many joints of other sorts. It was not at all
unusual in passing down the principal streets to
come upon one after another of outdoor gambling
games. Here would be an improvised roulette wheel
set up at the edge of a board sidewalk. Down the
street a few steps one might come upon a blackjack
game, a shell game or a faro table. The air was
crisp, and these games were moved frequently to
take advantage of the warm sunshine. A gamester
might be seeen lugging his apparatus across the
street to a more favorable spot, where, his new stand
established, he would place his six-shooters on the
table before him and start haranguing the passing
crowd to stop and seek their fortunes. A good many
rough and tumble fights occurred around these out-
door gaming tables.

Until this time very little had been done toward
establishing the places that would supply the soberer
and more substantial needs of the people.

I was for establishing myself immediately in
business, but Charlie persuaded me to accompany
him to Oklahoma City to look the situation over
there. We remained there several days, and Charlie
decided to stay. He soon opened a furniture store
there and prospered. I returned to Guthrie and, after investigating the business opportunities of the
place for several days, I bought a half interest in a
general merchandise store. I also purchased the
building we were to occupy, and I'll never forget how
proud I was to see my name in big letters before my
own business. My partner was a man named Baldwin and, because we seemed to understand each

other, it was not long before we succeeded in building up a good trade. Our store was one of the most
pretentious in Guthrie and we were the first to in-
stall plate glass show windows. After a few weeks
when things had started moving along fairly well,
I returned to Kentucky to be with my wife at the
birth of our first child. My visit was short as I was
anxious to get back to Oklahoma to prepare a home
for my little family. In January, 1890, I sent for
them, and my wife's mother accompanied her to our
new home. I met them in Kansas City that I might
enjoy their first impressions and reactions as they
entered the strange country. The train stopped for
a while in Ponca City in the Cherokee Strip and a
number of Indians loafed about the station platform.

My women folks were thrilled and, I think, a little
frightened, but Mrs. Nix put up a very brave front
and I was thankful that she was a true pioneer woman and not a hysterical creature to be frightened
by the difficulties that were sure to be ours. I established my family in the rooms above the Baldwin &
Nix store where we lived comfortably for several
months.

Shortly after my wife's arrival we were aroused
one night by a pistol bombardment in front of the
building. It seems that our plate glass windows had
been too great a temptation to a crowd of rowdy

cowboys, and they had determined to shatter them
with bullets. I quickly slipped into a few clothes
and grabbed my six-shooter on the run. Mrs. Nix
ran after me. As I reached the steep wooden stairway I could hear the clatter and shatter of those
precious plate glass windows. My Kentucky ire was

aroused and I was ready to fight a small army. As I came out upon the street one or two friends rushed to me, and my wife was soon struggling to keep me from precipitating a bloody fight.

"Come on, you dirty cowards, let's fight it out!" I yelled madly. The cowpunchers looked at me for a moment, and one or two of them grinned sheepishly as they put the spurs to their bronchs and dashed away. It is probably a most fortunate thing that Mrs. Nix and my friends interfered, for the drunken cow-hands could easily have killed me in my tracks if I had started anything. It was a harrowing experience for Mrs. Nix but her courage never faltered. I was very happy a few months later to be able to move my family into a new home in a quieter part of town. But the three large rooms of our first western house seemed palatial to us, and we were prouder of that place than we ever have been of the finer homes we have enjoyed since.

One of the most fortunate friendships I ever made—one that has ripened and mellowed with the passing years—was with a man who represented, compositely, all of the best manly qualities the Indian Territory had produced. Oscar Halsell was a Texan who had been forced north as the tide of settlement moved into his Texas ranges. He became one of the Indian Territory's best known and most prosperous cattlemen. He was a man of extraordinary moral character and of unusual intelligence. When he saw the leading events that presaged the passing of the cow ranges, he immediately determined to adapt himself to the new situation and to aid in the development of the country with all his resources. When he saw a number of his cow-hands bitterly resentful toward the settlers and the towns, joining outlaw bands, he never failed to use his influence to turn them straight. Some of them were sensible enough to listen to his advice and they became useful citizens. Others could not tolerate the thought of giving up the freedom of the ranges and, though they always remained loyal to their friend Halsell, they persisted in following their foolish and futile bandit careers. Halsell was loyal to them as long as they lived and regardless of what they were charged with having done. He understood their temperaments, and he always said they were unfortunate victims of circumstances over which they had no control.

"They're just foolish, spoiled boys," he used to tell me, "and they're too good to let go to waste. I wish I could help them to get off on the right foot. They'd be good men."

Oscar Halsell has been criticised by a few misunderstanding people because of his friendly feeling toward a number of the outlaws, but they did not realize that he had ridden the ranges, eaten and slept with these former cowpunchers, and that he knew their good qualities, while others seemed to know only their bad. I have always admired the man's loyalty, and from the beginning I was grateful for the circumstances that seemed to be leading us toward common interests and a more intimate business association.

* * *

Our Guthrie post office had been housed for some time in a small temporary building that was inadequate to the needs of the community. Dennis Flynn, postmaster, had been authorized by the department at Washington to negotiate for a permanent building that would take care of the needs of the growing community for a number of years to come.

He entered into an agreement with a citizen named I. S. De Ford, who owned a corner lot adjoining my store. De Ford was a town character who speculated a little bit in real estate and he made a good deal of his money at the gambling tables. He had earned quite a reputation as a fighter and many thought that he was a man to be feared. This reputation seemed to have its effect upon De Ford's opinion of himself for the man had developed a quarrelsome nature.

When he entered into the contract with Postmaster Flynn he started construction work on the new building. I strolled out of the store one morning and found a number of workmen excavating and cutting back beneath the foundation of my store building, endangering its walls. I called the attention of the gang foreman to that fact and he told me that I would have to see De Ford as he had been instructed to do it that way. I discussed the matter with Mr. De Ford and he informed me in a very indifferent matter that the edge of my building was over on his property and that he proposed to dig the excavation where it belonged, regardless of what he might do to my building. I attempted to reason with him, explaining that if an error had been made in the government survey we should have it adjusted by the proper authorities as my building was but the width of my lot and if it was encroaching upon

his property the building on the other side was encroaching upon mine. De Ford was very nasty about the matter, saying that he had neither time nor inclination to be bothered and that he was going to proceed with the erection of the post office building.

This roused a bit of my Kentucky fighting spirit and I warned him as graciously as I could to order his men to stop the excavations that were cutting under my foundation. I then turned and went back to my store to await results. Immediately after noon I went out to see if my request had been complied with and found that no new instructions had been given to the foreman. His men were working and I became alarmed lest they should completely undermine the foundation of my building and cause the dirt walls in my basement to cave in. I went back into the store and returned in a minute with my forty-five. When the men saw me coming they seemed to lose interest in the work and without the least discussion they drifted away to other parts as if important business called them.

Quite naturally it was but a few minutes until De Ford came in a rage to learn why his men had quit their work so suddenly. I placed my gun in my pocket and stood waiting for him. As he drew near he ripped out an oath and shouted, "What the hell did you mean by ordering those workmen away from my property?" He came on toward me as if he were determined to wipe me off the face of the earth. His great body was trembling and his fists were clenched tightly. He was usually armed and I thought it would be safer to let him know that I had

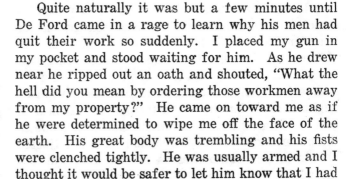

prepared for him so I drew my gun quickly and threw down on him. He came to an abrupt stop, his face chalky white as he gasped out, "For God's sake don't shoot, I'm not armed!"

A fellow citizen named Little who, by the way, was a friend of mine, stood near and I asked him to examine De Ford for weapons. De Ford cursed the smaller man as he went through his pockets and took a long hunting knife from him. I then handed my pistol to Little, and tore into De Ford in true Kentucky style. Before I had struck the second blow my partner, Ed Baldwin, was racing down the street shouting at the top of his voice, "Nix and De Ford are killing each other!"

Within ten minutes half of Guthrie was on hand and all reports had it that it was a fine exhibition. I have always been fairly modest about my own ability as a fighter, but within a few minutes I had so thoroughly put the finishing touches to De Ford that he was begging for mercy. I turned and walked into the store, and De Ford stumbled away spitting blood, nursing bruises and (I heard a short time later) muttering curses and threats. Within a few hours reports of his rash threats reached me. I was determined to have the matter completely settled and I made up my mind that I would find out immediately if the fellow had any more fight left in him or if he had just been doing some wild talking. Late in the afternoon of the same day I saw him standing on the corner a short distance from my store. I put on my hat and coat and strolled down the street toward him. As I passed close to him I quickly grasped his coat collar and thrust him back against

the wall of the building near which he was standing and said, "De Ford, is it true that you are not satisfied and that you are looking for me?" The man's lips trembled and he dropped his head without saying a word. He stood there completely nonplussed and after hesitating a moment I turned and walked back to the store. Next day De Ford sent word to me that he was willing to arbitrate our dispute over the boundary line and the matter was soon settled satisfactorily. The entire community seemed glad that someone had taken a few tucks in De Ford's ego and, incidentally, I gained many new acquaintances who later became warm and lasting friends. The affair so thoroughly convinced the community that they had no reason to fear De Ford as a man-killer that he was somewhat humbled before the Guthrie people. From that time on, although he still remained so much a bully that he never failed to pick a fight whenever he got outside his own community, he did a good job of letting me alone, but always speaking in passing. Years later he came to see me in Joplin, Missouri, where I was in business. Sitting at my desk one day I heard someone speak to me and, looking up, was much surprised to see De Ford standing there fumbling his hat nervously.

"Hello, Marshal," he began timidly, "you never expected to see me, did you?"

I got up and extended my hand. De Ford dropped his head and his eyes couldn't quite meet mine as he shook my hand in a half-shy manner.

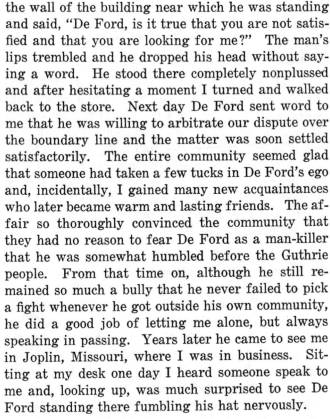

"I am on the hog, Marshal, I don't suppose I have any right a-comin' to you, but——."

"That's all right, De Ford," I replied although

Top—Former Chief Justice Frank Dale, U. S. Territorial
Court. Center—Former Justice Henry W. Scott.
Lower—Justice A. G. C. Bierer.

Dale, Brown & Hoyland
Attorneys and Counselors at Law

Frank Dale
Harry F. Brown
Robert W. Hoyland

Dale Building

Trial, Corporation and General Practice
All Federal and State Courts in Oklahoma

Guthrie, Oklahoma,

May 16, 1928

Honorable E. D. Nix,
Central National Bank Bldg.,
St. Louis, Missouri

My dear Nix:

You have advised me that you are compiling a brief history of the conditions in the Territory of Oklahoma during the period you so ably filled the position of U. S. Marshal. At that time I was Chief Justice of the Territory and in assuming such position I inherited a condition of lawlessness which was appalling. I took the matter up with you and in as much as the bandits were well known, I suggested that the proper thing to do was to kill them off, as we had lost several fine officers in a pitched battle with the outlaws at Ingalls. We called in a number of our best marshals who were instructed to take no chances with those bandits naming the men connected with the Doolin Gang. In six weeks the bodies of nine of them were brought into Guthrie for identification and the rewards offered by the railways, express companies and the banks.

I have often thought that perhaps the orders I gave were the only ones of record in the United States, dealing in such drastic manner with an intolerable condition of outlawry. I am very glad you have undertaken to hand down in history the efforts put forth while you were U. S. Marshal to exalt justice and to protect the public against lawlessness.

I hope for your continued prosperity and with kindest regards personally, I am,

Yours very respectfully,

Frank Dale

FD/h

I could not feel enthused about the touch that I knew he wanted to make.

"Now, Marshal, I am jist—jist a-tryin' to git back to Oklahomy. I thought mebbe I might—."

Well, I gave him his fare back to Oklahoma and never saw him again.

A number of years later during an altercation with a man in an Oklahoma City hotel he fell headlong down a stairway, breaking his neck and dying instantly.

In March, 1890, I purchased Ed Baldwin's half interest in the store and by applying myself to the building of trade I was soon making enough money that I began to think of getting into a broader field than retail business offered. Oscar Halsell and I became very close friends and when, in the fall of 1890, we decided to enter the wholesale grocery business together, I congratulated myself upon having so desirable a partner. Although Halsell came into the business utterly inexperienced, his natural business instinct made him a valuable and helpful partner and I have always attributed a large part of my success in Oklahoma to the soundness and keenness of Oscar Halsell's judgment.

We developed a considerable business with the Indian traders and it was not long until the Nix & Halsell Company was supplying a broad territory.

Guthrie also prospered and grew until it took on the appearance of a permanent city with its stone and brick buildings and its comfortable homes.

When I first came to Oklahoma, Guthrie was governed by a board of managers chosen in a rather ar-

bitrary manner by a few of the better element of citizens. The Territory had no organized government and each individual was a law unto himself. Banks had been established by individuals or partnerships and were being operated without the slightest legal control or restriction. I think it was remarkable that during this period not a single defalcation was committed and not a cent was lost by depositors in one of these crude banks. I like to tell this to those who would say that early Oklahoma was settled by a pack of scapegraces who had left former homes involuntarily. Coming from the strict moral influence of my Kentucky home life I would have been quick to notice the shortcomings of the business men of early Oklahoma, and I must say that I found these men to be of as good breeding and as sound moral character as I have ever met in any community.

The better element of men became very clannish and every frontier community was blessed by the efforts of these small groups who were loyal and honorable to the core and whose good influence comprised the very fabric of our community ideals and ethics. Some of these fine fellows would have had considerable trouble describing, in good English, the moral principles for which they stood; but they had character and the backbone to enforce their own conception of right.

The women of the pioneering period cannot be praised too highly for the high-minded manner in which they approached most difficult social and family problems—their homes were crude, and they lacked most of the comforts and conveniences they had known before coming to the new country. The environment for several years was of a sort that seemed to threaten the very welfare of children, yet these pioneer mothers were able to overcome all these precarious conditions with unparalleled courage and with a strength and depth of character that has stamped itself upon the generations that have followed.

Soon after I arrived the town of Guthrie was organized along conventional lines and C. B. Dyer was elected mayor. In May, 1890, a territorial government was formed and George Steele, formerly of Indiana, was appointed governor. The form of government and the statutes of the State of Arkansas were adopted as the legal basis for the territorial government. In the fall of 1891 Guthrie had her first bank failure, the Commercial Bank closing its doors because of the failure of a banking connection in Kansas. I was appointed receiver and was required to give a bond of four hundred and fifty thousand dollars. This was quite an enormous responsibility for a young man of thirty but, assisted by the wise counsel of friends, I disposed of the affairs of the unfortunate organization very successfully.

Oklahoma was progressing rapidly in every way. Settlers were producing paying crops and business was prospering. The bandit problem, however, had become acute, hampering the development of legitimate business and making it almost impossible for money or merchandise to be successfully transported through the territory. The bandits were robbing trains, banks, stores and the isolated farms of settlers. Reports were going out that Oklahoma was a

precarious place to live and progress was arrested at the very time when the territory needed new people and new capital. The citizens were becoming impatient with the officers who seemed unable to cope with the situation. We all realized that something had to be done, but doing it was a difficult matter.

Must the settlers of the new territory bow to the will and power of the brigands?

CHAPTER IV

THE RISE AND FALL OF THE DALTONS

True, there was a streak of Younger blood in their veins—and the Youngers had achieved a great deal of outlaw notoriety—but Louis and Adeline Dalton's family of boys and girls also bore the blood and breeding of many generations of honest, industrious people. It is not unusual that a family should produce one black sheep—or even two—but what fluke of circumstance caused four of Louis Dalton's sons to turn outlaw? Was it a cruel disillusionment of some sort? Was it an unfair or unkind act of some representative of the organized society they seemed to hate so bitterly? Was it an inherent, criminal instinct, the animal nature—a heritage,

perhaps, from the Younger strain? The reader's guess will be as good as mine.

Louis Dalton was a Kentuckian and had served in the Mexican War. In 1850 he removed from Kentucky to Jackson County, Missouri, where he later married Adeline Younger, the charming daughter of a prominent farmer and a cousin of the Younger Brothers, whose notoriety rivaled that of the James boys. Louis Dalton and his wife settled in a modest home and led the lives of people who were worthy of better sons. In 1860, Dalton removed his little family to a farm near Coffeyville, Kansas, where the younger children were born and where all grew up.

In 1884, his eldest son, Frank, went to old Indian Territory and he was commissioned as a deputy United States Marshal, with headquarters in Fort Smith. He became widely known as a brave and trustworthy officer. His young brother Bob, fascinated by the wild life of the territory, came to visit Frank and was with him in 1885 when Frank was slain in a gun-fight with horse thieves. This was young Bob's baptism of fire and it is said that he fought like a veteran, making his escape from the thieves after a wild chase during which lead fell about him like rain.

Another son, Bill, drifted to Montana, then on to California where he established himself among substantial people and entered politics. He had barely lived in the State long enough to qualify as a citizen when he was elected to the State legislature.

The other Dalton boys had developed a wanderlust, and the little farm home in Kansas could no longer hold Gratton and Bob. Young Emmett was also fretting to be out seeing the world, but his father induced him to stay. Gratton had gone to California, but he returned home when Frank was killed. Going to Indian Territory, following the urge to be on the go and to find excitement, he accepted an appointment as a deputy United States Marshal. For a few months he made a very good officer and his bravery would have distinguished him if it had not been for that peculiar streak of deviltry that, at times, seemed to dominate his better nature.

Although Bob could not have been more than nineteen or twenty, he was soon appointed a deputy United States Marshal, with duties in the federal courts at Wichita, Kansas, and at Fort Smith, Arkansas. Later he served as chief of police for the Osage Indian Nation.

Young Emmett was staying at home, although he was impatient to be enjoying the thrilling experiences his brothers wrote about. Early in 1889, Louis Dalton died. His grief-stricken widow, unable to remain on the little Kansas farm, with its haunting memories, induced her children—Emmett, two older sons and two daughters—to join her in trying for a claim in the Oklahoma run. They were successful and established themselves on a fertile farm near Kingfisher. Her eldest sons—who were not to share in the notoriety of their younger brothers—married and located on nearby farms. Her daughters also married well and, with sheer force of character and integrity, they lived honorably through the period when it seemed their younger brothers would disgrace them.

Emmett soon left home and joined Gratton and

Bob in the Indian territory. Emmett's outlaw career was to be short, but very eventful. Emmett Dalton was fearless and he loved excitement, but he lacked the bloodthirsty bravado of the successful bandit. Perhaps he had inherited too much of the substantial quality and character of his father and mother.

Although Bob and Gratton were officers, they had been engaging in a number of minor depredations against the property rights of settlers and, shortly after Emmett joined them, the three stole a herd of horses and drove them to Kansas, where they sold them. With the proceeds Gratton and Emmett left for California and Bob returned to the territory, feeling sure that he was not suspected as a horse thief.

Early in 1891, an unsuccessful attempt was made to rob a Southern Pacific express train at Tulare, California. The express messenger surprised the bandits with a fusillade of shots that defeated the robbery, although, in the melee of wild shooting, the fireman was killed. The Dalton brothers were accused of the murder and attempted robbery and Gratton was captured. It was at that time that Bill attempted to use his political influence to get Gratton out of this trouble but the situation threatened to compromise his position and he was forced to abandon his efforts, although it is possible that he assisted his brothers in a quiet way. Gratton was tried and convicted, but he succeeded in escaping as he was being transferred from the county jail to the state prison. Emmett, who had remained in California, hoping to aid his brother, joined Grat and they returned to Oklahoma. The Southern Pacific offered a standing reward of $6,000 for their capture and, naturally, they were being sought by officers everywhere; particularly were their old haunts in Oklahoma being watched.

Young, impulsive and fired by the success of their California escape, the two joined their brother Bob who had already made plans to form an outlaw band and who had recruited Bill Doolin, Dick Broadwell, Bill Powers and Black Faced Charlie Bryant. Bill Doolin had worked as a cowpuncher for Oscar Halsell for some time and he left the Halsell ranch but a short time before, determined to become an outlaw. Broadwell and Powers were also ex-cowpunchers, and Black Faced Charlie Bryant was a peculiar character who had drifted in from no one knew where and who had very little to say about his past. Somehow, somewhere, his face had got dangerously near an exploding gun and he had received powder burns that had left splotches of burned black powder beneath his skin. This accounted for his being called Black Faced Charlie. They had made plans for a series of wholesale robberies that would surpass anything ever attempted by any of Oklahoma's earlier bandits. After numerous insignificant depredations, young Bob developed a plan that he hoped would establish the Daltons as super-bandits.

As they laid the groundwork for their daring exploits, the outlaws combed the territory for the best riding stock they could find. Soon after the organization of their band, the Dalton gang made a raid on a colony of Missourians who had settled near Orlando on Beaver Creek. Eight or ten horses were stolen, and the bandits made a dash back toward

the Indian Territory. A posse was quickly organized that followed the horse thieves to a point near
Twin Mounds in the Territory. The trail growing
warmer, the posse divided to search the dense timber
along the bank of a creek. Two members of the
posse, William Thompson and W. T. Starmer, a cousin of George G. Starmer, later one of my deputies,
were ambushed by the outlaws who hid behind a pile
of driftwood. The possemen dropped to the ground
quickly and attempted to conceal themselves behind
stumps while they poured a deadly fire in the direction from which the bandits' shots had come, but the
outlaws were too well sheltered to suffer damage, and
within a few minutes Starmer lay fatally wounded
while Thompson made his get-away. When Starmer's body was examined it was found that he had
been hit by three bullets so well aimed that any one
would have killed him. His own Winchester was
empty, indicating that he had fought to the last
cartridge.

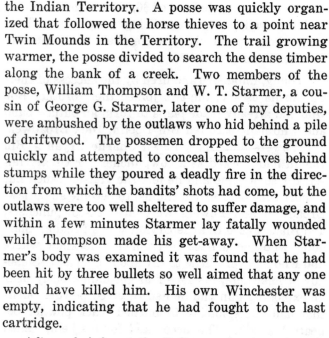

After a brief rest the Daltons set out westward,
seeking a place of greater security for the undis-
turbed development of their next immediate plans.

Red Rock, Oklahoma, was a little Indian trading
station built upon the rolling red clay prairies in the
Cherokee Strip, and so isolated that even today the
State highways do not touch it and the Santa Fe
trains hoot disdainfully as they whiz by. The depot
was situated about a mile from the town, and it was
here the bandits could work quickly without fear of
interference by the officers of the little community.

At nine o'clock on the night of June 1st, 1892,
the Dalton gang rode into a deep washout near the

railroad and near the Red Rock station. Leaving their horses concealed here, they waited in the shadows for the arrival of the southbound Santa Fe passenger train. As the small wood-burning engine labored into the station and came to a stop, a blanketed Indian with a squaw and two papooses alighted.  The telegraph operator ran to the engine to give the engineer his orders, when Black Faced Charlie Bryant and Dick Broadwell dashed past him and leaped into the cab of the locomotive. An armed guard sat on a pile of wood on the tender eating a sandwich. The surprise attack so demoralized him that he gave a hysterical jerk at his gun, causing sticks of wood to roll beneath him and he sprawled across the coupling into the cab of the engine at the feet of the two bandits who quickly disarmed him. The express  messenger and his guard had just been congratulating themselves that there were no shipments to be put off the train at Red Rock, and they went on placidly with a game of checkers. When the command came for them to reach for the sky, the checkerboard fell from their trembling knees and the checkers rolled all about the car. They were looking into the guns of Bill Doolin and Gratton Dalton. Back in the passenger coaches, Bob and Emmett Dalton and Bill Powers were herding the frightened passengers out onto the station platform. With the express messenger and his guard disarmed and bound, Grat and Doolin looked about for the large safe that was supposed to contain several thousand dollars in currency. There had been a slip somewhere, for they only found a small box-like safe with a chain attached to one of the handles. They dragged this to the door and threw it out on the platform. After quickly relieving the messenger of his keys they opened the flimsy door of the little iron box and found a single pack containing two or three hundred dollars in currency.

While Bob, Emmett and Powers were forcing the passengers to give up their valuables, Black Faced Charlie left Broadwell in the engine to hold his prisoners there while he ran back to assist the others. In passing the station window, he saw the frightened face of the operator in the dim lamp light as his nervous hands trembled on the telegraph keys. Assuming that the operator was sending out news of the robbery, Bryant sent a bullet crashing

through the window, and with a moan the slender boy inside slumped from his chair. The telegraph instruments clicked frantically for him to complete his message.

Within fifteen minutes the terrified passengers were herded back into the cars and the train was on its way. The disappointed bandits slunk away with but a part of the booty they had hoped for.

There were great official stirs, rewards were offered by the express and railroad companies and desperate attempts were made to finally wipe out the Daltons, who were becoming a menace to Oklahoma's march of progress, but the outlaws disappeared as if they were spirit creatures who had no material bodies to conceal and all searches were fruitless.

Within a short time, Black Faced Charlie appeared at a cowboy dance near Hennessey, Oklahoma, and before the evening was over he had started an altercation with a cowman from the western part of the Cherokee Strip and was considerably worsted in the affair, receiving a wound that sent him to bed under a doctor's care.

Deputy United States Marshal Ed Short heard of the affair and went to Hennessey seeking Bryant. He located him easily in the home where his wounds were being treated and, entering his bedroom, he was able to overpower and handcuff the outlaw before he could get to his gun which was concealed beneath his pillow.

In those days it was necessary to transport our prisoners to the nearest large cities where adequate jail facilities were available.   These outlaws were desperate men.   It was not safe to attempt to hold them in the flimsy structures that served as jail houses in the young towns that had grown up in this new country.

The next morning after Bryant's capture Deputy Short arranged to take him to Wichita, Kansas. On this trip, Short's lack of caution, or perhaps it was his over-confidence, cost him his life. The prisoner was handcuffed with his hands in front instead of behind him, and when the train arrived he was placed in the express car. After a short time, Short handed the outlaw's six-shooter to the express messenger and asked him to guard his prisoner, saying that he wanted to go back into the passenger coach to see a friend. The messenger casually placed the six-shooter in a pigeon-hole above his desk and went about his work. The outlaw watched his opportunity, and as he saw the messenger intent in his work he slipped up behind him and grabbed the six-shooter with his hand-cuffed hands; covering the messenger,

he was backing toward the sliding door of the car where he expected to make his escape when Deputy Short re-entered. Bryant whirled quickly, facing Short, his manacled hands aiming the gun clumsily as he blazed away at the deputy. Short staggered, seriously wounded, drawing his gun as quickly as possible. The express messenger ducked behind a stack of freight. Before the duel between these two men of undaunted nerve had ended both six-shooters were empty and the two combatants lay in pools of their own blood, dying.

The train was then drawing into the station of Waukomis, Oklahoma, and the deputy and the outlaw were taken from the splintered express car and laid upon the platform. Conductor Collins kneeled beside the dying officer. . . . "Ed, is there anything I can do for you?" Short tried to force a grin as he answered feebly: "I hope . . . . I got that snake he sure got me . . . take off . . . my boots . . . Collins . . . . and send word to my mother."

A short distance away lay the outlaw who but a few moments ago had had life and vitality in such measure that he had regarded death as that strange, intangible thing to be considered as being far in the future—now, but a few brief minutes later, he lay gasping, his life blood gurgling from many open wounds.

A young man walked to his side and stooped to speak to him—"Aren't you Charlie Bryant?" The outlaw nodded his head weakly as he recognized the young man as a boyhood friend. Bryant then made that strange request that seldom came from the lips of dying gunmen: ". . . . I . . . . can't die with

my boots . . . . on . . . . won't you . . . ." The
young friend stooped and tenderly removed his boots
and promised to frame a respectable story to be sent
to the desperado's mother.

Ed Short's untimely death was but another lesson
to the territorial officers, proving to them that they
must not under any circumstances give an outlaw
prisoner a chance for escape.

The rest of the Dalton gang had apparently
dropped out of existence. Several weeks passed
without the officers' receiving the slightest clue as to
their whereabouts. Then in the latter part of July
they appeared over in the Cherokee country near the
Arkansas line where they perpetrated one of the
most daring train robberies that had ever been attempted. They knew that a considerable shipment
of money was being made on a Missouri, Kansas and
Texas passenger train on this particular day; and

they also knew that the train was being heavily
guarded by a force, augmented by Indian police. In
spite of the discouraging prospect for success, the
Daltons lay in wait for the train near a little station
called Adair. As the train came to a stop, the bandits attempted to capture the guards, who poured a
heavy fire upon the robbers. With undaunted nerve
the robbery of the mail express car and the passengers proceeded during one of the hottest gun battles
that ever took place upon such an occasion. The
Dalton gang succeeded in carrying away all of the
valuables and money and several of the Indian police

and passengers were wounded. A physician who
lived in Adair was killed. It was never learned
whether or not any of the bandits were wounded; if

so, they were carried away and nursed to recovery by their companions.

Again the Daltons dropped out of sight and the officers and their posses were unable to find a trace of them. Now and then they would hear of some small depredation of which the Daltons were vaguely suspected. Encouraged by their successful robberies and escapades, young Bob Dalton's mad ambition was fired with a desire to commit a robbery so daring and so sensational that the entire country would be shocked, and that would establish the Dalton gang as more to be feared than the James boys or the Youngers had ever been. Having been reared near Coffeyville, Kansas, the Dalton boys knew the little town, its inhabitants and their habits intimately.

Young Bob decided that Coffeyville should be the scene of his *coup de theatre*. He had boasted to his impetuous followers that he would lead them to glorious accomplishments greater than America had ever known. They would rob two banks in the same town simultaneously. That would eclipse anything the James or Youngers had ever done. He visualized himself as a romantic hero and he developed a super-ego and an unreasonable confidence that was to lead him to his destruction. Bob felt that this next stroke must be the one that would establish his band's fortunes so soundly that they would be able to retire for a considerable time. Bob and Grat had been recognized in the Adair robbery, and the indig-

nation of the territorial officers and citizenship was seething. Sooner or later the Daltons would be captured. They realized this and laid their plans to get out of the country.

Top—U. S. Attorney Thos. F. McMechan. Bottom—U. S. Attorney Roy Hoffman, Brig.-General in world war.

BRIG. GEN. ROY HOFFMAN

PRESIDENT
RESERVE OFFICERS' ASSOCIATION
OF THE UNITED STATES

Oklahoma City, Oklahoma,

May 16th, 1928.

Hon. E. D. Nix,
Central National Bank Building,
St. Louis, Missouri.

Dear E. D.:

       I hear to my great satisfaction that you
are planning a write up of the early day history of
Oklahoma Territory.

       I have long hoped that some one qualified
would speak the facts about those times. The story
has never been told. There have been many hack
amateurs who have tried, but the face of those early
days is still unillumined.

       Strength to your Arm. No one should know
better how to do it. As United States Marshal during
those stirring days, you were in charge when the reign
of outlaw rule was abruptly terminated by the Winchester
and the courts of law. As prosecuting attorney for the
Government during your regime, I was in constant contact with your work and that of your deputies, and
know the great things you did in establishing the
law, peace and dignity of your State. So again I
say, stick to your job and work this out, and I
will help in any way that I can.

       Sincerely yours,

RH-s

On the morning of October 4th, 1892, the Dalton gang comprised of Bob, Grat and Emmett Dalton, Bill Doolin, Dick Broadwell and Bill Powers rode out from their Indian Territory hiding place in the direction of the Kansas line. Their six-shooters and rifles were oiled and loaded to capacity; their cartridge belts and pockets were filled with ammunition, and as their horses fox-trotted over the vague trail the men rode in a huddled group, discussing their plans in hushed tones. Doolin rode beside young Bob, serving as a sort of first lieutenant and offering such suggestions and warnings as an older man could give to daring and rash youth.

Late in the afternoon they crossed the Kansas line and, riding a few miles farther, they stopped and camped for the night. They built their fire in a secluded spot and held their consultations in whispers as if afraid the rocks and trees might over-hear and frustrate their plot.

Several cigarettes after dusk they spread their blankets and retired for the night, all but young Emmet falling into sound sleep. The boy was nervous . . . this affair didn't seem to him to be quite right. Perhaps he was developing more of a conscience than he would have admitted to the others. In the middle of the night he threw his blanket aside and walked nervously about the little camp. His nerves were on edge. Bob stirred in his blanket and called: "That you, Emmett? . . . You had better be sleeping." The boy sat down on his rude bed and waited for his brother to go back to sleep. He then dragged his blanket over near Bob's sleeping form and lay down. His brother's peaceful snoring

seemed to reassure him; he soon drifted away into sound slumber.

Before daylight the bandits arose and prepared a light breakfast; the bitter, black coffee warmed them and stimulated their spirits for the task that was before them. At about seven o'clock they rode out of the camp toward Coffeyville, expecting to arrive there soon after the banks had opened and before there were many people on the streets. It was one of those invigorating fall days that seem to sharpen the mind and to exhilarate the body to an eagerness to attack whatever experiences the day may bring forth. There had been a light frost or two, and the ground beneath the trees was covered with brown and pink and gold leaves. The short grass beside the trail was beginning to turn brown and the earth was moist enough that the horses raised very little dust.

During the night Doolin's horse had wrenched a foot in some manner and was limping painfully. As they passed a small ranch, it was Bob Dalton's suggestion that Doolin fall back and try to rustle a new mount for himself, for it was imperative that the bandits be able to make a rapid departure following their robbery. Doolin turned away from the trail and the others rode on toward Coffeyville.

"I'll be there not more'n fifteen or twenty minutes behind you boys. I just seen a chestnut sorrel geldin' in a field outside the timber there that looks like he might step. It won't take me long to toss a rope over him."

Many old-timers have said that Bill Doolin tried to persuade Bob Dalton that he was biting off more than he could chew. Did Bill Doolin loiter behind because he preferred not to have a hand in the Coffeyville affair? Anyone familiar with the indomitable courage of the man would have known that his reluctance was not due to fear. Perhaps he used better judgment than Bob Dalton was capable of exercising.

As the horses trotted along Bob Dalton adjusted a heavy false mustache and goatee to his smooth face, and handed a false beard to Emmett to conceal his features. Grat's face was covered by a long, shaggy growth of beard, while Dick Broadwell and Bill Powers wore no disguises of any kind since they were unknown in Coffeyville.

As the riders drew near the town's borders they halted in the road to wait a few moments for Doolin. Young Emmett Dalton was sent riding back to the top of a hill to see if Doolin was following. He rode back to the group, reporting that he could see nothing of the other man. Bob Dalton was impatient and after a very short wait he touched his horse with the spurs, saying: "We can't waste any more time waitin' for him. This has got to be done quick. Come on."

Shortly after nine o'clock the five men rode at a slow trot into the principal street of the town, the three Daltons abreast and Broadwell and Powers following. As it was an ordinary sight for cattlemen to be riding in and out of Coffeyville during this period, the bandits attracted no unusual attention. They were mounted on their best horses and their heavy Mexican saddles were decorated with the spangles and carvings that cow men in that period

so vainly affected.   On the sides of their saddles
hung large hair-covered pockets, each carrying several six-shooters.   Behind the saddles, their slickers
were compactly rolled.   Their Winchester rifles were
concealed beneath their coats.   To the casual ob-
server they seemed to be unarmed.   Their broad-
brimmed hats were drawn well down over their
faces, and they looked neither to the right nor to the
left as they approached the town square.   Here they
turned to the right and rode half a block, disappearing into an alley where they tied their horses.   After
some moments they walked out upon the principal
business street of Coffeyville.   A few teams hitched
to farm wagons stood at the hitching rails up and
down the street and here and there were cow ponies
standing as if they were anchored by the loose bridle
reins that touched the ground.   A housewife, basket
on her arm, bustled out of a door of a meat market
and brushed Emmett slightly, disarranging his false
beard.

They proceeded down the street passing farmers
and citizens.   One merchant, looking a little more
closely than the other passers-by, saw at a glance
than the men were disguised and he immediately suspected that they were bank robbers.   He concealed
himself in a doorway and watched until three of
them, Grat Dalton, Powers and Broadwell, entered
the Condon Bank.   At about the same moment, Bob
and Emmett went into the First National Bank.
Walking furtively past the Condon Bank, the merchant saw Grat Dalton pointing a gun at the cashier's head.   The frightened man ran down the street
for about half a block, then began shouting that the

banks were being robbed. Another citizen had followed the Daltons into the Condon Bank and witnessed the hold-up but, as he tried to leave, he was ordered to hold up his hands and he remained where he was.

The cry—"The banks are being robbed!" flew from door to door, up and down the streets, until the whole town was alarmed, and men came running with six-shooters, Winchesters and shot guns. Within an incredibly short time a fusillade of shots was being fired through the windows and doors of the two banks at the bandits. Through this fiery battle, the Daltons, by their sheer coolness and daring, seemed about to justify their boast that they would eclipse the exploits of the James boys and the Youngers. With bullets, crashing window glass and splintering wood flying about them, they went calmly about receiving the money that was being handed out to them by the frightened bank employes. Packages of currency and stacks of coin were thrown quickly into the bags they had brought for the purpose, and within three minutes the Daltons were ready to make their exit into the street—but they reckoned without the alertness and bravery of the Coffeyville citizens who were massed in the street and ready for battle.

As Bob and Emmett would have left the First National Bank they were met by a hail of bullets and the crash of falling glass. They turned back and made their way through a rear door into the alley, fighting viciously as they ran.

Grat, Broadwell and Powers were having their own troubles by this time. Powers had been hit and blood was gushing in a stream from his right sleeve. As they came to the door, Powers carried his six-shooter in his left hand and was still as calm as any man could have been. These three decided to fight their way out of the front door and through the crowd of citizens. As they reached the sidewalk Powers was hit again and he fell, gasping his last breath. A moment later Grat Dalton fell to his knees fatally wounded by a bullet from the gun of City Marshal Charles T. Connelly. With the figure of the City Marshal dancing before his blazing eyes, Grat Dalton raised his pistol and fired the shot that killed Connelly. Two citizens, Lucius M. Baldwin and George B. Cubine, rushed to aid Connelly, and Broadwell felled the two of them—killing them instantly. Broadwell made a dash through the alley for his horse, followed by a half dozen citizens. He had mounted and was putting the spurs to his horse when a full charge of buckshot and a bullet from a Winchester struck him at about the same time. With the blood gushing from his mouth and with one arm shattered, he clung to his horse and dashed out and over the road by which the bandits had entered the town. A mile or so away his dead body was found by the roadside, the horse standing beside it.

As Bob and Emmett attempted to escape by the back door of the First National Bank, a citizen named Charles Brown rushed toward them and Bob drilled him squarely between the eyes. A moment later as they were about to reach their horses, Emmett heard a groan behind him and saw Bob fall into the alley's muck. Emmett quickly mounted his horse and rode back to where his brother Bob lay dying. He reached down and took hold of Bob's hand and tried to raise him to the horse behind. While he was trying to rescue his brother, Emmett Dalton was struck in the back by a heavy charge from a shot gun at close range. He released the dying man's hand, reeled in the saddle and fell to the ground.

Within fifteen minutes from the time they entered the banks, four of the outlaws were dead, and a fifth, Emmett Dalton, had been captured, with one bullet through his right arm, another through his hip and a sprinkling of buckshot in his back.

The bodies of the four dead bandits were taken to the jail where they remained until the mother of the Daltons arrived, accompanied by their two older brothers. Emmett was taken to a hospital and when he had recovered sufficiently was removed to the jail at Independence, Kansas. When quiet was restored, it was found that the robbers had taken eleven thousand dollars from the First National Bank and twenty thousand from the Condon Bank. All of this money was returned to the banks with the exception of a twenty dollar bill which was never found.

The Coffeyville raid was as disastrous to the Dalton gang as the Northfield raid had been to the Youngers many years before. It was the end of the Dalton gang in the southwest, but it was not the end of the reign of the outlaws. Bill Doolin who, but for a queer turn of fate, might have died an inglorious death with the Daltons, was destined to become one of the most vicious outlaws Oklahoma was ever to know.

Doolin had succeeded in stealing the thorough-

bred horse and he had proceeded on toward Coffeyville. As he drew near enough to see the smoke from
the chimneys of the Kansas town and to see the sunlight glinting from the roofs, some peculiar intuition
caused him to linger and watch as if he were waiting
for something—a vague something that he could not
have described. Presently, he saw a horseman racing toward him in a cloud of dust. The man drew
up as he approached Doolin and so great was his
excitement that his words were almost incoherent.
He told of the tragedy that had happened in the
streets of Coffeyville and Doolin learned the fate of
his companions.

Realizing that there was nothing he could do, the
cowboy bandit responded quickly to the instinct for
self-preservation. He knew that his connection with
the Dalton gang was suspected and even known to
some people, and he did not know how soon a posse
might be on his trail. Perhaps the Coffeyville folks
would believe that all of the gang had been wiped
out and would make no search—perhaps they would
not. He could afford to take no chances.

Within twenty-four hours the entire country
would be roused and an intensive search would begin
for all the men who were known to have had the
slightest connection with the Dalton band. Miles
away on the bank of the Cimarron was a haven of
safety, but between Doolin and that haven were
many obstacles. The outlaw had been fortunate in
finding so fit a mount for the gruelling ride that was
before him. As soon as the frightened informer
from Coffeyville had disappeared down the dusty
road, Doolin wheeled his steed and dashed away to-

ward the Kansas-Indian Territory line. That much of the ride must be made in daylight and he must dash on until darkness fell to shield his first breathing spell. Never once was it necessary to let the spirited thoroughbred feel the steel of his spurs. This sort of horse would run until he dropped in his tracks. Once or twice Doolin reined up to let his horse wet its lips in a muddy stream. The animal's neck, flanks and hips were covered with salty foam, and its strides grew trembling and uncertain before dusk finally fell. After a rest of two hours Doolin pressed on for the rest of the night.

As daylight broke he found refuge in a deep ravine and behind a great pile of drift-wood. The horse was led about a half mile beyond the man's hiding place and hobbled, where he was left to graze during the day. Doolin made his way stealthily back to his blankets and slept as only an exhausted man could sleep, until darkness fell again. That night Doolin crossed the territory like a flying wraith— flitting by ranch and farm like a ghostly rider saddled upon the wind, reeling off mile after mile until he reached the old rendezvous of the gang—a cow ranch on the Cimarron, twenty-five miles west of Tulsa.

Doolin had plans, and they were to be brought into effect while he rested there.

CHAPTER V
BILL DOOLIN TAKES THE SPOTLIGHT

I have often wondered just how much confidence one should place in Bill Doolin's story about the crippled horse. Doolin was an ambitious man,—as outlaws' ambitions go. He told a number of friends that he had remonstrated with Bob Dalton concerning his very daring plan to rob two banks at one time—and he intimated that there had been a little friction over this matter. Certainly he was a man of more mature judgment and he was probably very resentful at Bob's insistence. Perhaps there was a conflict between the selfish ambitions of the two men. A man of Doolin's type would naturally have admired the daring and youth of the Dalton boys— and it was quite likely that he aspired to supersede young Bob in leadership. Perhaps if Doolin had led the band into Coffeyville and they had concentrated their efforts upon the robbery of one bank, the result

would have been much less tragic. At any rate, Doolin remained behind. We can only conjecture as to why . . . perhaps his own story is true. While Bill Doolin was an unlettered man, he had natural faculties for leadership that might have been turned in a legitimate direction with most substantial results, but the blood of the outlaw seemed to dominate.

During the period of his lonely concealment at the little ranch on the Cimarron, his active mind laid the plans for what later became the most vicious outlaw gang the Southwest ever was to know. The qualifications which make for fame or notoriety manifest themselves in most unexpected places.

Bill Doolin had been born to a poor but honest backwoods family in the State of Arkansas. His father, Mack Doolin, reared his children as respectably as his limited understanding and the poverty of the home environment would permit. The son, Bill, was a very popular young man among the people of his home community. He had a commanding, magnetic personality that seemed to overshadow his limited education and the crudeness of his backwoods ways. As a young man, he went to Oklahoma where he worked for a considerable time as a cow-hand for my friend, Oscar Halsell. Halsell was very fond of the young man and was deeply hurt when Doolin insisted upon taking up the life of a brigand.

*   *   *

After a few weeks at the ranch on the Cimarron, Doolin moved to the old outlaw rendezvous near the edge of the Creek Nation. He had already determined in his own mind just who should become a part of the band he had planned. Here at the outlaw cave he would find it easy to get in touch with the men he sought. Upon his arrival he was much surprised to find Bill Dalton on the ground.

Here was another victim of the Coffeyville tragedy—a man who had attempted to build an honorable career but who had been so demoralized and discouraged by the blow the Dalton name had received following the Coffeyville raid that he had decided to flee from his position as a member of the state legislature in California to the outlaw haunts of his dead brothers in the Indian Territory. The blow had been a severe one, and had so shattered the hopes and ambitions of Bill Dalton that he became a craven creature little resembling the splendid man he had been.

Perhaps Doolin was resentful at the presence of this member of the Dalton family who might jeopardize his own plans for completely dominating the new outlaw band. Some peculiar quirk in the minds of these outlaw leaders caused them to visualize themselves as romantic heroes. They were extremely jealous of the peculiar prestige that belongs to such predatory characters. They basked in the doubtful glory of the lurid publicity they received as if it were the mellow sunshine of an early spring day. Their egos grew and expanded until they became unbalanced, distorted mentalities—capable of much that was brilliant and of a great deal that was animal.

Bill Dalton, however, seemed to entertain a certain respect for the ability and experience of Bill Doolin—and he soon convinced Doolin that they should join hands and carry out their plans together. Dalton was willing that Doolin should lead the new organization in all its exploits. He would serve as an aide and endeavor to be as helpful as possible. It is surprising to know just how closely these fellows' planning processes resembled those of a group of business men engaged in legitimate enterprise.

Doolin first communicated with George Newcomb and Bill Raidler, close friends who had worked with him on the Halsell ranch. Newcomb, better known as "Bitter Creek" and also as "Slaughter Kid," was the son of a very highly respected family living at Fort Scott, Kansas. When he first came to the Southwest country he had worked on the cattle ranges of the Slaughter family. It was here that he was called the "Slaughter Kid." Bill Raidler was a Pennsylvanian, and a man of very unusual talents. He had come of a very fine family and had received a splendid education as a young man. The cattle ranges fascinated him, and he worked for Oscar Halsell for a number of years—being from time to time given a great deal of responsibility. The wire fences and small farms had made such inroads upon the Oklahoma ranges that these men were being forced to seek other occupations and, as I have mentioned before, they were very resentful toward the progress which was forcing them aside. They might curse the vicissitudes of the cattle business for all they were worth—but they were ready to fight to a bitter end any attempt to force them out of it.

Within a short time the gang was joined by Roy Daugherty, alias "Arkansas Tom," Dick West and Ol Yountis.

"Arkansas Tom" had always seemed a peculiar paradoxical character to me. I had occasion to learn a great deal more of the intimate details of his life than I ever knew of the others—and his story touched me deeply. He, like Doolin, was born in the State of Arkansas. His parents were religious people, and two elder brothers had been educated for the ministry. His mother died when he was ten years old, and after a time his father had married a nagging wife who made life too miserable for the sensitive boy to be able to tolerate his home life any longer. When he was fourteen he ran away to the Indian Territory where he found a place on the little ranch on the Cimarron River where Doolin had visited so many times. The boy had learned to admire the bravado qualities of Doolin and he believed he would like to emulate the deeds of his hero. Somehow, outlaw tales when they are told before a glowing fireplace have a fascinating appeal to the young mind. No doubt, Arkansas Tom had heard Doolin and his cohorts relate many thrilling tales in the little ranch house. He was especially excited over Doolin's wild ride following the Daltons' Coffeyville raid, and a few weeks later, when he learned that Doolin was recruiting a gang at the outlaw cave in the Creek Nation, he quickly outfitted himself and hastened to the place, where he begged to be allowed to join the band.

Little Dick West was a homeless waif who had drifted to Texas in his early 'teens. He had been knocked about from pillar to post, washing dishes in greasy restaurants and working for his board as a roustabout with cow outfits. He was a ragged un-

dersized creature and tough as pig-iron. No one knows what was responsible for his peculiar inhibitions against sleeping under a roof.

"I was born on the open prairie and I'll live thar. A house is jist a place to hole up and git cotched fer somethin' ye ain't done."

When he was sixteen the foreman of the Three-Circle Ranch picked him up on the streets of Decatur, Texas, and took him to the ranch in Clay County where he worked until the next spring. Oscar Halsell was just starting north with his herd of cattle and horses and he hired the boy to wrangle the *caballad*.

Halsell located on the south side of the Cimarron, thirteen miles from where Guthrie now stands, and established the HXBar Ranch. Little Dick worked on the ranch for Halsell until the opening of the country in 1889. He was a fairly reliable boy so far as his work was concerned, but wild as a March hare. His peculiar habit of rolling up in his blankets and sleeping when other punchers were seeking warm houses and cozy beds stood him in good stead on several later occasions after he had joined the outlaw band of Bill Doolin. If the officers attacked the rendezvous of the band—Little Dick was never found inside and was always able to make his getaway. On one or two occasions when he did come into conflict with the officers he jumped in the air yowling like a wild cat, with both guns spitting fire. The officers learned to know that he would never be taken alive.

Very little is known regarding Ol Yountis except that he had relatives living in Oklahoma and that he had a rather checkered career.

Photograph of E. D. Nix (1894).

BIERER & BIERER
ATTORNEYS & COUNSELORS AT LAW
GUTHRIE, OKLAHOMA

A G C BIERER   A.G.C.BIERER,JR.

May 15, 1928

Hon. E. D. Nix,
Central National Bank Bldg.,
St. Louis, Missouri.

My dear old friend Nix:

I am exceedingly pleased to know that you are preparing a history of those strenuous days of the early nineties when you were U. S. Marshal and I was Associate Justice of the Supreme Court of Oklahoma.

The run into the Cherokee outlet in September 1893, was the most strenuous contest for free homes in the richest part of the U. S. that America has ever witnessed. It brought about the greatest strive for supremacy that has ever been witnessed outside of the arena.

Your service as U. S. Marshal required not only a fearless executive but a high class of diplomatic conduct because, the human side of the equation, with men of that sterling character who went into and peopled the Cherokee outlet could not be handled by the iron rule without bullets and death, and those situations tried the nerve and ability of your splendid administration, and the deputy U. S. marshals of that high class exhibited by Bill Tilghman, Frank Canton, Frank Lake, Charles Colcord and your own brother, William Nix, all of whom were always faithful in their discharge of duty.

I am glad to assist you in this enterprise.

Yours very truly,

A G C Bierer

AGCB:DH

Shortly after the organization of the Doolin-Dalton gang, and while other members of the gang were arranging their affairs to join the outfit permanently, Bill Doolin, Bill Dalton, "Bitter Creek" Newcomb and Ol Yountis made a foray across the line into Ford County, Kansas, where they robbed a bank at Spearville of several thousand dollars. This occurred in November, 1892.

The outlaws then scattered to confuse the pursuing officers—Dalton riding toward his mother's ranch near Kingfisher, Doolin and Newcomb racing toward the gang's cave in the Creek Nation, and Yountis making his way toward the home of his sister near Orlando, Oklahoma. Yountis, being poorly mounted, made slower progress in his escape and he furnished the trail that led a Kansas sheriff to Oklahoma. As Yountis neared the boundary between the Cherokee strip and Oklahoma, his horse was just about exhausted and, lacking the cold steel nerve of Doolin and the others, he became frantic in his haste to put as much distance as possible between himself and Spearville. His horse had become so weak and was staggering so much that he was forced to dismount and lead the animal.

As he stumbled along foot-sore and weary, he encountered a farmer who was riding a very good horse. The farmer stopped and in a very friendly manner offered to aid the fugitive outlaw, when Yountis demanded that he dismount and exchange horses with him. The man resisted and without further discussion Yountis shot, killing the farmer instantly.

Yountis mounted the dead man's horse and raced

toward his sister's home about fifteen miles away. It was here that he hoped to hide out until all possibility of his being connected with the Spearville robbery had blown over.

The killing of the farmer raised a great deal of indignation in that community, and within a very few hours a posse of neighbors was searching for the killer. At this time Sheriff Beeson of Ford County, Kansas, arrived on the scene and finding the outlaw's exhausted horse, he was convinced that the murder had been committed by one of the Spearville robbers. This event furnished the trail that led the Kansas sheriff to the home of Ol Yountis' sister. Without visiting the place he convinced himself that the outlaw was hiding there and, not having legal authority to make an arrest in the Territory, he proceeded to Guthrie, about thirty miles south, to get the assistance of the United States Marshal's office in an attempt to capture Yountis.

Deputies Chris Madsen, Heck Thomas and Tom Houston accompanied the sheriff—the party being in charge of Madsen. They rode out of Guthrie in the evening, arriving at the farm house near Orlando just before daybreak the following morning. They placed themselves at strategic points surrounding the house, where they would be protected from observation, and waited.

Just as day was breaking a man emerged from the house, a pair of six-shooters buckled about his waist and a Winchester rifle resting in the crock of one arm. The fact that he was so heavily armed and that he moved so furtively convinced the officers that this was the man they were seeking. As he moved toward the barn he walked within a few feet of a stone wall behind which Heck Thomas was concealed. Thomas raised up quickly.

"Throw up your hands! You are under arrest!"

The outlaw replied with a flaming Winchester blazing away at Thomas almost before the last word of the officer's command had been spoken. Thomas ducked quickly and the outlaw's first shot was followed by a rat-a-tat-tat of explosions from his rifle that almost equalled the speed of machine-gun fire. The wild volley of fire aroused the household, and the outlaw's sister ran into the yard screaming hysterically.

"O Ol, run! For God's sake don't shoot him!"

The officers would gladly have taken their man alive but he had no intention of being so taken. Heck Thomas had changed his position behind the stone wall, and he raised to fire at the bandit just as the man's sister ran between them, causing him to hesitate. Yountis was disconcerted by the presence of his sister and his firing was wild. At this moment Chris Madsen stepped from behind a corner of the barn about fifty feet away and fired the shot that felled the outlaw. The terrified sister flung herself on the body of her brother as he lay writhing and clung to him, moaning with pitiful grief. The officers approached and found that Yountis had emptied his Winchester in that brief second or two. Undoubtedly the stone wall saved the life of Heck Thomas. Yountis was too hard hit to offer further resistance, and he was disarmed.

"Too damn bad I didn't get one of you devils before you done for me!" the outlaw said crisply through clenched teeth as he tried to stifle his moans. As he lay there cursing, the officers lifted his sister and gently led her to the house where she was placed in charge of other members of the family.

Realizing the seriousness of the man's condition, the officers transported him to Orlando where he was given medical attention but in spite of all that was done for him he died that night. Concealed in a belt about his waist was found $4500 of the money that had been taken from the Spearville Bank, which was later identified by officers of the bank and was returned to them by order of the court.

*   *   *

The Guthrie boom had ended, and the community had settled down to substantial growth. The town had been selected as the capital of Oklahoma Territory and had become the business center of the new country. Schools and churches had been established and the community life of the people was much the same as of any other complacent American town of that period.

The development of the country as a whole was suffering a great deal from the operations of the bandits who were interrupting the functioning of those two factors so essential to civilized progress— transportation and communication, and were disrupting and demoralizing many communities by their murderous raids upon banks and business institutions. Insurance companies had not entered the Territory and it was not possible to protect one's business and property against the depredations of the outlaws. The situation had become so precarious and destructive that it became imperative that the best manpower of the territory should devote itself to the elimination of the outlaws.

The wholesale grocery business of Nix and Halsell, as well as that of our competitors, was prospering and expanding. I had made a number of trips to the Indian trading points and had succeeded in developing some very nice business for our firm, but general conditions discouraged any attempt on our part to establish a larger sales force that would intensively cultivate the business of the small inland towns in the territory. Such business transactions would involve not only the traveling of the men themselves but the hazards of transporting merchandise and of safely carrying in our collections which, in such transactions, would run into many hundreds of dollars. We often thought we would like to undertake such a campaign of business expansion, but we felt as did the other business men of Guthrie. . . We could not afford to take the chances until the outlaw problem had been solved.

My handling of the affairs of the defunct Commercial Bank had given me many valuable business and political acquaintances. My own business and the affairs of the bank had been administered so satisfactorily that the people seemed to place a great deal of confidence in my executive ability. It seems that my friends had been considering my appointment to the office of United States Marshal long before they had suggested such a thing to me, and I was rather surprised when M. L. Turner, a prominent banker, and two or three other business men came to my office one day to propose the matter to me.

"Nix, the future of Oklahoma Territory is being seriously jeopardized by the numerous outlaw gangs that are operating without restraint," said Turner. "This country needs a man as United States Marshal who understands how to conduct the affairs of that office in a businesslike manner and who is fearless and daring enough to plan the sort of campaign against the law-breakers that will wipe them out. We have decided that you are the man."

While I felt considerably flattered that these men should have entertained such a high opinion of me, I was flustrated at their proposal. It seemed that it would be absolutely impossible for me to consider such a thing. I had my own business to take care of —and I hardly wanted to throw the burden of responsibility upon my partner, Oscar Halsell, as I would have to do to a great extent if I were to accept the duties of United States Marshal.

At this first visit I refused pointblank to consider such a proposition. This group of citizens, however, not to be turned aside, called upon my partner, Halsell, and discussed the matter with him—requesting him to urge my serious consideration of the matter. Oscar Halsell came to me and said that he felt that as citizens we owed as much of our service as we were able to give to the general good of the new country and that if I would consent to apply for the appointment he would do his part by relieving me of a large share of my duties in our wholesale grocery business.

No man ever had a more desirable partner than Oscar Halsell, and his persuasion, together with my absolute confidence in his integrity and his ability to

handle our joint business affairs in a manner that would be entirely satisfactory to me, caused me to tell the committee of citizens that I would accept the appointment if President-elect Cleveland desired to give it to me after his inauguration.

The citizens immediately started getting indorsements from leading business men of Guthrie and the Territory, and accumulated as fine a collection of credentials as any man could hope to have. I then visited Washington, calling on President Cleveland and his Attorney-General to discuss territorial conditions and my application for appointment to United States Marshal. While I was in Washington a heated contention developed regarding the appointment of a territorial governor and I was told that I might have this appointment if I would accept it. The warring factions were willing to compromise upon me. Because a very good friend of mine was a contestant for the place, I refused to become involved in the matter. Immediately following the inauguration of Cleveland my appointment was made and confirmed, notwithstanding that there were forty-two applicants for the same position, some of whom had made strenuous efforts and used a great deal of influence to get it. At the age of thirty-two, I was the youngest man who had ever been appointed to such a position up to that time.

I little realized just how strenuous a life I was to live for the next few years, nor how gruesome a trail of blood my organization would be forced to leave behind in its battle to exterminate the outlaws and establish law and order.

CHAPTER VI
BUILDING A FIGHTING ORGANIZATION

I was a very young man to have accepted such a responsible office, and during the first few months my own consciousness of its seriousness and magnitude made me feel that a heavy load had been placed upon my shoulders. Although I came of a family that for several generations served the people in official capacities, I was entirely without experience or training for the job that was before me. Perhaps this was a good thing; for, instead of approaching a task as an experienced man of that period might have done, I sat down in my office and analyzed its problems as I would have done with any business proposition.

I realized that first I must perfect an organiza-

tion of the sort of men whose characters were above reproach, whose judgment would be of a sort that would never compromise the dignity or prestige of the United States Government and whose cool daring and bravery would surpass that of the men they would be sent out to defeat. Supplementing this field staff, I must have an office force that would be able to handle the records of the office and to meet the public in the same gracious manner that we had always used in our other business.

During my visit in Washington I had a conference with the Department of Justice officials and had pretty thoroughly informed myself as to what would be expected of me in Washington, and as to the manner in which the routine of my office should be handled. The department agreed with me heartily that I should have a force entirely adequate in number to handle the very serious outlaw situation. I was told to use my own judgment and to build my organization to whatever size I deemed proper. When I intimated that I would probably need one hundred and fifty field men, not a word was said in opposition, although this was more than double the number of deputies ever allowed a United States Marshal in the history of the United States.

In addition to ridding Oklahoma of bandits, it was to be my duty to find proper quarters for United States courts that would be established in the territory, to equip them, and to provide adequate protection for their functioning. I was also expected to curb the destruction of government timbers, and the operation of whiskey peddlers on the Indian reservations and to protect Indian lands from invasion.

One of my first acts was to appoint John M. Hale as my chief deputy. Hale had had considerable experience as an Indian trader in the Osage Nation. Although he was even younger than myself, I knew him to be a man of honorable principles and unquestionable bravery. A Virginian by birth, he possessed an equilibrium and a depth of character that made him an ideal choice for the duties to which he was appointed. After he had established himself in his position he was soon rated by the Department of Justice at Washington as one of the most capable chief deputies in the service. He had been in the Territory a considerable time and I placed a high estimate on his ability.

My father, S. S. Nix, had joined me some months before and, because his business qualifications and experience as an officer in Kentucky seemed to better qualify him for the duties of chief clerk than any other man who was then available in the Territory, I immediately appointed him to this position. Our deep mutual affection made me realize that no other man would take so sincere an interest in assisting me, and I was glad that I was able to add my father to my organization.

W. S. Felts, a young man of exceptional ability as an accountant, was taken from one of the Guthrie banks and was made cashier and head of the accounting department.

Hale had as an assistant a very versatile young man named Sam T. Wisby—and J. K. McGoodwin was made assistant chief clerk. These, together with two stenographers, comprised my office force.

We then approached the most serious matter of

selecting a properly qualified staff of field deputies. Upon these fellows would hinge the failure or success of our efforts. I hope I do not seem to reflect upon modern officers when I say that I did not follow that old adage: "It takes a thief to catch a thief," although I have known of a good many officers who have proceeded upon this theory in the selection of their assisting force. First, although I had never been an extremist, I concluded that I would permit no man to hold a position on my field force if ever, under any circumstances, he used intoxicating liquors to excess. I considered nothing more dangerous to the public than to give a man authority to carry a pair of forty-five six-shooters and a Winchester and allow him to drink whiskey to excess. Personally, I did not use it at all. I don't care to pose as a moralist, nor do I look with favor upon hysterical crusades that pretend to have the public good for a goal but which, in many instances, are nothing more or less than vehicles for private exploitation and gain.

With the assistance of friends who were familiar with all parts of the territory under my jurisdiction, we compiled a considerable list of eligible men and began the task of sifting it carefully and choosing the organization that was to play a most important part in Oklahoma's march of progress. Our judgment must have been fairly good, for practically every one of my leading deputies later became successful and prominent in Oklahoma politics or business. While a great deal of the glory that follows accomplishment seemed to be concentrated upon a few of my best known deputies, I had a large num-

ber of others who were just as efficient in their work and who discharged every duty with honor to themselves. I might, say, incidentally, that out of about fifty thousand prisoners committed to the United States jail at Guthrie during my term of office, with possibly ten thousand more giving bond, it is not hard to see that there was plenty of work for the entire staff. Bill Tilghman, John Hixon, Chris Madsen, Frank Canton, Heck Thomas, C. F. Colcord, Forrest Halsell, Ed Kelly, Frank Rinehart, Jim Masterson (brother of the celebrated Bat Masterson), W. E. (Pat) Murphy, George Starmer, Frank Lake, John Hubatka, Jack Love, Gus Hadwinger, E. W. Snoddy, F. W. Langly, W. A. Ramsey, Steve Burke, Joe Severns, W. M. Nix, W. O. Jones, Frank Cochrane and Sam Bartell were just a few of the men who did outstanding work during my administration. The fact that I mention these by name does not imply that there were not many more of the hundred and fifty men who served under me who deserved to be lauded for their efforts. I wish space were available to name every man of them and to relate specifically their deeds and to let the reader know just how much I appreciate the important part they played in the success of our work.

I felt especially fortunate in getting such men as Tilghman, Hixon, Thomas, Madsen and Canton to head my campaign against the outlaws. Every one of these men had had a broad experience that equipped him for this job. Tilghman had been scout, Indian fighter, buffalo hunter and peace officer, and he was always a frontiersman as long as there was a frontier.

He was born at Fort Dodge, Iowa, in 1854, and his parents moved to Kansas in 1856. When he was sixteen years old he left home and went to southwest Kansas, which was then a wild, hazardous frontier. He was a government scout during the Cheyenne-Arapahoe Indian War in 1874 and fought through the campaign of 1878 when Dull Knife and his followers escaped from the reservation at Fort Sill, where they had been held captive by the government following the Custer massacre at Little Big Horn in 1876. The Dull Knife band had pillaged and plundered its way through the northwestern Cherokee Strip, Kansas and Nebraska, on the way back to the hunting ground of their fathers in the Montana country. Tilghman's home and all of his possessions were burned or carried off by the marauders.

Tilghman was at Dodge City when the town was first surveyed and he saw it grow into the wildest of all frontier towns. He was Marshal of Dodge City during three years of its bloodiest history and established there a reputation for fearlessness that remained with him all his life. While here he became the intimate friend of the famous Bat Masterson and of Bill Hickock. The three spent many hours in an inclosed lot back of a notorious saloon practicing with the pistols, and contesting against each other for high records on difficult marks. Tilghman became as good a pistol and rifle shot as the West ever knew. He was under-sheriff of Ford County, Kansas, and during that time captured some of the worst desperados of the Southwest. He came to Oklahoma in the run of April, 1889, and remained to carve a niche for himself in the State's Hall of Fame.

Tilghman was one of the handsomest men I ever knew—six feet tall, he weighed about one hundred and eighty pounds, and every ounce of it was sinuous muscle. His kind blue eyes and his open countenance reflected good will and friendliness to all he met. I have never known a man who regarded his enemies more kindly than did Bill Tilghman—and I have never known a man who fought his enemies more bitterly or more effectively than did Bill Tilghman when circumstances demanded it. Looking into his soft blue eyes, it was very hard to believe that the same eyes had looked down the barrels of flaming six-guns and rifles and dealt death to a great many men. During his service as my deputy, more rewards were paid to him for captures than were ever paid to any officer in the same period of time in the history of the United States.

Tilghman had a most casual, dry manner of relating an experience. He was a natural story-teller, and he had a knack for developing dramatic climaxes, then abruptly halting—leaving his listeners to form their own conclusions. If they pressed him he usually supplied the missing information with just a word or two so aptly chosen that his story was vividly completed. I remember his tale of an experience he had on a buffalo hunt.

"A young fellow named Tom Scott and I had gone down into the Cherokee strip to kill a few buffalo. The father of this young fellow Scott had been killed by Indians some time before, and Tom had sworn that he would kill an Indian to avenge his father's murder. We hadn't been out more than three or four days when we camped one night in a

little draw, hobbling our horses and turning them loose to graze. The place was so well protected that I reckon we must have been a little careless about our guns, for we went to sleep leaving our Winchesters standing against a tree nearby and our six-shooters thrown over our saddle horns near our heads.

"When we woke up next morning our horses and guns were gone, and there were moccasin tracks all around our little camp. We sure had slept well that night. It was a long walk back to Dodge City but I figured the quicker we got there the safer our scalps would be. So we hit the open prairie in a bee-line for civilization.

"We hadn't walked more than two or three miles before I noticed a couple of Indian bucks mounted on spotted ponies, watching us from a short distance away. I was pretty much scared for we had nothing on us but our knives and I could see they had rifles. They kept circling until finally I told Tom we had better stop and wait to see what they were going to do.

"As we stood still watching them they rode toward us. About forty feet or so off one of the bucks, who was riding the prettiest spotted pony I ever saw, asked me in sign language who we were and where we were going. Thinking they might belong to the gang who had stolen our horses, I decided we had better stall and tell them we were looking for some stray mules. The son-of-a-gun insisted that he knew right where our mules were, and that if we would follow them into camp he would see that we got them back. The situation was looking pretty precarious

Guthrie, April 27, 1889. See gambling groups.

Guthrie, Oklahoma, April 27, 1889.   See groups at gambling games.

to me—but there didn't seem to be anything to do but to follow the bucks into camp.

"Meanwhile, I sure was admiring that good-looking spotted pony and wishing that I had him between my knees, Dodge City bound. Scott was pretty well scared, but the little son-of-a-gun had a lot more nerve than most tenderfeet I'd ever known. Pretty soon we came to a stream that was too deep to wade and, after looking us over good and discussing the matter some, the bucks decided to let us get up behind them and ride over, and I whispered to Scott and told him—'Now is your chance—use your knife!—while we rode on out into the water, each one of us fingering his buffalo skinning knife. . . .

"You know, Marshall, that was as good a spotted pony as I ever rode. . . . I got twenty-five dollars for him in Dodge City . . . . that was a big price in those days."

"But Bill," I exclaimed excitedly, "what became of the Indians?"

Bill looked me over for a second before he replied in a drawling voice: "Oh, the Indians! . . . . why, when I turned around and looked downstream I saw them bucks floating off with the current."

He told me another experience he had with a noted gambler at Dodge City when he was marshal there. It seemed that there had been a fight in a gambling house, and this gambler had shot a boy who was standing near. The bullet had lodged in the boy's spine, leaving him paralyzed. In order to help the young fellow who was destitute, Tilghman used his influence in settling the case by having the gambler pay the boy eight thousand dollars, which

he seemed very glad to do, and he professed a great deal of gratitude to Tilghman for helping him to settle the matter out of court. Let Bill tell the rest of it:

"A few days later I was walking down the street and as I passed an alley I noticed this gambler slipping around behind a stack of boxes . . . and about that time he took a pot-shot at me. . . . I thought that was a peculiar way for him to be showing his gratitude."

I waited for a moment for Tilghman to complete his story—then I asked impatiently: "Bill, what happened to the gambler?"

Bill looked at me slowly for a moment, then said as he turned away: "Oh, the gambler! . . . A coroner's jury said it was justifiable homicide."

* * *

Chris Madsen was the most cosmopolitan of all of Oklahoma's pioneer officers. He was born in Denmark and served a term in the Danish army and later in the Franco-Prussian war. He then went to Algiers as a member of the notorious Foreign Legion where, after a time, he heard news of the Indian wars in America that appealed so strongly to his adventurous spirit that, in the year 1870, he set out for the shores of the new country, going west immediately upon his arrival. He served for some time as a scout and also gained considerable knowledge of the ways of the West while hunting buffalo. In 1875 he joined the United States Army and was soon made Quartermaster Sergeant of the Fifth Cavalry. Later he had charge of the Indian scouts in Wyoming and in the Indian Territory. He participated in the Indian campaigns in Arizona and against the Sioux and Cheyennes in Wyoming, Nebraska, Dakota and Montana. In 1877 he had a part in the campaign against Nez Perces in Idaho and Utah—fighting on down through the conflicts with the Southern Cheyennes, the Bannocks and the Utes. When President Arthur made his trip to Yellowstone Park in 1883, Madsen served as his personal guard on the trip from Ft. Washakie, Wyoming, to Yellowstone. In 1889 he settled on a homestead near El Reno, Oklahoma, and attempted to establish himself as a farmer. That life was entirely too tame for him, however, and he soon accepted a commission as Deputy United States Marshal under Marshal William Grimes. I considered it my very good fortune to be able to enlist the aid of so experienced and brave a man as Chris Madsen. Notwithstanding that he and I differed in politics, he became one of my staunchest friends and one of my most dependable deputies. No man ever stood higher in my estimation and I rejoice in the fact that his old age finds him virile and active and that he is still able to render valuable service to the United States Courts at Guthrie and Oklahoma City.

Captain Heck Thomas, the third of the three—Tilghman, Madsen and Thomas—who were to become widely known as the Three Guardsmen, was a Georgian and a man of such breeding that he was a polished gentleman even under the most strenuous of circumstances. At the age of twelve he had served as a courier in the Thomas Division of the Stonewall Jackson Brigade. Following the Civil War, and while still a very young man, he migrated

to Texas and, in spite of his youth, soon received an appointment as a member of the Texas Ranger forces. His undaunted nerve and his keen judgment soon established him as a man to be feared by law-breakers. At one time he was highly commended and paid a reward of five thousand dollars by the governor of Texas for the single-handed capture of two desperate outlaws—the Lee brothers. Governor Ireland declared that this feat was one of the most remarkable in the entire history of the ranger forces —and it established Heck Thomas as an outstanding law-enforcement officer. He was later induced to accept an appointment under Judge Parker of Fort Smith, Arkansas, who presided over the most famous criminal court the United States has ever known.

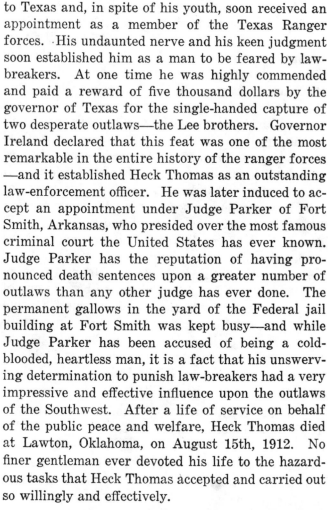

Judge Parker has the reputation of having pronounced death sentences upon a greater number of outlaws than any other judge has ever done. The permanent gallows in the yard of the Federal jail building at Fort Smith was kept busy—and while Judge Parker has been accused of being a cold-blooded, heartless man, it is a fact that his unswerving determination to punish law-breakers had a very impressive and effective influence upon the outlaws of the Southwest. After a life of service on behalf of the public peace and welfare, Heck Thomas died at Lawton, Oklahoma, on August 15th, 1912. No finer gentleman ever devoted his life to the hazardous tasks that Heck Thomas accepted and carried out so willingly and effectively.

Frank Canton established a reputation as a fearless officer that gave him an honored place in the regard of Oklahoma citizens. Four governors have honored him with appointments as Adjutant General.

John Hixon was selected because of the extraordinary experience he had as a pioneer officer on the Kansas frontier, and later in early Oklahoma. Although he was one of my opponents for the appointment as United States Marshal and he and his friends waged an energetic campaign for the position, I held him in the highest respect and was only too glad to be able to add him to my staff. He proved to be a valuable officer and a true friend.

Bud Ledbetter was a deputy under Morton Rutherford, the United States Marshal in charge of the eastern Indian Territory district, with headquarters at Muskogee. Because of the man's fearless qualities and his splendid interest in the things our district had set out to accomplish, I deemed it wise to give him a special commission with full authority to represent my office in any emergency that might arise. Ledbetter is one of the few old-timers still living; he is sheriff of Muskogee County and one of the oldest officers of the Southwest. He has met many of the bad men of his day face to face with six-guns spitting fire—and has always come out victorious. His deeds as United States Marshal have always reflected honor and credit to his office.

Charles F. Colcord, a Kentuckian by birth, was a frontiersman who had passed through several precarious years. He was thoroughly seasoned to the arduous demands our work would make upon him. He was also one of my opponents for the appointment and he would have made a splendid Marshal. I was only too glad to have him accept the appoint-

ment as deputy in charge at Oklahoma City. He later had an important part in the development of Oklahoma City, and is today one of that city's highly respected and wealthy citizens.

J. S. (Steve) Burke had been in the insurance business in Guthrie for some time, and a combination of circumstances had caused this young fellow to become discouraged and morose. I appreciated the splendid qualities of the chap, and had attempted in numerous ways to assist him in getting back on his feet and away from some of the bad company he had been associating with. When the time came to appoint my deputies, I gave careful consideration to Steve Burke and decided to give him an opportunity to prove his merit as a member of my staff. I am glad to say that I was not disappointed. While this narrative will only relate one or two of Burke's personal encounters with outlaws—particularly his part in the capture of the two girl bandits—his daring exploits were many and he had a number of hand-to-hand conflicts with desperadoes. In spite of Burke's exceptional bravery and his willingness to swap hot lead with a law-breaker when it seemed necessary, the man had a heart big enough to encompass and understand all the woes of sinful mankind, and he often grieved over the strange fate that had distorted the minds and characters of men who had splendid qualities but who were peculiarly led into the mesh of the bandit gangs. When my term expired, Burke took up evangelistic work and made a great success. He very often told his congregations a very frank story of his early dissipations and of the influence my friendly help had upon the shaping of his later life. His intimate knowledge of the ways of crooks and outlaws made him a most interesting and convincing talker and, just a few years ago, he died as he would have chosen to die . . . . while standing on a platform addressing a large religious gathering at Paris, Texas.

It would be possible to tell interesting things of the lives of all of my deputies—but I feel that I must be getting on with my story and that I must forego the personal pleasure I would have in recalling intimate details concerning all of these old friends.

Immediately upon the selection of my staff of deputies, I called them together at Guthrie where we held a three-day conference, establishing our policies and laying our plans for a campaign against the outlaws. I looked upon the group of men I had gathered about me as an organization of business men with a very definite obligation to deal fairly and honorably with everyone—citizen or outlaw— who was to come in contact with our department. In addition to laying down some very iron-clad rules as to the personal conduct of the men, we discussed and decided upon the policies we would always follow in our dealings with criminals. I urged the men, for their own good, to never forget that in many cases they would would be going up against some of the wildest characters of the frontier country and to always make sure that they safeguarded their own lives and the lives of respectable citizens. These things were to come first, although they were also asked to remember that even outlaws are human. We must always give the other fellow the benefit of the doubt and extend him a helping hand if he

seemed disposed to accept our good graces. I considered lack of courtesy and gentlemanly bearing a very serious offense. In my opinion, the man with a smile was more to be feared when it came to a test of real nerve than the would-be man-eater. I gave them positive instructions as to what I considered to be just and right in protecting themselves in their dealings with known bandits and, while I was very emphatic in urging them to use their guns quickly upon the slightest provocation, I ordered that they make every effort to avoid shooting a person charged with a minor crime—even though he should try to make his escape. I am pleased to say that during my administration not a single man was killed who was not a notorious lawbreaker. I wanted my men

to have the drop on the other fellow before they commanded him to hold up his hands and consider himself under arrest, because this order was invariably disregarded by the bad men, provoking a lightning attempt to murder the officer. I wanted to make sure my men should shoot first. In all of my dealings with some of the worst desperados the world has ever known, I know of but few who have ever submitted to arrest without a gun fight.

My officers were especially urged to thoroughly examine their prisoners for fire-arms and other weapons. When a man is charged with a crime against

the United States government—even though it be a minor one—he is apt to consider it a serious matter and to become very much excited upon his arrest. Such men, under the spell of fear, should be watched very carefully, as an overlooked gun or knife has caused the death of many an officer who failed to properly disarm his prisoner. I was especially emphatic in my instructions that under no circumstances should third degree methods be used in extracting confessions or other information from our prisoners. Never once during the period of my administration did I fail to comply with the request of a prisoner who wished to talk to me, and by kind treatment I got a great deal more valuable information from these unfortunate men than any third degree could extract. There is a tendency to regard the average prisoner as a person devoid of finer sensibilities and of character. Many of the men who passed through my charge during this period proved to be admirable characters who might have succeeded in many respectable walks of life.

I think it remarkable that my force of deputies was able to handle a total of approximately sixty thousand prisoners, many of them gun-men of the wickedest type, with a loss of but five officers. Throughout my term of office I communicated regularly each week with every deputy on my staff, informing them of all our office had learned that might increase the effectiveness of their work.

Charged with the seriousness of their responsibilities and with an unfaltering determination to rid Oklahoma and the Cherokee Strip of its bandit gangs, my men dispersed to their assigned positions to take up the campaign.

CHAPTER VII

A NEW EMPIRE IS FOUNDED

While I was very busy effecting my new organization the outlaw depredations seemed to have lulled temporarily. Bill Doolin and a few members of his gang did slip over the line to Cimarron, Kansas, and rob a bank there, securing about thirteen thousand dollars in cash and some other valuables. They fled back to their redezvous in the territory—a place so well concealed that it served them to advantage during many weary months of futile search for them by officers.

Their cave was large enough to hide at least twenty-five horses and to shelter from twenty-five to fifty men; it was a very comfortable place—cool in the summer and warm in the winter.

By this time the gang had been joined by Charlie Pierce, Jack Blake (alias Tulsa Jack) and Dan Clifton (alias Dynamite Dick), former cowboys who, because of their daring, became formidable additions to the band.

Somehow the news that the United States Marshal had organized a young army consisting of a hundred and fifty brave deputies caused the outlaw bands to lay low for a while, for which I was very thankful, because the government had just placed a great deal of responsibility upon my office by putting us in charge of the opening of the Cherokee Strip to settlement, which would occur on the 16th day of September following my appointment in May, 1893.

It would be hard for mere words to describe the circumstances and conditions that contributed to the great magnitude of the preliminary planning that must be done in order that the run for claims might be held under perfect control and rendered as peaceful and amicable as possible. The Cherokee Strip consisted of 5,698,140 acres of what has proved to be the richest land ever offered by the United States government to ambitious and enterprising settlers. According to the government survey there would be 35,613 claims, and it was estimated that there would be half a million people registered and lined up about the borders of the Strip to contest for these claims. My part in this great undertaking is one of my most gratifying recollections since I was able to see and have a part in the passing of the last wild, romantic frontier.

The peculiar thrill of the rough life and indomitable courage and desperate deeds of many thousands of people, all animated by that strange indescribable inner urge that causes men and women to leave happy homes in civilized settlements to undertake the arduous task of taming a wild country and bringing its resources under the control of their minds and hands, kept my interest aflame.

I wish that I might write the proper eulogy for these brave pioneer men and women. I am very glad that one of Oklahoma's leading oil magnates of today has given his thought and resources to the erection of a monument to Oklahoma's pioneer women. As long as such men as E. W. Marland—a typical American business leader—can pause in their busy lives to give grateful thought to those who, with their lives and blood, laid the foundation for our modern civilization, we need not fear that the ideals and the altruism of American business have been lost in the mad rush for money.

My close contact with pioneer life, with the hardships endured by women and children, housed in crowded dugouts and rough shanties, perhaps gave me a deeper appreciation for the part these pioneer women had in the opening and development of our country.

I appointed one thousand special deputies to assist in the orderly handling of the tremendous crowds that would surge to the boundary lines of the Strip to await with breathless impatience the signal that would release them and send them seething and fighting toward the land they aspired to own. My men were to patrol the entire boundary between Old Oklahoma and the Cherokee Strip. Immediately upon the opening, we were to take charge of the entire newly-opened area, including all new town-sites. Hence the necessity for this large force of men.

While the details of planning this immense affair were being wound up, Bill Doolin and his gang, during the month of August, broke their two or three months of quietude when they rode wildly into the little town of Wharton (later named Perry) a few minutes before the arrival of a Santa Fe south-bound night train. By this time they were so well organized and they had developed so perfect a routine for the handling of crews and passengers during a train robbery that within fifteen minutes they were riding off toward the Osage Hills with several hundreds of dollars in money, a considerable lot of registered mail and with the money and valuables of the surprised passengers. Their haul in cash from the express car would have been much greater had they chosen to rob one of the day trains, for by this time the express company was making its larger shipments during daylight and under heavy guard.

Following the robbery the gang flew quickly to its cave in the Creek Nation, and my own force was too busy with the affairs of the Cherokee Strip opening to be able to give a very hot pursuit. We were impatient for the opening to be over, for we could then concentrate our thought on the round-up of these outlaw gangs. The Wharton robbery was flaunted in our faces as if Bill Doolin were attempting to ridicule the new marshal and his "little army." Naturally, it did not please us very much—but our hands were temporarily tied.

As the sixteenth of September drew near, I completed the organization of the special deputies we had employed, and assigned them to their positions along the border between the Cherokee Strip and old Oklahoma—the entire length of which was to be patrolled by my men. For a week before the opening the crowds poured in from all over the United States and it was with a great deal of difficulty that they were restrained from breaking over

the lines and going in to take the choice land before
the appointed time.

Some few did manage to break through the lines
and to conceal themselves on choice claims. Several
killings grew out of the efforts of these Sooners to
take advantage of the more honorable contestants.
I remember that one of my deputies reported shortly
after the run had taken place that he had found one
man occupying a claim that he could not possibly
have reached in the short time that had elapsed
since the signal had been fired for the run.   The
deputy prowled about the little camp, looking for
evidence that might prove the man to be a Sooner.

"Look at that hoss over yonder," the suspected
man exclaimed.   "Cain't you see he's been through
the mill?"

The deputy walked over to where the horse stood
covered with lather.

"He don't seem to be pantin' much," the deputy
remarked as he touched a finger to the horse's neck.
The officer then touched the tip of his tongue with
his finger. The horse had been lathered with laun-
dry soap!

Needless to say, this Sooner was led away from
the claim he had staked and it was soon occupied by
a family that had actually made the run.

There were men mounted on fine race horses,
carefully grooming their animals for the run; there
were families in substantial wagons drawn by sleek,
fat horses and mules; there were poor souls, their
dilapidated wagons crammed with dirty children and
drawn by starved beasts that were poorly fitted to
contest against the strong men and animals who

would take the lead; there were penniless drifters, afoot, and there were carts, buggies and wagons so dilapidated that one expected them to fall apart at any moment like the Deacon's One-Hoss Shay. One's heart went out to some of the poverty-stricken families who had been buffed by a cruel fate for years before, accomplishing nothing and accumulating nothing, who had come to this border with the gleam of hope in their eyes, believing that at last their fortunes were to take a turn and they were to be able to fasten themselves to something of tangible material value upon which they might base their fortunes. All were optimistic, but the greatest optimists were those poor devils who hadn't a ghost of

a chance to prevail against the mighty hordes of strong men, but who, in spite of all this, were giving their best to the attempt. There were old men and women who should have been comfortably resting in civilized communities, free from the cares of earning a livelihood. Many of them were penniless, with wasted years behind them, and they were here to make a last attempt to accomplish and accumulate something for themselves. Failure for these poor old souls meant the blasting of the last spark of hope they had and their absolute dependence during their remaining years upon the alms of more fortunate people. One's heart ached for them as they waited

in their broken-down carriages and wagons, old fellows here and there bluffly pretending that they were not afraid to enter any sort of contest with youth, when one knew that they were already half afraid and half defeated by the many failures they had known. Somehow, civilization is a remorseless

Building of Half & Half Acre under U.S. Protection, May 26.

Guthrie, Oklahoma, May 26, 1889. On account of many contests building was under protection of the Government.

Guthrie, Oklahoma, June 3, 1889.

thing and the wheels of progress were not mindful of the lives they ground into the dust of the trail during this great Southwest-ward movement.

In spite of all our efforts to weed them out, the vast crowds contained hundreds of thieves and thugs whose only motives were to attempt by various means to rob the home-seekers of the limited money and valuable property they were carrying into the Strip with them. Then there was the gambling and whiskey selling element that would have succeeded in frustrating all of our plans for peace if my men had not been eternally vigilant in forestalling the plots of these human leeches.

Knowing that the first two or three days following the opening would see many serious disputes over the possession of claims and town lots, and realizing how this sullen, ill feeling would be irritated and amplified by liquor, I personally visited the representatives of prominent breweries who had planned to have their saloon open and going in Perry and in the other towns on the first day. I reasoned with the brewery representatives, pointing out how extremely hazardous it would be to open their joints before the people were amicably settled, and telling them very definitely and frankly that I would confiscate all of the shipments they sent in to the restricted territory before their licenses and permits had been officially granted. I must say that they fell into the spirit of the thing very splendidly, and that I had no trouble whatever with them. I feel the fact that liquor was not easily obtainable during the first few days was responsible for the peace and order that prevailed in the new territory.

Arrangements had been made with the railroad companies to run special trains into the Cherokee Strip bearing homeseekers. I took personal charge of the loading of the trains at Orlando near the border line between old Oklahoma and the Cherokee Strip. The Santa Fe had provided three special trains, each engine coupled to a line of coaches almost a mile long. These three trains were placed in such a way that none but myself knew the order in which they would pull out from the town. I gave the train crews special instructions to move very slowly in order that the people entering the Strip by rail might not have an unfair advantage over the claim-seekers who were traveling afoot, horseback or in wagons and carriages.

The immense crowd at Orlando was loaded in a most orderly manner. I think the knowledge that more than a thousand deputy United States marshals were guarding the southern border had a psychological effect that kept our hordes in a congenial and harmonious state of mind.

It was anticipated that Perry, formerly Wharton, would become the most important town on the Santa Fe Railroad in the new territory, and everyone was anxious to get to Perry as quickly as possible to stake town lots.

While I was very busy supervising the loading of the trains, my attention was called to a young man on crutches who stood back as if afraid to enter the press of the crowds and fight his way to the train. I decided that the young man would never succeed in finding a place on the crowded cars and I determined to help him. I touched him on the

shoulder—"Young man, come with me—I'll take care of you," I said—and I took him down to the engineer of the first train going out and requested that he be allowed to ride in the cab of the engine, although positive instructions had been given that no one would be allowed to ride on the cow-catcher or any part of the engine; thus this young man was the first, excepting the fireman and engineer, to reach the heart of the Cherokee Strip and the town-site of Perry by train.

He was representing a group of daily newspapers and my assistance enabled him to get a splendid first-hand story of the opening of the Cherokee Strip. I met the young man a day or two later in Perry and he introduced himself as Edward Hooker and expressed his sincere gratitude. It is a queer coincidence that more than thirty years later, after I had established my home in St. Louis, my son should become associated with him in a large advertising agency.

I started the first two trains from Orlando, and rode into the Strip on the last car of the last train. Dozens of men and boys clung to the sides and tops of the coaches like flies. Occasionally one would jump or roll off, or someone would rush out of the coach and jump to the ground to begin a search for the government's survey stakes that marked the corners of 160-acre homesteads. As I stood upon the platform of that railroad coach and looked out over the vast prairies, I viewed a picture so stupendously breath-taking that its vivid details will never leave my memory. In each direction as far as I could see was a sea of surging humanity, struggling, fighting,

racing toward the homesteads they hoped to acquire.
Many hundreds of them were doomed to disappointment—and quite naturally these disappointments led
to conflicts that caused a great deal of bloodshed.

As our trains pulled into Perry and our passengers fought their way out through the doors and
windows of the coaches, we found that approximately 35,000 people had concentrated in this little
settlement within the brief period of two or three
hours.   Men, women and children were rushing
about excitedly — families separated.   There were
but six thousand town lots available in Perry and
half a dozen claimants were clamoring for each one.

"Did you get a lot, Bill?"

"Hell, no! . . . I staked one, then found three
other buzzards already had it staked. . . . Too many
people here . . . not enough lots to go around."

As I walked toward the center of the town I
found two young men whom I had known in Guthrie
who were about to shoot each other in a dispute over
a lot.   I immediately disarmed them and impressed
upon them that the value of the lot could not be
compared with the value of their lives.   One of them
suggested that they allow me to arbitrate the matter
of their claims, and they agreed to leave the matter
to me.   Each of them placed his stake on the dis-
puted lot and I promised that I would look into it
some time during the afternoon as soon as the crowd
had adjusted itself and things were moving a little
more smoothly.

I placed Bill Tilghman and Forrest Halsell in
charge of the peace officers at the land office which
was being swamped by the rush of people who

wanted to be the first to file on their claims. Other competent officers had been placed at the offices in other towns in the Strip and every effort was made to handle the problem as systematically as possible and with absolute fairness. Hundreds of disputes made the tasks of the land office recorders most disagreeable and perplexing, and it took great vigilance on the part of peace officers in charge to keep down bloodshed.

A few hours later when I found time to investigate the claims of the two young combatants, it was discovered that their lot lay in the middle of the street! This fact automatically cancelled both of their claims and they departed arm in arm, good friends.

When one considers that the government had staked out six thousand lots in Perry and that there were more than thirty-five thousand people contesting for possession of these lots, I think it most remarkable that the day should have passed without bloodshed. There was not one killing at Perry, and there were few disturbances resulting in so much as a fist-fight. Officers were mingling with the crowd constantly, admonishing one here and there and attempting to establish a friendly, congenial atmosphere that would cause everyone to enter into the spirit of the occasion and contribute to the maintenance of order.

The other communities on the Santa Fe and Rock Island Railroads that were under the charge of my deputies were just as peaceful, and I am happy to say that while a great many murders were committed on this day in various parts of the Cherokee

Strip, not one occurred in the towns my force was patrolling.

In the establishing of law and order in the new territory, one of the first essentials was the organizing of the United States Courts. Two very able Oklahoma barristers and judges were placed in charge of the Cherokee Strip—Judge A. G. C. Bierer was given the eastern half with headquarters on the Santa Fe Railroad at Perry, and Judge John L. McAtee was put over the western half with headquarters at Enid on the Rock Island. Judge Bierer appointed my brother, W. M. Nix, as assistant clerk of his court, where he served until I later appointed him managing deputy of the Perry district.

With the opening of the Strip, it was necessary to reassign members of my force, and I placed Jack Love in charge at Woodward, Gus Hadwinger and E. W. Snoddy at Alva, W. A. Pat Murphy at Pond Creek and W. A. Ramsey at Kingfisher. These men worked in close cooperation with the Federal judges and United States attorneys in their districts, giving proper attention to the service of papers, the accumulation of evidence and the maintenance of order in the courts. A number of field deputies were assigned to work with them in the remote parts of the district.

Many of the bandit gangs had become so well known in Oklahoma that they had moved into the Cherokee Strip, believing that they would be able to operate with more freedom among the new settlers, who were not acquainted with them. By this time judicial and business affairs of the Cherokee Strip had settled down to a very peaceable and satisfactory routine, and my staff was able to concentrate its thought and effort upon the campaign against the outlaws.

Following the robbery at Perry (or Wharton), Bill Doolin's men had gone into hiding for a very short time. When we next heard of them they had robbed a bank at Southwest City, Missouri, where they secured fifteen thousand dollars. In a hot fight with citizens they killed former State Auditor Seaborn and were successful in making their get-away. Bill Doolin was shot in a foot but his injury was too slight to cause any delay in the gang's dash back through the territory. They rode swiftly on their way, swooping down upon the little town of Pawnee on a sunny fall day during the noon-time quietude, and holding up a bank. They made a quick get-away with about ten thousand dollars in cash.

Immediately following the Pawnee robbery we received information in Guthrie that they planned dashing into our town and pulling off a bank robbery before the new marshal and his deputies would have time to realize that they were there. We made special preparation to receive them but for some reason they did not show up.

From here they fled to Texas, and within a short time we received information that they had robbed a bank in the northwestern part of the State, securing the considerable sum of fifty thousand dollars.

Bill Doolin, during this period, was conducting his exploits in a very spectacular manner—flitting from one crime to another and disappearing so successfully and entirely following each hold-up that no trace was found of him until the gang bobbed up in a new place and executed a new robbery. I think he believed that such whirlwind methods were confusing the new marshal and his "little army"—as he loved to style my force of deputies.

CHAPTER VIII
THE FIGHT AT INGALLS

It would be hard to find a better setting for the hilarities of outlaws than the little town of Ingalls provided. Situated in the edge of the Creek Nation away from railroads and beaten trails, Ingalls was so remotely located as to cause the occasional traveller to wonder why the town had ever been established in the first place. The ruins of the deserted town stand today, and it is still possible for the curious investigator to dig bits of battered lead from the rotten wood of the dilapidated buildings. Weeds stand waist high in the streets. The old Trilby saloon is perhaps the best preserved building now standing there, and one can step inside its ramshackle walls and find signs that will help him visualize the gun battles that have taken place there.

In the heyday of Bill Doolin's career, Ingalls was a sort of pop-off valve for him and his men. They might have to travel stealthily and avoid the community settlements in the interims between their spectacular hold-ups, but here they could blow the lid off;—they owned the town, figuratively, and when Bill Doolin's outlaw band marched into Ingalls every joy-making device was set going full speed.

The notorious cave of the band was located not far from Ingalls. It was during an attempt to trail the band to this rendezvous that one of our scouts learned of their frequent visits to the little town. Mary Pierce operated a hotel in a crude two-story building, and spent her days planning new diversions

103

for the men who were fattening her bank roll. There were always three or four ladies of joy on the premises. The proprietor of the Trilby saloon contributed his bit to the periodic festivities of the outlaws and, taken as a whole, Ingalls was a happy-go-lucky village. So little legitimate business was transacted here that the residents of the community had practically no contact with the sort of people who might have informed the officers of the presence of the outlaws here.

Finally, however, we got word that the Doolin gang was spending three or four nights a week in Ingalls and we organized a posse to investigate. Bill Tilghman had planned to lead the group of officers, but he had broken an ankle and was confined to his home in Guthrie. John Hixon was placed in charge of the expedition and Lafe Shadley, Tom Houston, Dick Speed and Jim Masterson (a brother of the noted Bat Masterson) were assigned to accompany him. A number of other possemen were selected and deputized and, outfitted with supplies to last several weeks, this heavily armed force moved out toward Ingalls, determined to exterminate the Doolin-Dalton gang if they could be found.

The officers and possemen had disguised themselves as hunters and as they drew near the vicinity of the outlaw haunt they camped and hunted for a few days, sending two scouts to investigate the lay of the land at Ingalls. Two or three days passed and the scouts reported that the gang had ridden into the town during the early forenoon of a crisp fall day and had placed their horses in the livery stable, and that they had separated, some going to the Trilby saloon and others to the Pierce Hotel. Hixon made immediate preparations for a siege and dispatched a message to John Hale and W. M. Nix who were attending court at Stillwater about fifteen miles west, requesting they join the outfit within a few hours.

The posse traveled in two covered wagons, the men carefully concealed beneath the flapping canvas in order that they would attract as little attention as possible. Shortly after noon of the same day the scouts reported, the two covered wagons drew near the edge of the little settlement. Hixon ordered the teams stopped in a ravine protecting them from view of Ingalls and instructed his men to quickly prepare themselves for a battle. The wagons carried a considerable supply of guns and ammunition, each officer buckling two belts of cartridges about his waist and filling his pockets with other ammunition; and each posseman had two six-shooters and a Winchester well supplied with ammunition.

Hixon then set about as quietly and stealthily as possible to place his men in a strategic position to observe and prevent the escape of the outlaws, pending the arrival of Chief Deputy Hale and W. M. Nix, at which time he expected to launch the siege. Believing some of the outlaws were housed in the hotel, Hixon first placed several of his possemen at such points as to make it impossible for any one to escape. Just as he and his assistant deputies, Masterson, Speed, Houston and Shadley were being located so they would have good range on the Trilby saloon and livery barn, the attention of the outlaws was attracted to their queer actions and some one started

firing from the saloon, this firing precipitated a fight before the officers were entirely prepared. With bullets flying about the closely grouped officers there was nothing to do but to make the best of the situation and to attempt to defeat and capture the outlaws. The officers opened an intense fire upon the buildings and the Battle of Ingalls was on. Jim Masterson placed himself behind a small tree, and outlaw lead was tearing holes in the ground all about him. Considering that the sapling behind which he stood was very little more than half as thick as his robust body, it was remarkable that he was not killed. Hixon had thrown himself into a shallow ditch and was concentrating his shots upon the saloon from which most of the outlaws' bullets were coming, deputies Speed, Houston and Shadley were in the thick of the fight but their positions made them better targets for the outlaws.

The fire from the saloon was temporarily stilled and the officers could see the commotion which indicated that some one had been hit. During the lull in the shooting from the saloon, the officers were alarmed at hearing bullets whizzing all around them from a source that seemed mysterious until they discovered that someone was firing from the second story of the Pierce Hotel. Then another fusillade from the saloon began and, under its protection, Bill Doolin, almost dragging the wounded Bitter Creek, raced across the street from the saloon to the livery stable. As they drew near the entrance to that building, Doolin cried out and staggered dropping Bitter Creek to the ground. Both of them scrambled on hands and knees into the shelter of the stable. They

were soon followed by Bill Dalton, Red Buck and Dynamite Dick, who zig-zagged across the street like a pack of Apache Indians in their efforts to dodge the officers' bullets. They reached the stable safely and began a hot barrage from that point.

The outlaws now had the advantage and the officers found it necessary to expose themselves and shift their positions if they were to be able to shoot effectively. Deputy Houston attempted to run to the shelter of a tree and was instantly killed by a bullet from the hotel window. Lafe Shadley ran toward the livery stable and succeeded in dropping behind the carcass of a horse that had been shot, from which point he was able to pour a hot leaden fire into the stable.

Over at the Pierce Hotel the women folk, including Rose of Cimarron, Bitter Creek's sweetheart, had taken refuge in an upstairs room adjoining that from which a rain of bullets was pouring. The crude building had no stairway to the second floor and the only means of getting up and down was by a ladder that leaned against the exposed side of the structure. Peeping stealthily through a window, Rose saw her sweetheart, Bitter Creek Newcomb, tumble into the sand before the livery stable when Doolin was shot. Hastily buckling two belts of cartridges about her waist and grasping a Winchester, she ran to the only exit, almost maddened with a determination to go to the assistance of her lover. By this time the officers were bombarding the hotel and it was impossible for the girl to leave by way of the ladder. She and Mrs. Pierce hastily knotted quilts together and within a few minutes Rose had slid through a window to the ground on the sheltered side of the building. Without regard for her own safety, she ran across the lead-swept street toward the livery stable. The inherent chivalry of the officers must have caused them to hold their fire until the women had reached the stable, although they realized that she was carrying another *gun* and additional *ammunition* to the outlaws.

Inside the stable Doolin was preparing for their escape. His own wound had dazed him and only his iron nerve sustained him as he staggered about, giving orders. He and Dalton would keep the officers covered while Red Buck and Dynamite Dick were to assist the woman outlaw and her wounded lover in mounting their horses and to ride away with them from the back door of the stable, protecting their escape. Doolin and Dalton kept up a continuous fire through the wide cracks in the side of the building.

Dick Speed started to run across the unprotected street to where Lafe Shadley lay behind the horse's carcass. Doolin, reeling weakly, took a shot at Speed and missed, then knelt, steadying himself against the side of the building and taking careful aim. His second bullet struck Deputy Speed squarely between the eyes and the officer fell without an outcry.

The officers were able to see that part of the gang was escaping through the back door of the stable, but the fire continued from the upper window of the hotel and they were forced to remain behind their poor shelters, unable to attempt to frustrate the escape. When the others had gone Doolin and Dalton quickly mounted their horses and followed, dashing away at full speed. When they had ridden

Stage station between Guthrie and Kingfisher, June 4, 1889.

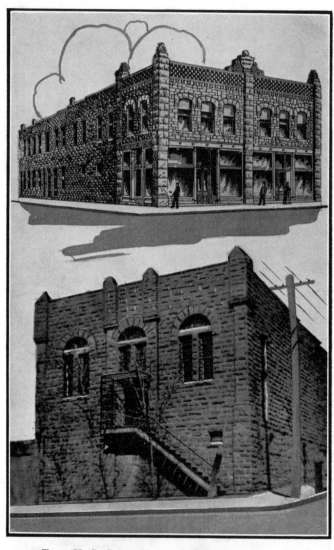

Top—U. S. Court Quarters. Lower—U. S. Jail,
Guthrie, Oklahoma.

about a quarter of a mile they caught up with Red
Buck and Dynamite Dick.

"Where's Rose and Bitter Creek?" Doolin demanded.

"Hell! we ain't got time to fool with them," Red
Buck exclaimed as he thrust the spurs into his
horse's belly.

A shot flashed from Doolin's gun and a bullet
pierced Red Buck's hat. The outlaw pulled his horse
to its haunches and whirled about, facing his leader.

"You damn yellow-striped cur, come back here—
we are not leaving them behind."

Deputy Lafe Shadley had seen Bitter Creek fall
from his horse and Rose had quickly dismounted to
try to aid him. Shadley, holding his Winchester in
position, ran toward the fallen man. At this moment Bill Dalton approached on his return to look
for the wounded bandit and, seeing Shadley before
the officer had noticed him, he shot, killing the
deputy instantly. Doolin, Dynamite Dick and the
cursing Red Buck arrived on the scene and Dalton
assisted in placing Bitter Creek on his horse, Rose
mounting her horse and Red Buck and Dalton sup-
porting Bitter Creek on each side while they raced
away from the scene of the battle. The officers, being unmounted, could not follow.

The fleeing bandits seemed to have forgotten the
comrade in the hotel who continued his shooting
from the upper window. The officers joined the
posse and quickly surround the hotel, determined to
capture the man or men hidden there. However, the
accomplishment of this thing was more difficult than
it seemed. The concealed outlaw was able to cover

the ladder entrance perfectly and there was no other way to get up to him. It would be necessary to either starve him out or to make him exhaust his ammunition before it would be possible to enter the place.

By this time Chief Deputy Hale and W. M. Nix arrived and the officers held a pow-wow while keeping the building covered to prevent the outlaw's escape. The intrepid Jim Masterson seemed to offer the best solution to the problem. Reaching inside of his shirt he pulled out three sticks of dynamite which he had concealed for such purpose if needed.

"This will bring them out, although we may have a little trouble gathering up the pieces," Masterson observed as he picked up a handful of rubbish and started toward the building. Within a few moments the officers had gathered a heap of trash and had placed it on the sheltered side of the hotel while two or three of them kept the outlaw occupied with an intermittent fire upon his hiding place. Mrs. Pierce, the proprietress of the hotel, peeping from her hiding place, saw what the officers were planning, probably to burn the hotel, and ran out pleading with them not to destroy the place, saying it contained everything she owned and it was her only means of livelihood.

"Who's up there?" Hixon demanded of her.

"Just one man, Arkansas Tom."

The officers impressed upon her the fact that her life and property was at stake if she misled them in any way. She again confirmed the statement that only one outlaw was in the building. Deputy Hixson turned to her and said: "Mrs. Pierce, it is up to you to have him surrender. Bring him down with his hands in the air if you can, otherwise we are going to blow him into the sweet subsequently."

The frightened woman went to the foot of the ladder and called to the outlaw, then climbed up and went inside. Within a short time she came to the opening and called to the officers that the man would surrender, and Arkansas Tom led the way down the ladder followed by Mrs. Pierce. He was soon securely shackled, the only prisoner taken in the bitter Ingalls battle.

Hixon and W. M. Nix climbed the ladder and investigated the room above, taking charge of Arkansas Tom's firearms that had been left in his hiding place. They reported that the room was literally shot to pieces, bullets had pierced and shattered practically everything within the place and it was miraculous that Arkansas Tom was ever brought out alive.

The men were dispatched to look after the teams while the others stood guard over the prisoner since it was possible that the other bandits might return to aid their comrade. This did not happen, however, and within a short time the two covered wagons were driven into the little town and the bodies of the dead officers were lifted into one of them. Arkansas Tom, securely shackled, was placed in the other conveyance and the little cortege made its way toward Guthrie.

Chief Deputy Hale and Nix were soon in their buggy rushing to Stillwater where they quickly organized a posse to chase the outlaws. Deputies George Starmer, Steve Burke, W. O. Jones and three Indian scouts joined them and they were soon on the

best mounts to be had equipped for a real battle if possible to overtake the Doolin gang.

By early dawn the officers were in Ingalls and on the trail. About twenty miles southeast of Ingalls they found the outlaws had stopped at an Indian settlement where Doolin and Bitter Creek dressed their wounds, got some coffee and then rushed on in the southeastern direction toward the Osage hills.

About four o'clock in the afternoon the officers reached the Arkansas River and after crossing this stream it was impossible to find their trail again. We learned later, after the arrest of Doolin the first time, that on reaching the Arkansas River they had traveled north along the edge of the river for at least two miles to throw the officers off their trail, and made their way to the Dunn Ranch, rather an exclusive hiding place.

As it was late in the evening the officers decided to return to Stillwater. In the meantime our office had instructed the deputies at Pawnee and Pawhuska to be on the lookout for the gang.

Fate seemed to be dealing the face cards to the bandits. Three brave officers had lost their lives on this great battle and no serious damage had been done to the escaped outlaws. Our prisoner was perhaps the least important member of the gang for he had less of the really bad criminal qualities.

At the time of his capture Arkansas Tom was just twenty years of age. His brief career as an outlaw had lasted slightly more than a year. When the handcuffs had been placed upon his wrists he turned to Mrs. Pierce and said:

"I surrendered on your account. I would a heap rather they had killed me or burnt me alive than to have give up like this." The woman shed a few crocodile tears and the outlaw was made to feel that he had been quite heroic.

A short time later Arkansas Tom was tried in the court of Chief Justice Frank Dale. The incident at Ingalls had so aroused the ire of Judge Dale and his determination to assist in the extermination of the bandits, that he gave me a most unusual order, perhaps the only one of its sort ever given by a federal judge. "Marshal, this is serious," he said. "I have reached the conclusion that the only good outlaw is the dead one. I hope you will instruct your deputies to bring in dead outlaws in the future. That will simplify your problem a great deal and probably save some lives."

At the conclusion of Arkansas Tom's trial, Judge Dale gave him a fatherly lecture.

"Young man, I hope that this experience will be a great lesson to you, that when you have served your sentence and come out to take your place among the men of the world you will lead an upright life and try to be a man."

I began squirming in my seat, fearing that Judge Dale was about to assess a very light sentence. We all sympathized to a certain extent with the young prisoner, but the facts in the case were of a sort that made leniency impossible. Was Judge Dale going to allow his sentiment to sway his judgment?

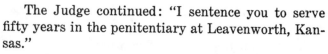

The Judge continued: "I sentence you to serve fifty years in the penitentiary at Leavenworth, Kansas."

This was sort of anti-climax to the fatherly lecture. If Arkansas Tom were to serve his sentence he would have passed seventy years of age upon his release, and it was hardly possible that he would remember Judge Dale's advice about living an upright life after so long a time.

Chief Justice Dale had something of an ironic sense of humor. He realized that crime conditions in the new country had become so serious and were so vitally affecting the welfare of respectable people that sometimes rather severe punishment was absolutely essential. On one occasion a young man was brought before him charged with stealing, and Judge Wisby had made an impassioned appeal for leniency, basing his pathetic plea upon the youth of the lad and the fact that he had been led astray. Judge Dale turned to him and said: "How old do you say your client is?"

"Just twenty-one, please, Your Honor," the attorney replied hopefully.

Judge Dale settled back in his chair and studied for a moment. . . . . "Twenty-one . . . hum-n-n-n . . . . your client is past the age of maturity and should know right from wrong. I will just give him an extra year for being led astray so easily."

Arkansas Tom had served fourteen years of his sentence when his brother, a minister of Carthage, Missouri, came to my home in St. Louis to solicit my aid in getting a pardon. He brought a report of

Tom's perfect conduct at the penitentiary. Time had mellowed my feelings in the matter and, remembering his youth and his loyalty to the widow Pierce in his surrender, I decided to use my influence in his behalf. I secured the help of other United States officers who were associated with me in his arrest and conviction, and we were successful in having him released on parole.

He returned to Oklahoma where he was employed in the store of an old friend. Later he visited me in St. Louis and I helped him to get a position as an accountant. He was found to be very accurate and reliable. Many of my friends met him and they were very much interested in him and his past history.

The Daily Oklahoman of Oklahoma City commented upon my interest in Arkansas Tom: "When Mr. Nix learned of the outlaw's sincere effort to establish himself, he knew the imprisonment had accomplished the work for which it is destined, and the former officer's heart went out to the man whom he had hunted down. He arranged for a meeting with him. When the two met they grasped hands, looked into one another's eyes and solemnly pledged friendship—the one, rich in the world's estimation of riches, offered to the other, poor and anxious for a helping hand, the opportunity he needed to again become a man among men."

After working out of St. Louis for a year he returned to Oklahoma City where he was employed by Bill Tilghman for two years. Later he returned to Joplin, Missouri, and Galena, Kansas, where some of his people lived and, to our great surprise and disappointment, he became involved in a bank robbery at Neosho, Missouri. He was convicted and sentenced to the penitentiary at Jefferson City. After serving his term on this charge he again returned to Joplin and within a short time he was alleged to have held up a bank at Asbury, Missouri, and was killed by Joplin officers when he resisted arrest. It seems that after he got from under the influence of Tilghman and myself his mania for the wild life dominated him, and it eventually cost his life.

CHAPTER IX
I TAKE A LESSON IN HANGING

At about this time, young Henry Starr appeared on the Oklahoma scene and began a career that stamped him as the most unusual outlaw who ever lived. Starr was born at Fort Gibson in the Indian Territory in 1873. His father, George Starr, was a half-breed Cherokee Indian and his mother was a fourth-breed Cherokee. Henry grew up in the Cherokee Nation and at the age of sixteen became a cowboy. He was a young man of unusually good habits. He did not use tobacco, coffee or liquor. He was athletic in build and action and his friendly, intelligent black eyes and coal-black hair gave him the appearance of a young chap one might trust under any circumstances. Soon after his first robbery a reward was posted for his capture and a deputy sheriff named Floyd Wilson encountered the lad, recognizing him immediately. Both were on horseback and when Wilson ordered Starr to surrender they dismounted and faced each other, six-shooters in hand. Starr told Wilson that he would not submit to arrest as he did not believe he was an authorized officer and he suggested that the man go peacefully on his way.

"Throw up your hands or I'll kill you," Wilson commanded bruskly.

Starr regarded him for a moment, then spoke: . . . "I'm going to give you first chance . . . I'll lower my gun and let you shoot, then if I kill you it will be in self-defense."

The nervous and excited Wilson fired almost immediately and the bullet grazed the side of Starr's head. Starr's pistol then spat its leaden death, piercing Wilson's heart. The officer fired a second time as he fell but his bullet went wild. Starr mounted his horse and rode away. Within a short time he had been captured and, by agreement, pleaded guilty to a charge of manslaughter before Federal Judge Parker at Fort Smith, Arkansas, and was sentenced to twenty-five years in the Ohio penitentiary. After serving five years he was pardoned and returned to Oklahoma.

Shortly after the conviction of Henry Starr, I had occasion to accompany Bill Tilghman on a trip to Fort Smith, Arkansas, to which point we were transporting a group of prisoners. Here I met for the first time the famous hanging Judge Isaac C. Parker, whose court holds an unbroken record—both as to the number of men condemned and as to the extreme power that was vested in Judge Parker.

While the constitution grants the right of trial by
jury, the jurors in his court were selected under his
personal supervision—and it was not unlikely that
the Judge, in his zeal to rid the Southwest of its
notorious desperadoes, used extraordinary influence
to accomplish his very determined purpose.   Although Judge Parker's court was held in the State
of Arkansas, it had no jurisdiction over the criminal
cases in that State but was confined strictly to crime
committed in the Territory and No Man's Land.

For the first fourteen years of Judge Parker's
term of office, no appeals could be taken from his
court.   His decisions were final.   In 1889 this unusual power was modified by Congress, making it
possible for an appeal to be taken from his ruling or
decision, just as it could be done in any other court
of justice.   Parker seldom modified or qualified any
of his instructions to the jury in criminal cases.   He
demanded that they either hang or acquit.

During his twenty-one year term as federal judge
he sentenced one hundred and seventy-two men to
life imprisonment and ninety to be hanged.   I had
heard so much of him even before I left Kentucky
that I was glad of an opportunity to meet this extraordinary official.   Our visit in his chambers at the
court house was most cordial—and, strange to say,
I found him a warm-hearted, congenial man, which
caused me to wonder how such a distinguished
gentleman could adapt himself to such an unrelent-
ing attitude toward all criminals.   The fact that
Judge Parker's dealings were principally with vicious, hardened criminals probably accounts for the
fact that they all looked alike to him and that he had

little sympathy for the frailties of human nature. He was much interested in me and remarked that I was very young to be occupying such a responsible position which, considering the hazards and the magnitude of the position, seemed to demand the experience of a much older man than myself. In those days, a man was hardly regarded as qualified to hold a public office until he was past fifty. I was but thirty-two when my term of office began.

While in Fort Smith I took advantage of the opportunity to meet George Malledon, who had achieved a reputation as an expert hangman. He took a great deal of pleasure in showing Tilghman and myself the gallows that had been erected in the yard surrounding the federal jail building, upon which it was possible to hang six men at a time. I doubt if another such structure ever existed in the world. Mr. Malledon informed us that upon two occasions he had hanged six men at one time. Such executions were witnessed by thousands of people who came hundreds of miles to see them. We talk of the morbid curiosity of the present day as reflected in the glaring headlines of our newspapers; we need not feel discouraged about the decadence of civilization on this account; for the people of that period were just as morbidly curious as men and women could possibly be.

On hanging days they used to come into Fort Smith days ahead of the occasion, many of them camping and sleeping on the ground in order that they might have ring-side places when the trap fell. Malledon had the ropes used in these hanging specially made of chosen hemp fiber, woven by hand in

St. Louis. He showed us how he tied the knot to make it possible to break the neck of the victim instead of strangling him, which he considered a more humane way to hang a man. When the rope was adjusted around the neck, the big knot was placed under the left ear where it would lay in the hollow just back of the jawbone. When the trap fell and the man dropped through, the rope jerked the head sideways, cracking the neck instantly. Malledon said that by this method there was not a quiver, nor even a muscular reaction. The body would just sway and whirl slightly, and then it was still.

While it was a gruesome thing to me, I felt that I was obliged to learn as much as possible about hanging, for it might fall to my lot to carry out such an edict of the law. While the idea was repulsive to me, I preferred to be able to do it properly.

CHAPTER X

THE CASEYS FLASH AND DIE

My office had been getting a number of reports about the depredations of the Casey brothers who had taken a claim on Mustang Creek in Canadian County near El Reno. Two settlers living on claims adjoining the Casey farm had been murdered, and the populace and officers had suspected that the Caseys had committed the crime to get hold of the farms of their neighbors.

Deputy Chris Madsen, who was stationed at El Reno, took up the case in his quiet way and within a very short time he had gathered sufficient evidence to have two of the Casey brothers indicted. They were released on bond and immediately moved westward, settling near Arapaho in the Commanche-Arapaho country, from which new vantage point they sent out threats that they would not submit to trial

on the murder charge. One day, some time later, they imbibed too liberally and, with their courage stimulated by bad whiskey, they concluded they would come into El Reno and clean up Madsen and his crowd. They arrived heavily armed in a blustering fashion, and the citizens of the little town were soon aroused and excited. Madsen happened to be out of town for a few hours and when he returned the Caseys had gone. Upon hearing that they had been there he immediately notified Deputy Ferris of Yukon, about fifteen miles east of El Reno, asking him to be on the lookout for them. Ferris rode to the edge of Yukon to watch the incoming trail. When the Caseys approached him and he was about to question them, one of the brothers shot him from his horse. The citizens of Yukon immediately armed themselves and tried to catch the bandits. A fusillade of shots was exchanged and a running fight took place as the bandits fled toward the South Canadian River. Deputy Ferris, who was not seriously wounded, joined the posse in pursuit and they were successful in capturing Jim Casey. The other brother, Victor, escaped. The captive was bound hand and foot and taken to El Reno where he was turned over to Deputy Madsen. He absolutely refused to give his name or to acknowledge that he was one of the Casey brothers, but Madsen was able to identify him, and he was sure that the man who had escaped was another of the Caseys.

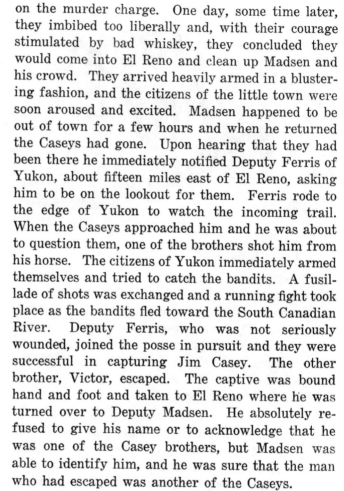

Madsen immediately organized a large posse, including some Indian scouts who volunteered to help locate the fugitive. After a fruitless search, the posse was returning to El Reno when they met a

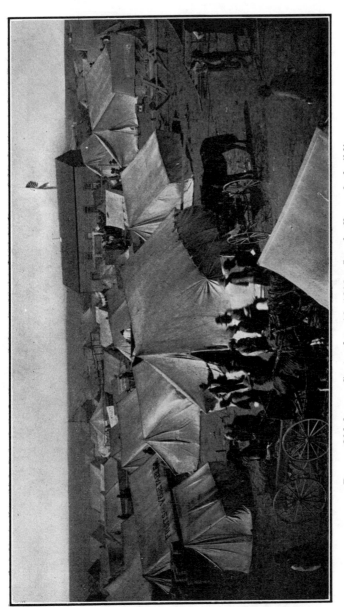

Perry, Oklahoma, September 16, 1893.   Land office only building.

Perry, Oklahoma, afternoon of opening, September 16, 1893.

young girl on her way home from school. She reported she had seen a man answering the description
of Victor Casey riding a dun horse and she told the
officers that the horse was hobbling with a crippled
leg that had been bound as if it had been hurt.

Upon his return to El Reno, Madsen found that
a mob was being organized to lynch Jim Casey who
was being held in the El Reno jail. Madsen immediately moved the prisoner to Fort Reno, where he
was placed in a military guard-house until the excitement had died down.

Madsen then decided to lead his posse to the home
of the Casey brothers' father and they set out upon
the tiresome trip, arriving at about daybreak the
next morning. As they drew near the Casey home,
they met the senior Casey with a load of bedding in
his wagon. Madsen concluded that the father of
the fugitive was taking supplies to the hiding place
of his son. The old man insisted that his name was
Rogers, that he lived at Thomas, Oklahoma, and that
he was going to visit his wife at Minco. The officers
pretended to accept his statements and rode on.
When they had passed a turn in the road, Madsen
quickly detailed two men to follow old man Casey,
while he proceeded with the rest of the posse to the

Casey home. Here they found the wounded dun
horse. Investigation proved that the horse had been
shot in the leg and by this time the animal could
hardly walk. In searching the house, the officers
found a pair of trousers saturated with blood and
they were convinced they were on the right trail.

The elder Casey must have become suspicious
that he was being followed, for he soon turned his

his team about and drove back to the farm. He
seemed greatly surprised to see Madsen and his
posse in the place. Madsen informed the old man
that they had found the wounded horse and that he

was sure his son was hiding somewhere near. Casey
denied the charge emphatically and Madsen threatened to arrest him for harboring criminals and to
take him to El Reno and throw him in jail. Old
man Casey remained obdurate, so Madsen took
charge of him with his wagon and team and forced
him to drive toward the home of his brother who
lived near. Madsen rode in front, with the posse in
charge of old man Casey and his team. They had
gone about a mile when Madsen saw a man approaching with two horses. The officer concealed

himself and his party and watched the man turn the
horses loose and go to a farm house nearby. They
followed him and learned that he was George Casey,
an uncle of the Casey boys. Madsen asked him
where he had been with the horses and he replied
that he had been after a load of wood, although there
was no wood about the place to indicate that this
was true.

"See here, Casey," Madsen exclaimed, "you know
where Vic Casey is hiding and if you know what is
good for you, you will lead us to him." The man
refused to tell anything and he was placed under ar-

rest and taken back to the home of the boy's father.

By this time a number of other members of the
family had assembled and the entire outfit was
placed under arrest and informed that unless they
gave up the fugitive they would all be taken to El
Reno and placed in jail on a charge of harboring

criminals. They seemed to believe that the officers
were bluffing and were very much surprised when
teams were hitched to wagons and they were loaded
in and started toward El Reno. After the party had
gone about three miles, old man Casey became convinced that the officers were serious in their inten-
tions and he called Madsen, saying that he would
lead the posse to the hiding place of Vic Casey if the
rest of the family would be turned loose. Madsen
left his posse with the family and, mounting old man
Casey upon a horse belonging to one of his officers,
he went with Casey. When they reached a point
near the hiding place Madsen commanded Casey to
go inside and bring his son out. The old man protested, saying that his son was armed and would
probably try to kill anyone who would try to come
near him. Madsen was insistent.

"No doubt he will recognize one of his own breed.
. . . . Go in and get him—now!"

Casey entered the place and in a few minutes appeared at the door assisting his son, who was not
able to put his weight on a wounded leg. Vic Casey
had to be carried to the wagon. The officers dressed
his wound as best they could and, releasing the other
members of the family, proceeded to Fort Reno with
their prisoner, where he was confined with his
brother.

When the case of the Casey brothers was called
to trial before Judge Burford at El Reno, Canadian
County, their lawyer succeeded in getting a change
of venue to Oklahoma City, Oklahoma County. They
were tried before Judge Henry W. Scott, convicted
and sentenced to life imprisonment. They were held

in jail at Oklahoma City pending an appeal to the Supreme Court.

During this interval, the Christian brothers, Bob and Bill, were arrested and placed in the Oklahoma City jail for murder and other depredations in the Eastern part of the territory. They were both young men about the same age of the Casey brothers and soon became fast friends. John Casey and the Christian brothers soon began to plan to break jail and they used Jessie Finley, an attractive young girl of about sixteen, who was a sweetheart of Bob Christian, to work out their plans successfully. Jailer Garver was an elderly man around fifty, absolutely honest and he could not look upon this attractive, innocent looking young lady with suspicion, and from time to time gave her more and more liberties thinking her harmless. But, nevertheless Jessie Finley was a "plant" and a skilled one at that.

Jessie's home was about thirty miles south of Oklahoma City and she visited the jail weekly bringing flowers, tobacco, cigarettes, food and delicacies. In the course of a few weeks her winning way enabled her to bring quantities of food to the Casey and Christian brothers. The final and fatal day was set for Sunday at which time Jessie brought with her an unusually large basket supposedly supplied with chicken, vegetables and delicacies. By this time she had the confidence of the jailer to such an extent that he extended her an unusual privilege and allowed a separate table to be set in one of the cells where the four outlaws ate their dinner with Jessie presiding as hostess, their jailer little dreaming that this basket was laden with four six-shooters

and a full supply of ammunition. The outlaws were successful in hiding the guns and ammunition without being detected by the gracious and friendly jailer. After the dinner was served and a short visit, Jessie left the jail and the city as well so as not to be on the ground during the later developments. The four outlaws returned to their cells and all was quiet. At supper time, however, when the jailer let the prisoners out to eat, the outlaws hung back until most of the prisoners were back in their cells. They then overpowered the jailer, took his keys, bound and gagged him, unlocked the jail door and at this point Victor Casey, whose wound was still afflicting him, refused to go, but Bob and Bill Christian and Jim Casey broke away without him. Bob Christian had the keys but halted long enough to lock the jail door and throw the keys on the office desk. They wished to prevent a general jail delivery for the reason it would cause excitement and jeopardize their chance for a successful escape.

The three immediately separated. Bob Christian soon mounted a horse near by which turned out to belong to Marshal Milt Jones and escaped with a hail of bullets flying all about him. Bill Christian turned toward Grand Avenue and fled on foot with the crowd following after him. On reaching the eastern boundary of the city he met a farmer driving into town in a buckboard drawn by one horse. Bill ordered him off the vehicle at the point of his gun, mounted the seat and swung the horse round and away he went as fast as the horse could carry him under lash. About two miles from Oklahoma City close to the northern bank of the Canadian

River, he left the vehicle and let the horse go wild and disappeared in the timber and undergrowth. So Bob and Bill Christian both made a clean get-away.

Jim Casey was not so successful. On reaching the middle of the crossing of Broadway and Grand Avenue, he encountered a young couple taking a pleasure drive in a one-horse buggy. He jumped in behind them and as he was giving orders to drive fast and keep straight ahead, Marshal Milt Jones with gun in hand ordered a halt which the driver obeyed. At this Jim Casey shot the marshal and he fell dead in his tracks. No sooner had this happened than another deputy was on the scene instantly firing at Casey and he fell out of the back of the buggy near the body of Milt Jones.

The jail break occurred between sundown and dusk and soon darkness enveloped the country which made it impossible for the officers to overtake the Christian brothers. The last they were heard of after their escape, they had joined the Cuban Army, remaining their until after the Spanish American War. From there it was stated they located somewhere in Mexico.

Victor Casey died a short time after the jail break and before his case was passed upon by the Supreme Court.

Jessie Finley paid the penalty for her part in the jail break.

Thus passed the Casey and Christian brothers who aspired to be bad men but were either too bad or not bad enough to succeed.

CHAPTER XI
CATTLE ANNIE AND LITTLE BREECHES

Bill Doolin and Bitter Creek Newcomb had recovered from the wounds they received at Ingalls and when we next heard of them they were seen near Hot Springs, Arkansas. Doolin later told me that he had planned to hold up a Hot Springs bank but that after looking over the lay of the land they decided against this venture. The town of Hot Springs was rather compactly built and the bank they wanted to rob was so located that an escape would have been hazardous. I think the outlaws were also influenced by the fact that the Hot Springs chief of police was a man who had served a good many years as an officer on the Kansas frontier and that he had a reputation for having administered doses of lead poison to several notorious characters in that country.

While the Doolin gang was on its way to Arkansas, my men had been following their cold trail several days behind them. On one occasion when it seemed the officers might be getting near the gang's hiding place, they met a heavily armed girl on the trail and they questioned her. They later suspected that the girl notified the Doolin gang that the officers were drawing near and that the bandits' flight to

Arkansas was caused by this incident.   However, this matter was never fully substantiated.

Deputy Burke had been hearing of a number of cattle and horse thefts and some petty stealing that was being done by a pair of girls who seemed to be hanging out near members of the Doolin gang, yet never becoming a part of the gang.   After a number of these reports had convinced Burke that the girls were actually outlaws, he set out to find them.   Here and there he would discover a theft or a case where they had peddled whiskey to members of the Osage tribe, but for some time he was unable to find a warm trail.   The girls were becoming very troublesome and it was evident that they were keep-ing in fairly close touch with the movements of my officers and passing their information along to the outlaws.   Soon we learned enough about them to know what they looked like.   The elder one, a girl about seventeen, had been dubbed Cattle Annie, and the small one had been nick-named Little Breeches. Wherever they were seen, they were heavily armed with pistols and Winchesters, and it was reported that they were pretty accurate shots.

They continued for some weeks to mystify my force, until Bill Tilghman and Steve Burke found a trace of them when they happened to be scouting on another mission.   They immediately took up the trail and located the girls at a farm house near Pawnee. As the officers drew near, Little Breeches ran out through the back door of the farm house and mounted her horse.   Tilghman followed, spurring his horse into a dead run.   Cattle Annie was not seen and Burke dismounted to search the house for her.

Tilghman's horse was a faster animal than the crow-bait Little Breeches was riding and he soon overtook her. She attempted to fire at him over her shoulder but apparently she was not accustomed to shooting from a running horse and her shots went wild. Here was a new problem for Bill Tilghman. He was the most chivalrous fellow who ever lived and he would not kill a woman under any circumstances. This female was pouring hot lead at him and he was too much of a gentleman to shoot back. Finally, exasperated, Tilghman unsheathed his Winchester and shot the girl's horse. The animal tumbled in the dust with a grunt, pinning the girl's leg beneath its carcass. The impetus of her fall threw one of her six-shooters a short distance away into the grass and, as she lay pinned beneath the horse, she could not reach her other gun. She struggled there, cursing and scratching in an attempt to reach the lost gun which lay just six or eight inches beyond her grasp. When Tilghman reached her side she was frantically pulling at the grass near the gun and screeching like a wild cat. She threw a handful of dirt into Bill's eyes, causing him a brief moment of pain. Tilghman picked up the gun, removed its shells and then lifted the carcass of the horse from the girl's leg. She came up fighting and scratching but he soon had her disarmed and under control. She had not been injured in the fall. Bill placed her on his horse and mounted behind her, riding back to see how Burke had fared with the other little catamount. Burke was easing up to a window, intending to peer through to see who was inside, when the head of the other outlaw girl was thrust out as she

looked nervously in the opposite direction of the officer. She had a Winchester in one hand and just as
she saw Burke and would have aimed the gun to
shoot him he caught her about the shoulders and
pulled her through the window. When her feet
touched the ground she made a wild effort to get hold
of one of her six-shooters but with Burke's strong
arms about her she was helpless. When the officers
joined each other Tilghman was still rubbing his
eyes and Burke had a long scratch across his cheek.

The girls were taken to Perry, Oklahoma, where
they were brought to trial before Judge Bierer who,
because of their age, sentenced them to the federal
reformatory at Framingham, Massachusetts. The
girls gave their names as Annie McDougal, alias Cattle Anne, and Jennie Metcalf, alias Little Breeches.
They were daughters of two poor families living near
each other in the Osage Nation. Their people were
uneducated, but were considered respectable. I remember that the father of one of the girls attributed
her wild ideas to the environment of some of the hi-
larious dances that were held in the Indian country
and to the influence of outlaws who attended these
functions.

When the jailer's wife had scrubbed the pair and
dressed them in attractive clothes, they appeared
to be very innocent country girls and they got the
sympathy of everyone who saw them.

Charlie Colcord and I made the trip to the reformatory with them. The long journey pleased the
girls a great deal, as their lives had been very much
circumscribed by poverty and the crude environment
in which they had been reared. The news associa-

tions had written a great many sensational stories about the pair and the people of Boston were greatly interested in seeing Oklahoma's girl bandits. When we arrived a large crowd awaited us and I believe the girls secretly enjoyed the publicity they received. They had been very little trouble on the way and we had been able to relieve each other in guarding them, so we had plenty of rest.

Judge Bierer had appealed to the instincts of the girls and I believe they were deeply impressed by his advice. The last report I had concerning them stated that they had ben discharged from the reformatory and that they had taken up settlement work in the slums of New York. I have often wondered what became of them and what they were able to make of their lives, in spite of their early handicaps and experiences.

CHAPTER XII

CATTLE THIEVES, COUNTERFEITERS AND WHISKEY PEDDLERS

The Doolins having gained a reputation for themselves as being the largest and most daring gang operating in Oklahoma at that time, it is quite natural that we gave a great deal of thought to their apprehension and destruction. Bill Tilghman, Heck Thomas, Chris Madsen, John Hixon and a number of my other tried and true deputies were concentrating their efforts upon this task. During their scouting trips they were successful in locating several other offenders who aspired to become well known outlaws, but whose operations had been confined to so limited a local territory that their desired notoriety had not materialized.

In May, 1894, Ben Cravens and William Crittenden stole twenty head of cattle from the Osage Indians and drove them to the home of a farmer near Perry who took the animals into the town and sold them to a butcher. Through the description of the stolen cattle that had been filed at my office, we traced them to the slaughter pen of the Perry butcher. W. M. Nix took the case, assisted by Steve Burke. They discovered that the Perry butcher had paid but half of the purchase price for the cattle and that the remainder was to be paid about ten days after the sale was made. Our officers kept a close watch for the parties who would come to collect the balance. In spite of the vigilance of the deputies, the outlaws managed to slip into town and visit the

137

butcher, who evidently reasoned that there was an opportunity to avoid paying the money over to the thieves and he made excuses about not having it, at the same time telling them that they were being watched by the officers. The outlaws drew their guns and forced the frightened merchant to pay over the amount he owed them, plus a small sum for good measure.

The angry butcher immediately advised United States Commissioner Ed Tebbe and he got in touch with Deputies Nix and Burke, who were soon pursuing the flying cattle thieves in the direction of the Osage Nation.

On the afternoon of the second day, little realizing how close they were to the fugitives, Nix and Burke spied two horsemen a mile or so ahead, just as they had turned toward a small sod house built on a steep slope that led to a canyon. The officers spurred ahead rapidly and headed off the two riders before they had reached the sod house, which would have been a formidable fortification for the outlaws had they succeeded in reaching it. Nix and Burke commanded the outlaws to throw up their hands, which they did, and Nix drew a bead on them with his Winchester while Burke searched them, relieving each man of a pair of six-shooters. As usual, the prisoners denied their guilt.

They were brought to Perry where the butcher identified them, after which they acknowledged their identity as Ben Cravens and William Crittenden. They were taken before United States Commissioner Tebbe and were ordered to be placed in the United Stats jail at Guthrie.

The officers had arrived in Perry with their prisoners after dark and a hearing was held the same night. There being no other trains to Guthrie until the next day, it was necessary for the officers to lodge the outlaws in the Perry jail. The jail was a pretty weak structure and, with the assistance of outside friends, Cravens and Crittenden escaped before morning. Deputy Nix immediately notified our office and we instructed the deputies throughout that part of the territory to watch for the escaped prisoners. Nix and Burke spent the day scouting the country but they found no trace of the outlaws.

In about ten days we received notice from the city marshal of Caney, Kansas, that Cravens was being held in jail there. Deputies Nix and Burke proceeded to Caney at once and took charge of the prisoner. On account of the lack of railroad facilities they were obliged to drive from Caney to Pawhuska in the Osage Nation, staying over night there and driving next day to Newkirk in the Cherokee Strip, where Judge Bierer was holding court. They had succeeded in getting Cravens to plead guilty and both the officers and their prisoner were anxious to have an immediate hearing of the case. It was a very warm day and the drive over the sandy hills to Newkirk was fatiguing. Cravens complained of the heat and Deputy Nix, out of the goodness of his heart, took the handcuffs off the man so that he might be more comfortable. A short time later they made a stop to water their horses and both Nix and Burke alighted to unfasten the check reins so that the animals might drink. A Winchester rifle lay on the front seat of the hack. Nix looked up just in

time to see Cravens make a lunge toward the rifle, when the officer threw his forty-five on him, commanding him to throw up his hands. The handcuffs were placed on his wrists again and without further difficulty the party arrived in Newkirk late in the evening and Cravens was placed in jail.

The Newkirk jail held quite a collection of bad characters, and that night guards were placed at all points of possible escape. In spite of this precaution, Cravens escaped again and disappeared as completely as if he had dissolved into the atmosphere. He had boasted that there was not a jail that could hold him. It seemed that he was about right.

Another wide search was begun. In the latter part of June an Indian informed us that Cravens was hiding in the Osage hills. Deputy Nix was immediately notified and he set out for Pawnee where he secured the assistance of Deputies Frank Canton and Frank Lake. The Indian who had brought the information consented to serve as a scout for the expedition and he went on ahead to attempt to locate the fugitive outlaw. A few days passed and the scout returned, stating that he had located the man at the home of a family of half-breed Indians. Under cover of darkness the officers set out for the place. When they arrived they surrounded the house and waited for daylight. They had hoped to be able to catch Cravens outside of the house where they might avoid a gun battle that would give all the advantage to the outlaw. The sun came up and some time elapsed, however, and no one stirred about the place. Deputy Frank Canton, who was noted for his cool daring, walked up to the front door and knocked.

Fine representation of early day settler.

Typical early day mansion.

A woman called: "Who's there?"

Ignoring her question, Canton commanded her to open the door.

"Go to hell!" the woman screeched, and Canton gave the flimsy door a hard kick with his heavy boot. The door flew open and there stood Ben Cravens, his forty-five in hand. The audacity of Canton must have surprised the outlaw for he did not offer to shoot before Canton had him covered and had commanded him to surrender. By this time the other deputies were at Canton's side and Cravens was disarmed. Again he was taken to Perry and this time he was placed under such heavy guard that he could not escape. Cravens pleaded guilty and was sentenced to a long term in the federal penitentiary at Leavenworth.

He almost immediately began his plans for escape. Two fellow-workers in the coal mines had joined him. On the morning of the day of his escape Cravens and his cohorts fell into the lockstep procession in the usual way and were taken to their work in the mine one thousand feet underground. When the prisoners had been distributed in the various tunnels Cravens and his two fellow-convicts worked their way gradually toward a guard who stood near the hoisting shaft. Turning suddenly on the man, they overpowered him and entered the car that would draw them to the surface of the earth, forcing the guard to give the hoisting signal. As soon as the unfortunate man had done this they knocked him in the head with a pick handle, killing him instantly and threw him off the car back down the shaft. With the guard's two guns they stood ready

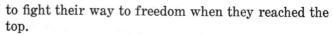

to fight their way to freedom when they reached the top.

The little spot of daylight above them grew larger until they were finally drawn out of the earth's blackness into the bright sunlight. It was a moment before their eyes could adjust themselves to the blinding daylight and, in this brief moment, the outside guards had discovered that they were attempting to escape. Led by Cravens, the prisoners dashed madly through the cordon of guards, shooting as they ran. In the fight that followed one of the prisoners was captured, another was desperately wounded, but Ben Cravens made his way to freedom. It was many years before Ben Cravens was re-captured and today he languishes at Leavenworth prison, serving the term that would have ended several years ago had he served it from its beginning.

Our force had felt rather badly about allowing Cravens to escape on two different occasions, but when we learned of his escape from the Leavenworth prison, our own embarrasment was considerably relieved for he had demonstrated that he was a most unusual jail-breaker.

Craven's partner, Crittenden, was not so very well known and our officers went rather leisurely about the task of finding him, fully confident that he would turn up and be captured without a great deal of difficulty. When we received word that he was hiding in the Creek Nation, Deputy Nix set out to find him and arrest him. Steve Burke and an Indian scout who was well acquainted with the Creek and Osage countries accompanied Nix and they soon found their man at a hide-out not far from the present location of Sapulpa. He resisted arrest and attempted to draw his gun. Burke was a little too quick for him and shot the pistol from the outlaw's right hand before he could pull the trigger. He surrendered gladly and was brought to Perry, where he pleaded guilty and accepted his sentence. I understand he is living in Oklahoma today and that his conduct since his release from prison has been above reproach.

* * *

Our Oklahoma City office had received a number of complaints about some of the depredations of Bill Blake and Andy Puckett, whom we thought to be associated in some way with the Doolin gang, but whose principal operations were confined to their own efforts. They were stealing cattle and horses, plundering in various ways and peddling whiskey to the Indians. When their identities were finally learned, District Deputy C. F. Colcord of Oklahoma City handed warrants to Deputy Sam Bartell and told him to either kill these outlaws or bring them in. It was known that they were making their headquarters in the Glass Mountains in Major County, but no one had been able to locate their rendezvous. When Deputy Bartell picked up a trail that seemed definitely to lead to the Blake and Puckett stronghold, he organized a posse and started out in that direction. Before they reached the mountains they learned that the outlaws were off on an expedition and they were able to follow their trail south into Dewey County. Nearing Munce, the officers unexpectedly encountered Blake and Puckett and a gun

fight ensued, during which Bartell's horse was shot from under him. No one was seriously injured and the outlaws escaped towards the Glass Mountains. Bartell quickly obtained another horse and led the pursuit, coming upon the outlaw camp at about four o'clock the next morning.

The deputy and his men tied their horses a short distance away and crept quietly into the camp. Blake and Puckett made a desperate fight, but they were soon overpowered, disarmed and shackled. They were taken to Oklahoma City where they were tried before Federal Judge Henry W. Scott and sentenced to the Leavenworth penitentiary.

*   *   *

Merchants all over the territory were getting hold of counterfeited silver dollars so perfectly made that it was hard to detect them from the genuine. It seems that they were being passed among the Osage Indians and that several thousand of them had already been placed in circulation throughout the territory. The government sent out notices to banks and merchants warning them against the spurious coins and we were beginning intensive work in an attempt to solve the counterfeiting mystery.

Deputy Marshal George G. Starmer was assigned to the job and he succeeded in finding a number of small operators who were quickly convicted, but the principal source of the counterfeit money continued to pour its stream of coins into circulation. Starmer finally located the hiding place of this counterfeiting organization in a large cave in the Creek country. Organizing a posse, he raided the place and captured a very complete layout of equipment, including a set of dies that were perfect. Quite a stock of counterfeit money was also confiscated and A. Maden and his wife surrendered without resistance. They were tried in Guthrie, pleaded guilty before Justice Dale and sentenced to ten years in the federal penitentiary.

*   *   *

Out of the sixty thousand arrests made by my force during my administration, it is strange that the incident regarding F. M. Baker, his wife and Bill Thomas should be so outstanding in my recollection, considering that these people were neither notorious nor desperate. United States Commissioner C. J. Wrightsman of Pawnee had issued warrants against them for cattle thefts and Deputy George Starmer was sent out after them. He organized a small posse and succeeded in locating the offenders near Catoosa. There was a brief fight but no one was injured and the outlaws made their getaway. A few days later they were located on Bird Creek on what was known as the Bill Halsell ranch. Their camp was surrounded at night and they were taken before they could resist.

They were brought before Commissioner C. J. Wrightsman at Pawnee for a preliminary hearing and committed to the federal jail at Guthrie pending their trials.

Starting for Guthrie in the afternoon following the hearing, it was necessary for Starmer and his assistant officer, Charlie Dugger, to hold the prisoners over night in camp when they reached Bird Creek. Beds were made on the ground near the wagon wheels and the captives shackled to the wheels

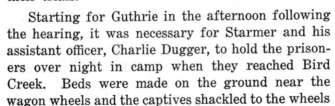

of the vehicle in such a position that they could not reach each other. The officers were pretty tired, having spent the preceding night in search for these outlaws before their capture and they slept soundly.

Just before daybreak Starmer heard a noise. He roused himself quickly and found that Baker had managed to get out of his handcuffs and was racing toward the creek. The deputy was immediately on his feet and after him. Baker jumped into the stream and Starmer began to shoot into the air about the man, hoping that it would scare the outlaw and cause him to surrender. He did not attempt to injure the man, for he had positive instructions from my office never to shoot a prisoner for an offense of this character. As soon as it was light enough to trail the man Starmer left Dugger to guard the others while he crossed the creek to make a search in the surrounding woods. He was unsuccessful and after a time returned to camp, setting out with Mrs. Baker and Thomas for Guthrie.

While she was being held in the federal jail the Baker woman sent word that she wanted to talk to me and I had her brought to my office. When she entered the room she started a tirade against my deputy, George Starmer, charging that he had stolen her husband's necktie and coat, then killed him while he was attempting to swim Bird Creek and that he had made no effort to locate the body. She ranted and raved and used considerable bad language, but I listened to her as any gentleman would listen to a woman and told her I would be very glad to investigate the case. When she was returned to the jail she immediately wrote a very bitter letter to the

authorities at Washington. Although it passed through my hands before it was mailed, I allowed it to go on without comment.

George Starmer had told me his side of the story and I placed so much confidence in what he said that I did not take the trouble to call him in to question him about it. A week or ten days later, however, I received a letter from the Department of Justice requesting a full report on the case. Starmer happened to be in Guthrie on the day it arrived and I sent word to him that I wanted to talk to him.

When he walked into my office I assumed a very serious manner and handed the letter over to him. "That looks pretty bad, George, what have you got to say about it?" I could see Starmer's color rising in his face as he read the letter and by the time he finished he was almost speechless. He looked at me and gulped a time or two before he could speak.

"Why, Marshal . . . . it's . . . . a . . . . damn . . . . lie!"

Of course, I knew it was a lie and I would not have questioned the veracity of George Starmer's first story to me—but this was too good an opportunity to pass up for having a little fun. I looked Starmer in the eye very seriously and said in a rather abrupt tone: "That may be true, George, but it looks to me like it is up to you to prove it. This woman tells a pretty straight story and Washington seems to be taking it seriously."

Starmer was absolutely nonplussed. It never occurred to him that I would question his story, and I could see that his dander was rising.

"Well, Marshal, what do you want me to do about it?" he said in an attempt at a matter-of-fact tone that could not conceal his nervousness.

"There's only one thing for you to do, George. . . If this man is alive, it's up to you to produce him."

Starmer looked at me a moment, then said: "Alright Marshal, give me ten days."

"Well, George—it's up to you."

Without a word he turned and left my office and I did not hear from him again until he walked in about a week later with F. M. Baker neatly handcuffed to his arm. This time he was grinning.

"Here he is, Marshal!"

I looked up from my work. "Here who is, George?"

"The corpse!" he exclaimed.

"What corpse? He looks like a pretty live man to me."

George refused to be flustrated by my question.

"This is the body of that man, Baker, his wife is raising so much hell about, and he's got on the necktie and coat!"

I looked Baker over seriously and turned to George. "How do you know it's Baker? We will have to bring the woman over from the jail to iden- ify him."

Starmer knew that I was prolonging the kidding and he refused to be bothered by my attempt at hav- ing a good time.

Baker was soon restored to the arms of his spouse and, from the reception he received at her hands, I have often wondered if he wouldn't have preferred to have been shot at Bird Creek. I have heard tongue lashings before, but hers eclipsed them all. Where had he been? What had he been doing? Why had he been doing it? Who had he been with? Eternal woman!

Starmer had located Baker at Vinita, Oklahoma, and had had no trouble in catching him and bringing him back. The three members of the gang were convicted and sent to the federal penitentiary. When my administration as Marshal ended, Starmer left the territory. It was almost twenty-five years before I saw him again. We met at St. Joseph, Missouri, where he held the office of Assistant Chief of Police.

George Starmer declares to this day that he knew all the time that I was just fooling him. He took the incident pretty seriously, though, and I know he heaved an immense sigh of relief when he got his handcuffs on F. M. Baker again.

*   *   *

In this connection I must tell of the most unusual case of John Crilley who was the prince of counterfeiters. His specialties were single and double "Eagles," being ten and twenty dollar gold coins of United States money. At the time in question, about the year 1894, he was seventy-five years of age, but in sound health with an abundance of vim, vigor and vitality. He owned a ranch in Pottawatomie County, a few miles southeast of Tecumseh, the county seat, right in the shadow of the sessions of the United States Court. He seemed absolutely fearless. He denied the charge in detail,

averring that he maintained his laboratory for ex-
perimental and scientific purposes. There was, at
this time, no chemist or scientist in Oklahoma who
could have matched him, even if expert testimony

had been resorted to. So the trial was conducted in
primitive fashion, confined to the mere question of
fact as to whether Crilley was guilty of uttering
counterfeit coin.

This fact was easily established as a number of
the eagles had been passed in Tecumseh, and those
who had received them from Crilley had identified
both the counterfeiter and the coin. Counsel for
Crilley asked for a change of venue from Pottawatomie to Oklahoma County, and it was in the latter
jurisdiction that the case was tried.

The credit for running down Crilley must be
given, almost entirely, to my deputy Sam Bartell.
Sam was what we might call a free-lance officer.
He never paid any attention to district lines. Once
given scent of a transgressor of the law, he would

follow him to the ends of the earth. While Crilley
was right at hand, no one ever dreamed that such
a harmless old man was capable of making gold
eagles. Not so Sam—Crilley had passed the coin,
and Sam was not satisfied with the explanation that
he had received it from some one else. He went to
the old man's home and demanded to be "shown."
Crilley showed him all but his laboratory, as Sam
said, everything from a "cambric needle to a thresh-
ing machine." Then came the underground laboratory, only the entrance with a little hut around it
visible above the surface. Sam soon located molds,
tools and equipment, besides a large sack full of the
single and double eagles. All of which were introduced in evidence and the case seemed conclusive,
but in Crilley's testimony when the defense put in
its case, this remarkable old fellow had the most
astounding array of explanations probably ever presented in a court room. Of course most of it was
ruled out as incompetent, but it had a profound effect
on the jury, what they could understand of it, as
well as all who heard the testimony.

During a lull in the trial, and while the defendant
was giving his testimony on the stand, Judge Henry
W. Scott, the presiding judge of the Court, suddenly
turned to Crilley and asked him if he had ever lived
or had been in Pawnee County, Kansas, to which
Crilley replied in the affirmative. The Judge then
asked if he ever remembered being near Fort Larned
in said county, to which he also replied affirmatively.
"Do you remember a long hill beginning near the
military grounds and running north in a gradual
slope for about two miles," queried the Judge.

"Yes," replied Crilley. "Did you ever drive a one-horse, two-wheeled cart up that hill, with a rough lumber bed on it?" "Yes, many times," Crilley answered solemnly. "Do you recall, on one of these occasions, that you stopped your horse and cart in the road, and two boys with mule teams came up behind you with their wagons loaded with cedar posts; that you held the road and made them pull around you up that hill?" "Yes, I remember that circumstance, and to the best of my recollection, your honor was one of those boys—and, in extenuation of my actions, I would like to add that I was standing behind the cart searching in the bed for something I thought I had lost, and giving the road to two boys heavily loaded never occurred to me until they had passed and gone. I have thought of and regretted the occurrence many times, and I trust it will not prejudice my case before the court and jury."

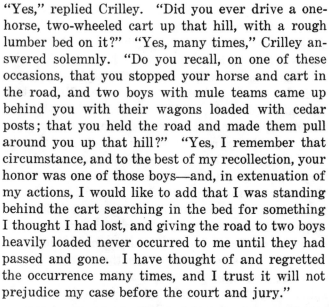

Quick as a flash, the Judge turned toward the jury and made the following statement: "Gentlemen of the jury, you will totally disregard all that has been said concerning the circumstance just brought out by the court. It was not proper that the court should have referred to it at all—it has in no way prejudiced the defendant with the court and it must not do so with the jury. I trust, too, that counsel will understand that it was not expected that any such development would result from the first simple question. The court will allow an exception if counsel for the defense desires to take it." Defendant's attorney very graciously waived any exceptions and the case proceeded as though the circumstance had never happened.

Needless to state that the jury brought in a verdict of guilty, but with it came a recommendation for mercy on part of the court, which the court exercised when judgment was pronounced. Judge Dale had given the simple counterfeiters of silver dollars ten years, but in sentencing Crilley Judge Scott very mercifully gave him but five years in the Kings County Penitentiary at Brooklyn, New York. When sentence was adjudged, the court room was crowded. All the other prisoners to be sentenced had been brought in before Crilley. Soon he was conducted in by Sam Bartell. As he came into the area of the railing, Crilley walked straight up to the Judge's bench, and laid down a fresh unopened box of cigars. This created a panic in the court room. The Judge beat his gavel frantically for order, but all to no

avail. The stampede kept up notwithstanding the court officers were trying to check it—and, without any reflection on the courage of the court officers, they were not lingering in the vicinity of that box of cigars, themselves. The explanation is that Crilley had created such an atmosphere during his trial, indicating super-knowledge of things in general, that when he laid the box of cigars on the Judge's bench, the crowd thought it was an infernal machine, and was getting out of the way before it exploded and blew everyone to atoms. By this time Judge Scott had seen the point. He picked up the box, pryed it open and showed the box of cigars. He turned it over to the bailiff with instructions to return it to Crilley after court adjourned, but it was quite likely that John Crilley had seen the last of his cigars. Judge Scott made no comment on the disturbance

more than that stated. The crowd returned to the court room and business was resumed, after having been so unceremoniously interrupted.

Judge Scott told me, after a lapse of years that, after he had moved to New York, he remembered John Crilley—his age and brilliant mind; that without solicitation he advised Crilley's attorneys that he would recommend a pardon if they would prepare the application. President Cleveland was still in office, but would go out the March fourth following. A personal letter to Cleveland explained all the circumstances, the prisoner's age, etc., but the President denied clemency, stating in his personal letter to Judge Scott, that he considered counterfeiting the most heinous crime under the government next to treason; that outside of treason no crime could be greater than counterfeiting the people's money, a crime that strikes at the very root of the trade and commerce of the Republic.

At any rate John Crilley did not get his pardon, and there is hardly a doubt that he died in the Kings County Penitentiary before his term of imprisonment expired. In some ways of viewing it this case is very pathetic, but from the view expressed by President Cleveland, a dangerous counterfeiter was stopped in his nefarious business forever, and the ends of justice satisfied unto the fullness thereof.

CHAPTER XIII
A DOUBLE ACTION SCRAPPIN'
DEPUTY

At about this time one of my young deputies, Warren Bennett, made a most remarkable capture when he found and overcame Rolla Kapp, a gigantic cattle thief. Bennett had trailed him for several days but the outlaw had succeeded in eluding him. The young deputy learned the location of the outlaw's home and found it on the desolate side of a sand hill about twenty miles from Pawhuska. The deputy watched the house for a whole day and until about midnight, and not a soul stirred about the place. Unrolling his blankets and hobbling his horse, Bennett crept up to the house and lay down on the porch before the entrance to sleep. The morning air was cool and pleasant and the officer was sleeping peacefully when he suddenly sensed danger and was awakened. Rolla Kapp, the cattle thief, stood over him, his pistol in his hand. Bennett gazed at him a second through half-closed eyelids, then with a lightning movement threw his blanket aside, drew his gun and shot the outlaw through the right wrist.

Kapp's pistol fell rattling to the floor of the porch and the cow thief quickly grabbed his other forty-five with his left hand. Bennett shot him through the left arm before the tip of his gun had left its holster. All of this happened so quickly that Bennett still lay upon the floor of the porch on his back, while the outlaw stood writhing in pain above him.

The deputy sprang quickly to his feet and snapped the handcuffs on Kapp's wrists. In spite of his painful injuries, the husky cattle thief was so enraged that it was remarkable that a man of Bennett's small stature was able to control him without being forced to kill him.

On the way to Pawhuska the pair met Deputy Vic Ellis of that town, who joined them on their journey.

Kapp was given a hearing before U. S. Commissioner, T. J. Leahy, of Pawhuska and was committed to the U. S. jail at Guthrie. Later he was tried before Judge Bierer at Pawnee, convicted and received a sentence of five years at Leavenworth penitentiary.

Having known something of the reputation of Rolla Kapp, I felt sure that he would not have hesitated for a moment to kill Deputy Bennett without giving him a dog's chance. This fact makes Bennett's feat all the more remarkable. When he sensed the presence of the outlaw standing over him and peeped with his almost closed eyelids to see who was there, he must have acted with lightning speed, for a man of Rolla Kapp's sort would not be slow with a gun himself.

Bennett was very modest about the whole affair and, although the papers got the story from Vic Ellis and praised Bennett highly, the young deputy insisted that it was a lot of foolishness. I remember his remark when I congratulated him upon his accomplishment. "Why, Marshal," he said seriously, "there was nothing extraordinary about it . . . . when I looked up and saw that cow thief standing over me with his gun in his hand, I knew it was me

Deputy U. S. Marshals. Top—left, Bill Tilghman, right, Chris Madsen. Center—Chief Deputy John Hale. Lower—left, John Hixon, right, Heck Thomas.

Deputy U. S. Marshals—Top—left, Jack Love, right, Frank
Rinehart. Center—Chas. F. Colcord. Lower—left,
John Hubatka, right, Sam Bartell.

or him.   I sure didn't want it to be me."   Sensing danger, a quick draw had saved him.

Bennett died a number of years ago but Vic Ellis, who has been prominent as a peace officer in Tulsa, Oklahoma, for eighteen years, still loves to tell the story of the exceptional bravery and alertness of his friend, Bennett.

CHAPTER XIV
THE RAILROAD AND THE PEOPLE CLASH

During the summer of 1894 the Rock Island Railroad bought tracts of land that adjoined their railroad near Enid and Pond Creek in the northern part of the Cherokee Strip and aroused the indignation of the citizens of these two towns by attempting to establish rival townsites within a mile of each of the towns. To strengthen its own position in the matter, and as a means to force citizens living on government townsites to move to the Rock Island townsites, the railroad company built depots on its own sites and refused to stop trains at either Pond Creek or Enid.

The situation grew more and more tense as the people became determined to continue the development of their property on the government townsites and to force the railroad to stop its trains to serve their communities. The railroad's land department had succeeded in selling a considerable number of lots and the situation had reached a deadlock, finally resulting in a near riot and an attempt by citizens to tear up the rails and destroy other property of the railroad.

While the government would naturally have sided with the people on the government townsites, the rash conduct of these folks forced the Department of Justice to action in order that the transportation of the United States mails might not be obstructed. Feeling in Enid and Pond Creek had become bitter

159

and most any little trifling incident might have turned the situation into a bloody battle with great loss of life. I had used my influence through my very efficient deputy, Pat Murphy, then established at Pond Creek, to adjust the matter—but our efforts were of no avail. The citizens of Pond Creek seemed much more outraged than the people of Enid. C. C. Daniels, a brother of the well known Josephus Daniels, was county attorney and, while he sympathized with the position of the people, he joined Deputy Murphy in trying to convince them of the futility of destructive tactics. The United States government could not permit interference with interstate commerce and with the mails.

Finally, after all efforts had failed to adjust the situation and an attempt had been made by citizens to wreck a Rock Island passenger train, I received a wire from the Attorney General of the United States to place the two towns under martial law, if necessary, to quell the disturbance.

Being closer to the situation than the government at Washington, I realized the fact that diplomacy and not a show of force would be necessary. I was convinced that if I gave out information to newspapers and set out with a trainload of men to enforce my authority, I would probably precipitate a bloody fight. I went into consultation with United

States Attorney Roy Hoffman, Justice Frank Dale and my chief deputy, John M. Hale, and we agreed that it would be better for me to take three or four trusted men and go to make an appeal to the better instincts of the citizens of Pond Creek, where the feeling was most critical.

In order that the people of that location might have no occasion to feel that I wanted to embarrass them, I gave out no news concerning the trip, but proceeded to their town as quietly as possible.

When we arrived at Pond Creek, Deputy Pat Murphy met us, telling us that the townspeople were prepared for battle. It seems that the railroad had intercepted the Attorney General's telegram and had informed the Pond Creek people that I was coming to place them under martial law. Murphy's life had been threatened because, in the performance of his official duty, he had been forced to take a strong position against the sentiment of the people. The people were thoroughly convinced that the government was taking an unfair attitude toward them and discriminating in favor of the railroad company.

After a brief conference I decided to go up town alone and, upon reaching the principal street, I found a hundred citizens lined up with Winchesters and shotguns in hand, awaiting what they thought would be an attack by a large group of deputy marshals. As I walked toward them I raised my handkerchief and drawing near I recognized S. L. Bradley, the county clerk and recorder, whom I had known quite well. Notwithstanding that he was a county official, he stood with his fellow citizens ready to fight to the end to protect their town from the greed of the railroad.

I motioned to Bradley and he stepped out of line and came forward to meet me. A moment or so later County Attorney Daniels joined us in our discussion of the situation. These gentlemen took the position that the government should force the railroads to

stop at the townsites that had been set aside by the government for settlement by its citizens. I agreed with them but explained to them that they were going at the matter in the wrong way, thereby forcing the government to take action to protect interstate commerce and the United States mails. I showed them the telegram I had received from the Attorney General and explained that unless some amicable understanding could be reached I would be forced to carry out the government's order and that there would probably be useless bloodshed. I also explained that I had not attempted to embarrass the Pond Creek people by giving out publicity regarding the situation but that I had come to them in a quiet, respectful way, hoping to be able to adjust conditions without being forced to the martial law order the government had given.

Bradley turned and made a short talk to the men who were lined up for battle, after which I was asked to talk to them. County Attorney Daniels followed by remarks, urging that the people follow my suggestion and give the government time to adjust their differences with the railroad company. The crowd, much to their own credit, fell into the spirit of the agreement very graciously.

I then told the citizens that I had warrants for about eighty of their people on charges having to do with obstructing the mails and interstate commerce. I told them that I had no desire to embarrass anyone and that if they would have their citizens appear before me as their names were called, I would check the warrants and allow each one to go on his own recognizance to appear before the United States

Commissioner at Kingfisher at a set time.   They agreed to this and I immediately sent a runner for my deputies to join me and take charge of the work. This little potential riot was terminated in a veritable love feast.   I was given a dinner at the hotel by a large crowd of the citizens.   Word had gone on to Deputy W. A. Ramsey at Enid as to what had been done and when I arrived there late in the evening he had a large crowd of Enid citizens gathered in the public auditorium to meet me.   The Enid people were very tractable.   I had warrants for about a hundred of their citizens and they were handled in the same way.

In a very short time the railroads decided to recognize the government townsites and render good service to the people of Enid and Pond Creek.   The charges against the citizens of both towns were dismissed without cost or prejudice.   It was probably very fortunate for all parties concerned that a way was found to handle this situation so amicably.

CHAPTER XV

TILGHMAN IN A DEN OF THIEVES

It was a bitter cold day in January: a cutting norther whined shrilly across the Oklahoma prairies, sweeping sleet and snow from exposed places and whirling frozen particles in the air as it dashed them madly along until they might fall in some sheltered spot. A thin crust of ice lay upon the breasts of sluggish creeks, their banks edged with compact miniature snowdrifts. The branches of the black-jack trees crackled in the wind; occasionally one broke beneath its frosty burden, shattering fine frozen bits into the lap of the vicious gale.

A covered wagon rumbled over the frozen clods of the vague trail, drawn by a pair of hungry, shivering horses. A grim-faced Indian urged the tired horses through the tempest. Charlie Bearclaw was as faithful a friend of the white man as the Indian race ever produced. He had served for a number of years as a scout for the United States Army and now was on the payroll of my office, having been engaged to pilot deputy United States marshals through the wastes and wildernesses he knew so well.

Bill Tilghman and Assistant Deputy Neal Brown rode behind the Indian, partly sheltered from the storm by the flapping canvas tarpaulin. Tilghman had received word that a rancher southeast of Pawnee near the Cimarron River was harboring members of the Doolin gang and assisting in some of their cattle thefts. The officers hadn't heard of the

Doolins for some time and Tilghman had little hope of finding them here, but he was determined to arrest the rancher he was seeking. Brown's teeth were chattering.

"It'll be a damn cold job fording the Cimarron, Bill."

"Well, it'll be a mighty lot colder if we don't get across it and headed toward Pawnee," Tilghman replied. "If it starts snowing again we'll never find our man."

A mile or so along they drove through a deep ravine and came out to see a thin wisp of smoke ascending from the chimney of a rude dugout about two hundred yards from the trail.

Tilghman called to the Indian: "Stop here, Charlie. You boys wait here while I run down to see what I can see."

The broncos humped their back and stood shivering, and Charlie Bearclaw filled his pipe as Tilghman walked through the storm to the dugout.

Not a soul was stirring outside the place, and Tilghman walked up to the door and pushed it open. At the end of the room a fire of blackjack logs crackled cheerfully in the wide fireplace. On both sides of the big room were tiers of bunks covered with hanging curtains. There were accommodations for fifteen or twenty men. The rancher sat in a chair before the fire, a Winchester across his lap.

"How far is it to Bee Dunn's place," Tilghman asked, while his sharp eyes were sizing up the layout.

"Find out for yourself," came the surly tone from the rancher, although Tilghman thought he caught a significant expression on the man's face, and was convinced he was affecting his unfriendly manner.

"All right, I will," said Bill agreeably. He was stamping his feet and rubbing his frozen hands and ears to stimulate circulation, all the while searching the large room for a sign that would reveal the cause for the rancher's surly manner. . . . "Say, this fire feels mighty good."

"It is hotter than that in hell," the man commented roughly.

As Tilghman was about to mention that he and his men would like to remain for the night, his eye caught a faint rustle of one of the curtains and he saw the tip of several Winchester barrels peeking their deadly eyes toward him.

The marshal assumed a nonchalant manner and tried to seem very much unconcerned but with lightning glances he was trying to determine if there were other guns pointing from the other bunks. For a few minutes there wasn't a sound except the howling of the north wind as it whisked fine snow through the unchinked cracks where it dropped in melting masses on the floor.

Here was a situation that demanded all of the coolness and chilled-steel nerve that Bill Tilghman's years of experience had given him. He talked on for a few moments without the slightest tremor of excitement in his voice. Finally he said to the ranchman: "Well, I guess we had better be getting up the trail—which way does a fellow get out of here?" he asked carelessly as he moved slowly toward the door.

"The same damn way you got in," the man snarled.

Will Dunn had recognized Tilghman when he first approached him, and while the wise officer had sensed such a thing, it was later he was assured he was talking to Dunn.

As Tilghman passed close by the bunks he could hear the breathing of several men. He did not hasten his step, nor look to right or left until the door closed behind him. He then wheeled about, drawing his two forty-fives and walked backwards until he had reached the wagon, his eyes set on the door of the dugout. Clambering in, he spoke to the Indian: "Give your nags the bud, Charlie." Turning to Brown he said, "Neal that dugout is lousy with outlaws just achin' for trouble. Before we tackle 'em we need help a-plenty."

Tilghman hurried to Pawnee where he found Chief Deputy John Hale, who had come to the little trading station to attend court. A large posse was immediately formed and the officers set out toward the scene of Tilghman's hair-raising experience. Early forenoon of the day following Tilghman's narrow escape, they neared the vicinity of the dugout. They approached very slowly, searching the landscape with field glasses. On a knoll a quarter of a mile from the habitation they made out the reclining figure of a man who was watching the place. The officers signalled, and Will Dunn, owner of the ranch, came running toward them and informed the officers that the outlaws had gone the night before. Dunn had feared that the place might be bombarded as the officers approached it and he had hidden out

to avoid being shot, and hoping to save his property from destruction.

It was from him that Tilghman learned how Bill Doolin had saved him from the cowardly fire of Red Buck Waightman. Tilghman also learned that Bill Doolin, Bill Dalton and six other outlaws had been hiding in the bunks of that dugout while he was there. Red Buck Waightman, the most desperate and inhuman man of the gang, had leaped from his bunk when Tilghman left the place, crying out that he was going to kill that "damn lousy marshal." He was only prevented by the interference of Bill Doolin and the ranchman, who had quite a struggle with the would-be murderer before they were able to subdue him.

Tilghman soon learned that the ranchman was Will Dunn and that he had assumed his hostile manner to convince the outlaws that he was not friendly to the officers.

Dunn had said to Red Buck: "If you shoot Tilghman there will be a hundred men on your trail inside of twenty-four hours."

Red Buck was viciously resentful toward his fellows. "You are a lot of damn cowards. Tilghman will be back here before sunrise with a big posse and we will be trapped like rats."

Dunn advised the bandits to leave the dugout at once, fearing an attack later. The bandits were worn and fatigued with hard riding and were badly in need of rest but, to avoid a conflict, they rode out into the storm, Red Buck still swearing and cursing at the others.

We realized that Dunn should not be censured for seeming to harbor the Doolin gang. His actions was only the result of the same fear that caused many other respectable citizens and cow men to give aid to the bandits much against their will.

Tilghman, appreciating Dunn's conduct, deputized Dunn as a posseman and a few days later when he came to Guthrie with Tilghman, as a further recognition, I gave him a commission as a deputy United States marshal on his word that he would assist us in wiping out the Doolin-Dalton gang.

ROBERT PHILLIPS

CHAPTER XVI

AN UNPLEASANT DUTY AVERTED

Early in the year 1895 Robert J. Philips, after a sensational trial in Judge Scott's court, was convicted and sentenced to hang after the killing of a farmer in the Choctaw Nation and stealing his team. His was the first death penalty to be assessed since my appointment and I was very much disturbed over the prospect of having to spring the trap that would break the criminal's neck.

While I had a pretty thorough instruction in the art of hanging men so that their necks would pop very neatly and effectively, the gruesomeness of the matter was magnified a great deal when it seemed that I was actually confronted with the responsibility of carrying out such an edict. I don't believe I am chicken hearted but somehow I just couldn't steel myself to the determination that I would see the thing through. Any sort of a legitimate alibi would have my enthusiastic approval.

The scaffold was built about a hundred yards from the federal jail. Philips had been very much fascinated by the progress of the construction work. A couple of other prisoners would give him a boost to the top of one of the steel cages in the jail where he could look out through the window and see everything that was done about the scaffold. When it was completed and the men were testing the strength of the rope and the mechanical action of the trap, they brought in a two hundred pound sack of sand to use as a dummy. Philips lay peering out through

173

the window. The heavy sack was adjusted to the noose and when the trap was sprung, the rope broke, the sand falling with a thud to the floor beneath the scaffold. The condemned man collapsed and went into a comatose state that puzzled our government physician a great deal.

When I heard of the incident I visited Dr. Smith and told him that while I didn't want to request him to give the man something that would kill him, I certainly hoped he wouldn't give him anything that would cure him. I was anxious to avoid an unpleasant duty. Within two days of the time set for the hanging, Philips died a natural death from nervous shock. It is the only occasion I can recall where I have rejoiced at the death of any man. I felt like celebrating.

My jubilation received a sudden shock a few days later when a man by the name of John Dawson was sentenced to be hanged. That gave me several days of anxiety and I was very much relieved when he succeeded in securing a reversal and a new trial that acquitted him. The officers on my staff were all convinced that Dawson was not guilty of the charge against him. He was an unusually pleasant fellow and conducted himself as a gentleman under all circumstances. I had so much confidence in him during his confinement in the United States jail that I allowed him to visit the bedside of his dying mother near Perry, Oklahoma. Dawson moved to Missouri and made good afterwards. I have seen him a number of times since his narrow escape from the gallows.

In this connection I am reminded of the case of John Milligan, convicted and sentenced to hang by Judge Henry W. Scott in the Oklahoma City district. Milligan was a colored man about twenty-four or five years of age. He had come to Oklahoma with a colored family from one of the southern states to work on their farm in Oklahoma County, which the head of the house had been fortunate enough to get in the opening of the country. The old colored man had a considerable sum of money which he carried in a belt around his waist. He would not even trust it with a bank.

This money aroused the cupidity of Milligan and he laid his plans to steal it. In doing so he aroused some of the family, so he proceeded to murder the whole family as he thought. However, a little seven or eight year old girl came to life, dragged herself to a neighboring family and told her sad and gruesome story. The story was investigated and pursuit of the negro began, which aroused all the peace officers in the Territory, in which many of my deputies took part so far as deemed proper in what seemed to be merely a Territorial case. After a few weeks Milligan was apprehended and put on trial with the result related above. The case was appealed to the Supreme Court of the Territory and the judgment of the court below affirmed, and the case remanded to said court for the execution of the sentence.

Judge Scott had fixed the day of execution of the negro and the event would have gone into Oklahoma criminal history with the other horrors of her early days, but for the fact that there arose from the fanatical element of the people of the Territory a hue

and cry against staining the fair name of this new land with a so-called legal hanging. Believe me or not, no State of the Union, considering its size and population ever set up a greater furor than occurred in this crime ridden land. One would have thought that, after the spilling of innocent blood in Oklahoma for years past, this would be the last place to inspire sympathy for such a bloody crime. But, bless you, men and women descended upon the Governor of the Territory, Governor William C. Renfrow in hosts. He did not know what to make of it. Not only that but every man of supposed influence was importuned to intercede with the executive power. As a matter of course my office was stormed, and I was amazed at some of my own friends who had joined in the parade to my private office to enlist my influences with the Governor at their behest. It was necessary for me to tell them very frankly that from what I knew of the case I felt the law should take its course. I did, however, on my own responsibility take the matter up with Governor Renfrow and Judge Scott. We discussed the case at considerable length, which satisfied me of the horrors of the crime more completely than it was reported in the newspapers or made to my office immediately after the murder occurred. Thus I washed my hands of the entire affair, leaving the issue for executive clemency where it belonged.

This did not in any way abate the activity of the clamorers for mercy to the poor ignorant negro. The proponents had set a mass meeting at the Hotel Royal at Guthrie and by some means had induced Governor Renfrow to be present. Supreme Court

was then in session and all of the Justices of the
Court were in the city.   Judge Scott was a guest of
the Hotel during the Supreme Court session.   The
leader of the male contingent was a man by the name
of John Furlong and, so far as the good women were
concerned all of them seemed to be leading in a solid
phalanx.   They had fought shy of Judge Scott until
the mass meeting was in full blast.   Then the Judge
was rounded up by the ladies, who must have given
way to that contingent of the aggregation out of his
general respect for women.   When he entered the
spokesman informed the Judge and all present that
the Governor had expressed a willingness to com-
mute Milligan's sentence to life imprisonment if such
action were recommended by Judge Scott, the trial
Judge in the case.   The applause was mighty.   Here
was the Judge.   Here was the Governor.   Here were
the many good men and women whose desire it was
not to stain the fair name of Oklahoma with blood.
If the law could be stayed a bill would be passed by
the next Territorial Legislature abolishing capital
punishment.   So the agitaters asserted.

The excited assembly was breathless.   What
could the Judge do but to say the word that would
save a human life from the gibbet?   Would he say
that word?   His remarks were brief.   "Mr. Chair-
man, ladies and gentlemen," he said solemnly.
"John Milligan, was indicted and tried in the District Court of the Third Judicial District of the Territory of Oklahoma for the murder of an entire family of his own people, except a little girl of seven or
eight years, whom he thought he had murdered also.
He had a fair and impartial trial before a jury of

his peers. This jury returned a verdict of guilty as charged in the indictment. Upon that verdict of guilty it was the duty of the court to pronounce judgment of death on the gallows. That judgment was pronounced according to law. The case was appealed to the Supreme Court of the Territory, unanimously affirmed by the Court and the case remanded to the court below for execution. Everything has been done and legally done but the execution of the judgment. Therefore, I feel it my solemn duty to refuse to make any recommendation or in any way interfere with the executive department in this case. Governor Renfrow is an honest, just and upright executive, and if the prisoner is entitled to executive clemency, it is his prerogative to so order. Thank you." Governor Renfrow after some consideration refused to grant clemency.

This was the end of the Milligan case, and the end of farther agitation. Milligan paid the penalty for his crime on the gallows in the Oklahoma County jail yard soon afterward, and this first legal execution had an instant effect in the lessening of crime which is a part of Oklahoma criminal history.

These experiences impressed me so deeply that I have refused upon a number of occasions since to serve on juries in cases where death sentences might be demanded.

*   *   *

CHAPTER XVII
THE VICIOUS RED BUCK IS OSTRACIZED

In the month of May, 1895, Bill Doolin led his swashbuckling gang to a point on the Rock Island near the little town of Dover in the El Reno district where they stopped a passenger train, robbed the express and mail cars and the passengers. I received a telegram from the Rock Island officials and immediately got in touch with Chris Madsen who was then in charge of that territory. With deputies Prather and Banks, two Indian scouts and two or three other men who had been recruited in El Reno, they loaded their horses into a box car and were quickly taken to the scene of the hold-up by a special engine and crew, arriving within a few hours after the robbery occurred.

They were soon on the trail of the bandits and just before sundown rode to the top of a rolling hill and looked down its slope into the camp of the train robbers.

At almost the same moment they were spied by the outlaws. The officers dashed forward in an attempt to get within firing range before the outlaws could reach their horses and escape. As the posse drew near, the bandits opened fire and a red-hot fight ensued. The horse of Tulsa Jake Blake was shot from under him and a moment later Red Buck Waightman's mount groaned and tumbled into the dust. Both the unmounted men raced toward a nearby clump of timber. One of their fellows, see-

181

ing their predicament, dashed back and Red Buck sprang up behind him just as Tulsa Jack fell headlong, fatally wounded.

After a thrilling pursuit of more than a mile, the outlaws entered some heavy timber and scattered, eluding the posse. Shortly after midnight they met again at a camp they had agreed upon. After a consultation, Doolin and Dalton decided the gang had better make a long ride and they set out in the direction of Woodward County in the Cherokee Strip.

The extraordinary crudeness and bloodthirstiness of Red Buck Waightman had been a source of irritation to Bill Doolin for some time. Doolin wanted to be rid of the man, but disposing of him was a delicate matter. It always seemed better judgment to let things ride, hoping that some day Red Buck would get a dose of lead either from the officers or from some fellow who might become aggravated at Red Buck's surliness.

Now the undesirable one rode along with the gang, mounted behind one of the other men and cursing the luck that had deprived him of his horse and saddle. He finally consoled himself with the thought that he would be able to steal a better horse before sundown, and hushed his raving.

Along toward noon they passed the home of a backwoods preacher. A little log cabin nestled comfortably in a group of shady trees and early spring flowers bloomed brilliantly in the small door-yard. Not far from the house stood a stockade-like stable built of poles, with a mud roof. Three or four lively horses trotted to the fence of the little barn lot and snorted as the strange horses of the outlaws drew near.

"By cracky, here's where I accumulate a horse!" Red Buck exclaimed as he jumped down from behind Bitter Creek and trotted down the lane toward the barn. The others waited at the road.

Red Buck went into the stable and after a moment came back dragging saddle, bridle and blanket. Releasing the lariat from the saddle horn, he uncoiled it and ran toward the corral.

At the same time the aged preacher ran out from the house, calling, "What are you doing there? That's my son's saddle and outfit—."

Before the tottering old man could finish his sentence Red Buck whirled and shot him dead. The outlaw then turned about and cooly proceeded to rope a horse and saddle it.

Bill Doolin had heard the disturbance, and he hurried to the scene. When he saw the helpless old man lying dead, all of his recent indignation was aroused but he managed to suppress the bitterness of his feelings as he turned to Red Buck: "Get on that horse, you damn fool, and let's get out of here!"

As the bandits raced their horses in an effort to put as many miles as possible between themselves and the scene of the murder, Doolin's determination to be rid of Red Buck grew until he finally called a halt. He leaped to the ground and the others followed, their blowing horses grateful for the breathing spell. Doolin's face muscles were twitching and he was having great difficulty in restraining his anger.

"Bring your saddle bags here, Bitter Creek."

The bags were brought and, without a word, Doolin proceeded to divide the loot from the Dover robbery, handing Red Buck his full share. Tossing the bags back to Newcomb, he turned coldly to Red Buck: "Now, let's see you drag your lousy, cowardly carcass out of my sight! If I ever see you again I'll kill you! You could have taken that horse and outfit without harming a hair on that old man's head. You are too damn low to associate with a high class gang of train robbers. Git!"

When they had disarmed the surprised Red Buck, they rode away and left him standing, mouth agape, staring after them in his surprise.

The gang immediately separated, agreeing to meet at a rendezvous near Woodward within a few days. About five days later they came together at this point twelve or fifteen miles east of the town of Woodward where they had found an ideal hiding place and a very good abandoned ranch house some distance from the trail. After resting a day or two, Bitter Creek Newcomb, Charlie Pierce and Little Bill Raidler rode into Woodward to look over the situation and see if it seemed possible to commit a profitable robbery.

They reached the town during the middle of the afternoon and rode up to a saloon. Tossing their horses' reins over the hitching rail, they entered the place. It was no unusual thing for pleasure-seeking cow hands to ride into these small frontier towns for a few hours of diversion and recreation, and the three bandits attracted no special attention. They separated for a while, Charlie Pierce going to look

for a girl he had known in Texas and Little Bill
strolling into the gambling room behind the saloon.
Newcomb drifted out to the street where he loafed
for a while, chatting with two or three of the citizens. Then he walked down to the depot and idled
very casually about until he had a perfect picture
of the place in mind. In some manner, he learned
that the evening train was supposed to bring a shipment of several thousand dollars for one of the local
banks. He reasoned that since the train would arrive late in the evening the money would be held in
the express company's safe until morning.

He walked back to the saloon, called Little Bill
from his game to have a drink and the two went out
to look for Pierce. They found him chatting with a
yellow-haired girl in a joint a few doors from the
saloon and had considerable difficulty in prying him
away.

The three mounted their horses and rode out of
the quiet little town. When they had ridden about
a mile, Newcomb stiffened in his saddle and became
alert. . . . "Say, pardners, I've got the information
we want. There ain't no sense in us riding fifteen
miles to get the others and then back again. We
can pull this by ourselves. What do you say?"

"Sure—suits us," the others replied.

When the three had ridden two or three miles
farther, they abruptly turned from the trail and rode
up a small draw that deepened as it left the road.
The twisting curves of the draw soon led the outlaws
to a point where they could not be seen by travelers.
Here they dismounted and sat down with their whis-

key and cigarettes to await the concealing shadows of night.

"We'll hit the town about ten o'clock," said Newcomb, as the others drew near to hear his plans. . . . "The money will probably be in the express office. I found out where the agent lives. We'll take him quietly and force him to unlock the safe. No complications, no fight, no trouble of any kind. Pretty slick,—eh?"

And thus the plan was carried out, so quietly, so effectively that the citizens of Woodward knew nothing whatever about it until morning. The express agent was seated in his comfortable home, reading. Newcomb had knocked at his door and, when the man came out, had thrust his pistol against his stomach, whispering: "Tell your wife you have got a little business down town. Don't raise a ruckus!" The man had been taken to the depot so quietly and unobtrusively that not a soul suspected what was going on, although the outlaws passed several citizens on the street.

The frightened agent opened the safe and bundles containing approximately sixty-five hundred dollars were handed over to the outlaws. The agent was then bound and gagged and left in the depot office. The bandits rode slowly down the main street of Woodward and out of the town without exciting the least bit of suspicion. As they reached the outskirts of the village, they spurred their horses into a run and made all possible haste for the camp, where the others waited.

They immediately informed their comrades of

their haul, and were much applauded for such undertaking by themselves.

The gang was soon on the go again, realizing that as soon as the robbery was known the officers would be one their trail.

It was early morning before the robbery was known to the officers. Deputy Jack Love notified my office, organized a posse and was soon on their trail. Love was an active and fearless officer but the outlaws had several hours the advantage and that part of the territory was used principally as a grazing country at that time and the officers had to depend upon overtaking the bandits, catching them in camp or in their hiding place. Love and his posse put in a strenuous day but failed to get in sight of the escaping outlaws.

The cave rendezvous of the gang in the Creek Nation had been discovered and the gang had established no new hiding place they considered to be absolutely safe. Of late, the officers had been able to keep pretty hot on the trail and Doolin and Dalton were worried. It seemed no longer possible to conduct their escapades with the wild abandon that had characterized their earlier depredations. They realized that they must be very cautious. The wound Doolin had received in the Ingalls fight, which at the time had seemed insignificant, was troubling him a great deal. The bullet had lodged near the base of the brain and was causing a pressure that was seriously affecting the man's nervous condition.

The cold-blooded killing of the old preacher by the murderous Red Buck had preyed a great deal upon Doolin's mind. He had no compunction about

killing an officer, or any other man, in a hand-to-hand fight where the breaks were something like fair, but the brutal shooting of this helpless old man had disturbed Doolin much more than his companions realized. This feeling together with his decline in health and spirit, caused Doolin to recommend that the gang disband for the time being with the understanding they meet at the Bee Dunn ranch in about fifteen days.

After some discussion the sixty-five hundred dollars taken in the Woodward robbery was divided among the members of the gang and they scattered again, agreeing to communicate with each other at the time and place agreed upon.

Doolin's wife and baby were known to be living somewhere in the territory. Although our officers were never able to locate them up to that time. Doolin went immediately to join them and to take a rest in an attempt to recover from his wound and cure his rheumatism. We later learned that Dalton went straight to the home of relatives in the country near Ardmore, Oklahoma. The other four went in various directions to follow their own notions for enjoying the fruits of their "toil".

Little Bill Raidler and Bitter Creek Newcomb took a trip to Chicago, where they spent their accumulated loot in riotous living. Chicago, however, was too fast for them and when they returned to Oklahoma they were flat broke. Little Bill bought a very expensive pair of silver plated six-shooters with ivory handles, embossed with scroll work and carved with figures of angels. These guns were taken from him later when he was captured.

Deputy U. S. Marshals. Top—left, W. M. Nix, right, W. O. Jones. Center—S. S. Nix. Lower—left, W. A. Ramsey, right, Forest E. Halsell.

Deputy U. S. Marshals. Top—left, E. W. Snoddy, right, George Starmer. Center—Joe Miller, deputy and jailer. Lower—left, T. C. Parker, right, Gus Hadwinger.

CHAPTER XVIII
THE LURE OF THE OUTLAW'S LIFE

Following the wiping out of the Casey gang, a couple of ambitious fellows named Bob Hughes and Jim Bourland decided that there was big money in the career of outlawry. Many wild tales had been told in the territory about the enormous sums bandits were getting away with. Bill Doolin was rated as a very rich man. These fellows decided to emulate him. They recruited Henry Silva, Felix Young and Jim Fuller and laid their plans for the first hold-up. They decided to stop a Rock Island passenger train at a bridge near Pond Creek in the Strip—and they flattered themselves that their plans had been so soundly laid that theirs would be the perfect crime. But there is an old saying about there being many a slip. The Pond Creek robbery was a fiasco. Hughes was killed by Bill Fossett, a special officer for the Rock Island, and the rest of the gang made their get-away without having secured a penny in loot.

Chris Madsen was instructed to take up the trail of the bandits and a few days after the hold-up Henry Silva and Felix Young were recognized in El Reno. Madsen was informed immediately and he located them in a gambling house. Silva surrendered without a fight, but Young tried to make his get-away through the back door of the joint.

Madsen turned the arrested prisoner over to a friend who stood near by and pursued the fleeing Young. The outlaw's horse had been hitched to a

189

post about two blacks down the street. Young had some advantage of the officer and reached his horse while Madsen was still a block away. The deputy commandeered a strong looking horse that stood at a hitching post near by and an exciting chase ensued. The bandit was not able to shoot effectively with his forty-fives, and Madsen's Winchester gave him the best of the deal. As Madsen drew near enough he fired, killing the bandit's horse and, as the horse tumbled into the dust, Madsen jumped to the ground beside the fallen man and disarmed him.

The two prisoners were transferred to the jail at Enid where they were held. Pending trial, Big Jim Bourland escaped into Texas, which was bad judgment on his part, for he had escaped from the penitentiary at Huntsville some time before and the officers were looking for him. He had not been in the Lone Star State many days until he was recognized and captured. After he had languished in the Huntsville prison for a short time, the federal government asked the State of Texas to release him and he was returned to Oklahoma for trial.

While Big Jim Bourland, Young and Silva were confined at Enid, they made their escape. Big Jim had not the instinctive nature of the ingenuous outlaw. Somehow it was impossible for him to elude officers for very long. Chris Madsen soon located him and returned him to jail. Madsen took up the pursuit of Silva and Jim Fuller, and discovered that Silva was supposed to be working in the mines in Colorado. The deputy went immediately to look for him and found that he had left for Wheatland, Cal., on account of a strike in Colorado. Madsen followed

him there and he succeeded in arresting him. The
man was convicted and sentenced to the federal penitentiary. Henry Silva, the only remaining one of
the Hughes-Bourland gang, disappeared completely
and was never found.

Big Jim Bourland was pardoned after he had
served a part of his term and he returned to Oklahoma, settling at Anadarko, where he became a respected citizen. He was a giant in stature and a
most genial fellow. He was later appointed a special detective and he assisted the officers of Oklahoma
in special work. He was absolutely fearless and
soon became a nemesis to law breakers.

On one occasion Big Jim informed Deputy Madsen that Kid Lewis, a brother-in-law of his deceased
partner in the outlaw venture, had associated himself with a young fellow named Tom Foster and that
the two were committing petty crimes in and around
Arapaho. These two young bloods must have suspected that Bourland had informed the officers about
them for they rode up to his home one evening and,
calling the man to his door, they shot him down without a word.

Madsen and a small posse had gone to Mountain
City on a special case and, upon learning of this last
murder and that Foster and Kid Lewis had gone in
the direction of Fort Sill, he immediately set out
upon their trail. Near the Fort the officers stopped
at a little red store along the trail and learned that
the two men had bought a supply of ammunition and
inquired as to the best way to get to Wichita Falls.
Madsen hoped to overtake them before they reached

the Texas line but was unsuccessful and he pursued them on into Wichita Falls.

As Madsen and his posse rode into town, he found the young outlaws in the midst of a bank robbery in which they had already killed the president and the cashier. A hot gun fight was on, but the outlaws succeeded in reaching their horses and getting away from the angry citizens. Madsen joined the Texas officers in the pursuit and assisted in the capture that took place an hour or two later. When the men were returned to the town and placed in jail a large mob was formed in the street, threatening to lynch them. The presence of the Texas rangers, however, seemed to put a quietus on the crowd and they finally dispersed.

Madsen started his posse back toward El Reno and, having some business in Fort Worth, took the train for that city, accompanied by Lieutenant Sullivan of the ranger force who, believing that peace had been established in Wichita Falls, was withdrawing his men and leaving the situation in the hands of local officers. When they had gone less than an hour the train was flagged at a little station and Lieutenant Sullivan was handed a telegram urging him to return at once. The officers were able to make close connections and they took the first train back to Wichita Falls. Madsen accompanied them.

When they reached the town and walked toward its business section they saw the shadows of two men swinging in the air from a telephone pole. The mob had disappeared and the gathering dusk was settling over the little town as peacefully as if nothing had happened.

CHAPTER XIX

THE FIGHT AT THE DUNN RANCH

After the robbery at Woodward I determined that we would wipe out the Doolin gang if I had to concentrate every man on my staff upon the task. We felt that we had them on the run and that if we would give them no opportunity to recuperate their strength and to add to their forces we would be able to prevent further robberies until we had them in prison or under the sod.

At about the time Bitter Creek and Little Bill returned from Chicago we received word from Will Dunn that these two outlaws had met Dynamite Dick and Charlie Pierce at the ranch of his brother Bee and the four outlaws had gone but would return in a few days. Deputy Bill Tilghman was joined by Heck Thomas and a substantial posse, they started immediately for Will Dunn's ranch. They found him in the dugout and were told that the outlaws were expected to reach the home of his brother, Bee, during the next twenty-four hours. The officers, accompanied by Will Dunn, rode to the home of the other Dunn immediately. Bee had not been informed of Will Dunn's appointment as a special deputy and he was very much surprised when the officers rode up to his home accompanied by his brother.

Tilghman and Thomas informed Bee Dunn that they had a warrant for him on a charge of cattle stealing and harboring outlaws, and that unless he cooperated with them in the capture of the outlaws, he would lose his liberty and possibly his life, as they

195

were determined to take the bandits regardless of cost. Dunn consented to aid the officers.

The Dunn ranch house was a two-story building with two large rooms downstairs, divided by a hallway from which a stairway led to one large room above. The upper room was fitted out with bunks, providing sleeping quarters for fifteen or twenty men. The building faced south and there were doors and windows in the north, south and west. The windows on the east side, both upstairs and down, had been broken out by a hail storm and were boarded up.

Because it was possible that the outlaws might approach from the east and it would not be possible to observe them from the inside of the house if they came from that direction, the officers decided to dig a pit a short distance from the house to conceal three of their number where they might stand guard and warn the others on the inside.

Heck Thomas, Bee Dunn and one of the possemen entered the pit which gave them splendid protection. Tilghman, Will Dunn and the remaining two possemen took their places in the house where they could cover all entrances to the building. The long wait began. The outlaws had apparently been delayed. The weather had been very bad and hard rains had flooded a number of streams so that the country was almost impassable.

On the evening of the third day, just as night was falling Bitter Creek Newcomb and Charlie Pierce rode toward the house from the north. The officers were ready and the outlaws were sighted while they were yet some distance away. The deputies had no idea how many men there might be, as the gathering darkness made the figures of the riders indistinct and it was impossible to tell if there were other members of their party a short distance behind.

As the two bandits neared the house, Heck Thomas called out . . . . "Throw up your hands, you are surrounded."

The two shadowy figures leaped from their horses and drew their guns. A flash of light from a belching Winchester revealed the location of the excavation in which the officers were sheltered and the two outlaws ran toward it, shooting rapidly as they ran. Then Thomas and posse aimed at the running shadows—bang!—bang! The two outlaws fell, fatally wounded. Charlie Pierce's head lay less than a foot from the excavation and Bitter Creek fell just behind him. They had proved true to their code—"Never surrender without a fight."

The bodies were placed in a wagon and two posse-men set out on the long drive to Guthrie, the other officers remaining to attempt to capture the remainder of the gang but it seemed that the outlaws' companions had either been warned or were not coming to the rendezvous for they did not appear.

It was our policy to have the bodies of dead bandits embalmed and held for several days that they might be claimed by families or friends. During this time hundreds of people viewed the remains at the undertaking parlors. I don't recall a single case where an outlaw was ever buried in the potter's field and I was usually very much surprised at the moral character and responsibility of the grieved ones who claimed the bodies of their wayward kin.

Bitter Creek Newcomb's father lived at Fort Scott, Kansas, where he conducted a very substantial business. My heart always went out to the relatives of outlaws and I did as much as I could to lighten their grief over the dead men and the attendant disgrace. Newcomb's father was a little resentful about the manner in which his son had been killed. He said he thought the officers hadn't given the boys much of a chance.

"Mr. Newcomb," I said to him, "have you had letters from your son since he became an outlaw?" The father answered that he had.

"Did he ever say in his letters that he expected to be taken alive?"

The father hesitated a moment, then replied, "No, he said that he would die before he would submit to arrest."

I placed my hand on the disconsolate man's shoulder and said: "My dear sir, I believe that explains the matter. I am deeply sorry for you, but my officers have their duty to perform. I think you understand."

The body of Charlie Pierce was claimed by a brother who lived near Paris, Texas.

Immediately after the killing at the Dunn ranch, Dynamite Dick and Little Bill Raidler, who were to have joined the others at Dunn's, separated and fled in opposite directions.

On an afternoon following, Deputies Nix, Burke and W. O. Jones were returning from Pawnee to Perry after an official trip. They stopped at a country store about twenty miles from Perry to buy cigars and chatted a while with the storekeeper. As they were leaving the store to return to their horses, a man rode up beside the officers' horses and dismounted.

Steve Burke immediately recognized Dynamite Dick, as he had seen him around Reeves Brothers' saloon and dance hall at Guthrie a number of times before the man had joined the outlaw gang, and he whispered to Nix and Jones as he drew his six-shooter. The outlaw made a quick draw but Burke fired, striking Dynamite Dick in the right arm just above the elbow. Officers Nix and Jones had shot almost simultaneously with Burke, one of the bullets taking effect and lodging near the bandit's lungs, the other one piercing the fleshy part of his hip and shattering a piece of the bone. He was disarmed, put into a wagon and taken to Perry.

At Perry he was placed in an express car and brought to Guthrie. I met the party at the train upon its arrival and assisted in taking the prisoner to the office of Dr. Smith, the government physician, where his wounds were dressed. Afterwards, the man was placed in the federal jail. In a few days he contracted pneumonia, probably brought on by the wound in his lung, and died. His body was claimed by his father who lived south of Ardmore, near the Texas line.

Having made such a good beginning after several months of futile effort to destroy the Doolin-Dalton gang, we directed our efforts to the apprehension of the two leaders, Doolin and Dalton, and the only three remaining members of the gang—Little Bill Raidler, Little Dick West and the brutal Red Buck Waightman.

CHAPTER XX

I TANGLE WITH CAP RED SHIRT

No one ever knew where Cap Red Shirt got his name. It seems that he had appeared on the Oklahoma ranges a number of years before my conflict with him and that he invariably wore shirts of such glaring red that his friends often wished for smoked glasses. He was never known to have confided to anyone as to his name or where he came from.

For years he was called plain Red Shirt and when he finally acquired a little ranch east of Mulhall, Oklahoma, and had a few hands working for him, they dubbed him Cap. He was about six feet two and powerfully built and was a very agreeable fellow until he got a few drinks; then he usually started hunting trouble. It seems that a number of the outlaws who had been killed were personal friends of his and we had often suspected that Cap Red Shirt had been connected in some manner with the Doolins.

When about half drunk he would whine and complain a great deal about the gross unfair treatment the outlaws had received at the hands of cowardly officers. My office had received a number of fictitious letters in which we were denounced as murderers. We felt sure these epistles had been written by him.

Early in June, 1895, Cap Red Shirt rode into Guthrie and went directly to Reeves Brothers' Saloon, where he spent an hour or two imbibing whiskey and boasting to the crowd about his fighting qualities and that he was going to make me bite the dust before he left town. He said I had been putting

the directions on the medicine some of the outlaws had been forced to take and that he was going to give me the same dope. Several friends came to my office to warn me but I paid little attention to it, regarding his boast as maudlin raving. I seldom carried a gun while around the office or my home and I didn't take the trouble to arm myself on this occasion. I was very busy handling some Washington correspondence and about eleven o'clock I stepped across the hall from my office to the United States Clerk's office to inspect some files.

As I stepped through the door I glanced up and there stood Cap Red Shirt leering at me. My father always said that the best defense is a surprising offensive tactic. Before the man had time to think or act I lunged for him and got him by the throat with my left hand, using all of my strength, for I realized that Red Shirt was a much stronger man than I. I closed down on his wind-pipe so quickly and severely that he was completely nonplussed and his tongue hung out. Meanwhile, I jerked his gun from its holster with my right hand and rapped him three times over the head with it. He slumped to the floor, completely out. Meanwhile, several citizens had rushed into the office and United States Clerk, Louis Pitts, came out of his hiding place behind a filing cabinet. He had heard Cap Red Shirt muttering threats just before I walked in and had expected a gun duel to the finish.

I refused to have Red Shirt thrown into jail but led him downstairs to the sidewalk in front of the federal building.

"See here, Red Shirt," I said, "I could throw you

into jail for today's threats, or on evidence we have that you have sent numerous threatening letters through the mail, or for harboring outlaws. I could have killed you with your own gun. I am going to do the fool thing and turn you loose. You've got twenty minutes to get out of town and if you ever come back, wear your buryin' clothes. Hike!"

The man seemed completely cowed and he turned and walked away without another word. Within a few minutes he was spurring his horse through the outskirts of the town and out onto the prairie toward Mulhall. I never saw him again after that.

He had had a wide reputation as a fighter but this little affair seemed to completely crush and embarrass him and from that time on he avoided all the friends he had known in Guthrie's saloons and dives. When I returned to Guthrie for a visit a number of years later I was told that he had been seen at Mulhall occasionally but that he had never come into Guthrie again. Evidently it was his pride and not fear that kept him away.

YEAGER - BLACK GANG

Dick Yeager, alias Zip Wyatt, alias Wild Charlie, was the dashing Romeo of the Oklahoma plains. He must have had more than his share of that magnetic quality that causes the ladies to lose their heads, for many stories have been told of his conquests among the plains women. At one time Yeager was associated for a while with a man named Winters, who had an attractive wife. Yeager managed to shrewdly calculate the husband's absences and to conduct an aggressive campaign for the favors of the lady. He

did his work so well that the fair one finally consented to ride away with him. She became his paramour until the fickle Romeo found a little biscuit-shooter in Galena and deserted the spouse of Mr. Winters.

Yeager's gang was often suspected of having had dealings with the Doolin gang but I am convinced that this was untrue. Dick Yeager and his gang confined themselves to postoffice robberies and cattle and horse stealing in the northwestern part of the Cherokee Strip. In late 1894, Yeager was accused of murdering a man who protested against the outlaw appropriating a fine saddle horse. A great many complaints came to my office from Woodward and Woods Counties. Ike Black, his wife, Pearl, S. T. Watson and Jenny Freeman made up the personnel of his gang and I have heard that the women often assisted in the depredations of the men folks.

Deputy Marshal Jack Love of Woodward County and Gus Hadwinger, F. C. Langly and E. W. Snoddy of Woods County had been kept very busy with other duties and very little progress was made in apprehending the Yeager gang. I finally decided to send Forest Halsell to Alva, in Woods County, with an assignment to stay on the job until he had run down this band of outlaws. Deputy Hadwinger joined Halsell in the organization of a posse and during July, 1895, they got word that the outlaws were camped in a clump of hills on a farm near Galena, belonging to a man named Dege. The officers stayed at the farm home for a day, hoping that some of the male members of the gang would come to the house. They disliked the idea of raiding the camp and tak-

ing a chance on having to shoot a woman. When no one showed up, however, the posse rode out into the hills to search for the camp.

As they drew near, they heard the shrill barking of a dog and a wagon rumbled over loose stones. The officers spread and waited for the wagon to draw near. Watson was driving the team. The two women were sitting in the wagon bed. Black sat in the back of the wagon, his legs dangling behind. Yeager rode along on a horse that was recognized as a stolen animal. The officers were at a serious disadvantage because they feared that their bullets might strike the women.

Halsell aimed carefully at Black and fired. The man cried out and grabbed his foot, then jumped from the wagon and ran into a slight depression between two sand hills. Both of the horses hitched to the wagon were hit, one through the neck and the other through the body. They were seen to stagger as the bullets struck them but Watson grasped the reins tighter and popped a blacksnake whip over them, urging them to faster speed.

Halsell and two of the posse men dropped out of the race to attempt to find Black. The others pursued the careening wagon and the mounted bandit through a hail of bullets. It was late in the afternoon and a heavy storm had gathered. Within twenty minutes from the time the outlaws were discovered, a torrent of rain was pouring down, lightning was flashing and thunder was rolling. The rain grew so heavy and darkness came so quickly that it was impossible to follow the trail of the fugitives.

The officers camped until morning, then took up
the trail. Halsell and his two helpers searched for
the footprints of the wounded Black. The other officers discovered that Watson, Yeager and the two
women had succeeded in crossing the Cimarron
River during the night. The posse crossed the river
and soon found the dead carcass of one of the horses
that had been wounded in the fight. At a little
ranch house nearby they learned that the bandits
had taken a horse to replace the dead animal and
had gone on in their flight. Black had succeeded in
rejoining the party. The officers searched all day
and camped again for the night on Gypsum Creek
about six miles southwest of Fairview. The trail
led on to a deep canyon, at the bottom of which little
Gypsum Creek trickled along.

Hadwinger took a pair of field glasses and scru-
tinized the surrounding country from a high point.
He finally made out the camp of the outlaws up toward the head of the creek. As they drew near, they
focused their glasses again on the camp and could
see the three men and two women and the vigilant
big black Spaniel breakfasting about a campfire.

It was one of those clear mornings after a two-
day rain had washed the atmosphere clean, when one
could see for miles. On the opposite side of the
outlaw camp was a tall round mound. It was
planned that Deputy Hadwinger and a part of the
posse were to circle around and come down from the
opposite side, sheltering themselves behind the
mound. Halsell and his men were to ride up from
the other side of the party and fire upon them, forc-

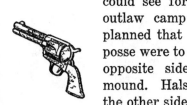

ing them to flee toward the hiding place of Hadwinger and his men.

By establishing two firing lines, the officers hoped
to compell the surrender of the three outlaws. Before Halsell could get his men into position to open
fire on the camp, the outlaws spied them and started
shooting, withdrawing gradually toward the deeper
recesses of the canyon and making it impossible for
Hadwinger and his men to shoot effectively from
their position near the mound. Near-by farmers
heard the shooting and came to assist the posse.

Realizing that it was dangerous to allow his men
to scatter lest they be ambushed from behind the
large gypsum boulders, Hadwinger took charge of
the search, leaving Halsell and two others to guard
the lower end of the canyon. The trail of the outlaws was soon found. It was easily identified by
the depressions made by the moccasin of Black's
wounded foot.

Halsell rode into the camp and discovered that
the men had left the women behind. They were
hiding in the bed of the wagon and he immediately
took charge of them.

The farmers who took part in the hunt were
strangers and it was hard to guess whether they
were friend or foe. The officers believed that they
were given a number of deliberately erroneous tips.
One of the local men ventured away from the searching party and was shot through the hat by Yeager.
Hadwinger fired at Yeager and it was later discovered that his bullet had shattered the outlaw's watch.

After this exchange of shots, night drew near,
and the farmers returned to their homes. It was im-

possible to follow the trail after dark. Hadwinger and his posse returned to the camp and found Halsell's men in charge of the wagon, Halsell having taken the women prisoners to a farm home near by. They found over a dozen bullet holes in the body of the wagon near where Black had been sitting when he was shot in the foot. His escape from worse injury and even death was miraculous.

Next day Halsell took the women prisoners to the federal jail at Guthrie. Hadwinger, assisted by Sheriff McGrath, Deputy Hildreth and a posse, continued the search relentlessly. Black and Yeager were surprised near Steer Hollow in Woods County and shots were exchanged. Two of the officers' horses were killed and the outlaws escaped again. Watson had disappeared and the chase was concentrated on Black and Yeager. The posse followed the trail up Cheyenne Canyon to a point near Richmond. The trail was difficult. Several times, without realizing it, the officers were within a quarter of a mile of the fugitives. The chase continued for about three days, when it was discovered that the outlaws were making rapid progress in an easterly direction.

On the sixth day the officers succeeded in killing Black in a running fight near Canton. His body was literally tattered with bullet holes. The man died with a chew of tobacco in his mouth big enough to choke a horse.

Yeager was also wounded. A bullet hit a scrub-oak tree which smashed it flat and it glanced, striking Yeager on the breast bone. The bone deflected the spent lead and it turned around under the man's arm and lodged almost in the middle of his back without entering the vital cavity. In spite of his wound, Yeager was able to elude the officers again.

Five days later the officers of Enid were notified that a suspicious looking party was hiding in a corn field in the country a few miles away. Deputy Sheriff Polk, of Enid, and City Marshal Smith of Hennessey went to the place immediately and, after searching through the corn field for a short time, found Yeager on a bare sandy mound where he was stretched out on the ground, face downward, lying perfectly still. The officers commanded him to put up his hands. He raised his head in a dazed way and without a second's hesitation reached weakly for his pistol. The officers fired two shots, both taking effect in his abdomen.

He was quickly overpowered and taken to the federal jail at Enid. Although we wanted to move Yeager to the jail at Guthrie, the bandit's condition was so bad that he never regained sufficient strength to make it possible.

Dick Yeager was a fine specimen of physical manhood. More than six feet tall, his unusual strength and courage made him a formidable enemy to all who opposed him. Only such extraordinary vitality as his would have carried him through the fifteen days he lived.

During the long chase after Yeager and Black the officers lost all trace of the man Watson. Some time later we heard that he reached the southwestern part of Oklahoma, near Anadarko, where he had been joined by a half-breed Indian named Esceness. Deputy Sam Bartell was assigned to capture Watson

and the half-breed.   After two or three days of trail-
ing, Bartell located the pair near the Clampton
Ranch on the Washita River about twenty-five miles
from Anadarko.   Esceness was killed in the fight
that ensued and Watson was chased for several
miles, the officers finally surrounding him and forcing his surrender.   Of the Yeager-Black gang, Watson was the only male member who lived to serve a
prison term.

The two women were given short terms in the
federal jail at Guthrie by Chief Justice Dale.

Kill Wentworth's Narrow Call

Kill Wentworth was always suspected of being
a member of the Yeager-Black gang, although we
had never been able to connect him with their escapades.   The man had a pretty black reputation but
the only actual information we had against him concerned the murder in the Osage country and the
theft of his team and wagon.   After a strenuous pursuit, Deputies Heck Thomas and Forrest Halsell captured the man and brought him to Perry, where he
was placed in jail.

The Perry jail was a notoriously flimsy structure at that time and the least carelessness on the
part of guards usually resulted in a wholesale jail
delivery.   Kill Wentworth escaped and was reported
to have headed for the Osage hills.   Heck Thomas
set out in that direction to search for him.

The day passed and, as the night's darkness
shadowed the little prairie town, an excited man ran
down the street calling to Deputy Forrest Halsell,
who stood before a lighted saloon talking to a friend:

"Kill Wentworth's down at Blondy's sporting house raising hell!"

Halsell set out in a run toward the place. Wentworth had so terrified the crowd in the joint that all had fled, leaving him in full possession of the reception room. Halsell pulled his gun and burst through the door. Wentworth stood behind a flimsy wood stove and, before the officer could speak, a bullet crashed through his pistol hand, knocking his gun to the floor. Wentworth was nearly drunk and, as he gave a lunge toward the officer, he struck the stove, knocking it half way across the room, soot pouring from the dangling stove-pipe, blackening everything.

Halsell's right hand was useless. Fortunately for him, he carried one of the large keen knives our field men found so many uses for, in a sheath on his belt. Grasping the knife in his left hand, Halsell lunged toward the furious Wentworth. Wentworth aimed his gun again, but Halsell was able to knock it aside and its shot went wild. With a sweeping stroke, Halsell dashed the knife across the man's stomach, literally cutting him open. In another moment the outlaw lay shrieking in pain and Halsell called in a number of excited citizens to help carry the prisoner to the doctor's office. Wentworth finally recovered, and was convicted and served a term for his many crimes.

CHAPTER XXI

THE TERRITORY GROWS TOO HOT
FOR DOOLIN

Bill Doolin had disappeared entirely. Our men were able to get no trace of him whatever and we were exerting every effort to find him. We had faint clues that we felt would lead to the apprehension of the members of the gang, but Doolin had become a mystery. Deputies Bill Tilghman and Heck Thomas, after weeks of weary searching, found the trail of Little Bill Raidler, which led them into the Osage Nation. From a friendly Indian they learned that he was hiding in the hills and taking his meals at Sam Moore's ranch, twenty-five miles northeast of Pawhuska.

Tilghman and Thomas went to the ranch house to await one of the visits of the fugitive outlaw. They soon learned the direction from which he would probably come and hid themselves near the faint trail.

On the evening of September 1, as the dusky shadows grew dense, Little Bill came whistling confidently up the trail on his way to Moore's for supper. He put his horse in the corral and walked in the direction of the ranch house. Tilghman stood in a shadow behind a corral post, and Little Bill passed so close to him he could have reached out and touched him. When he had gone a few steps farther, Tilghman called to him to throw up his hands. Little Bill whirled quickly, drew his guns and fired in the direction of the officer. They were not more than

213

ten feet apart but the outlaw missed his aim. Tilghman's Winchester spoke almost as quickly as the fire had flashed from Little Bill's weapons. Tilghman followed his first shot quickly with another and Little Bill fell, almost fatally wounded. He fired again as he pitched forward on his face.

The people of the ranch house came running out and assisted in caring for the wounded bandit. He was taken into the house and everyone thought he would soon be dead. They could not believe that the little pine-knot of an outlaw could survive such wounds. He put up a brave fight and the officers were soon able to bring him to Guthrie, where he was placed in the care of a government physician. Doctor Smith stated he had never seen a man survive such wounds.

Little Bill recovered in a short time. During the painful probing for lead and the treatment of his wounds, he was never heard to groan or murmur. After his recovery he was convicted and sentenced to the Ohio Penitentiary for ten years. After his term expired, he married and settled down, dying just a few years ago, after having established himself as a respectable citizen. His later life was greatly influenced by his intimate association with O. Henry while in the Ohio penitentiary. The famous writer, Little Bill Raidler and Al Jennings were inseparable companions while they were in the prison together.

Following the capture of Little Bill, I called Bill Tilghman, Chris Madsen and Charlie Colcord into Guthrie for a conference. Major Gordon W. Lillie (Pawnee Bill) happened to be in Guthrie and, because of his intimate knowledge of the Indian country, I asked him to sit in on the conference and to offer his suggestions. I had found his counsel valuable at other times. I felt that he might be able to contribute something of value to our planning.

We felt gratified that we had been able to demoralize the efforts of the Doolin gang and to put the survivors on the run. Tilghman, Madsen and Colcord were asked to concentrate their full time and thought upon hunting down Doolin, Dalton and Red Buck Waightman. Red Buck was reported to be hiding somewhere in the El Reno district. Madsen would go after him. Dalton was supposed to be somewhere near Ardmore in Colcord's district. Tilghman would free-lance in the search of Doolin, whose whereabouts were a mystery. Little Dick West was reported to have left the territory and we decided to give no further consideration to the job of hunting him down until the others had been apprehended.

An Indian scout who was acquainted with Bill Dalton's wife was called into the case and assigned to watch for her at Ardmore, as it was probable that she did her trading there. Shortly after that she was seen in Ardmore and followed to her home about twelve miles away. The scout immediately notified Colcord and his deputies and they hurried to the place.

The house was surrounded and watched for several hours. On the morning of September 25th, 1895, Dalton walked out into the yard and he was commanded to throw up his hands. He quickly drew his six-shooter and Deputy Loss Hart fired upon him,

fatally wounding him. The body was brought to Guthrie, his mother and older brother claiming it.

The mother of the Dalton boys was a dear old lady and she showed no bitter feeling whatever toward anyone on account of the killing of her son. I sincerely sympathized with her, for I knew just how deeply she felt the dishonor her sons had brought upon their name.

A day or two later I received word from Deputy Madsen that he thought he had Red Buck located. About October 2nd, 1896, they found this inhuman creature in a dugout near Arapaho. The marshal and a posse of citizens surrounded his place and when, a short time later, he came out to get a bucket of water he was commanded to surrender. He instantly drew his six-shooters from both his right and left scabbards. He was known to be an expert shot with both hands. The officers, knowing that they were dealing with the most desperate man of the entire tribe of Oklahoma bandits, shot before Red Buck's pistol could be raised and fired. He fell, fatally wounded. His body was also brought to Guthrie and, to our great surprise, it was claimed by as dear an old lady as I ever had known to be related to an outlaw. Mrs. Lucy Waightman was such a motherly character that I was greatly puzzled as to how such a demon could come from such a lovable mother.

*   *   *

Tilghman developed several leads regarding the whereabouts of Bill Doolin. It seemed that several of them were deliberately sent to us as blind clues. After a conference, we decided to try to locate the

Doolins through Mrs. Pierce, the hotel woman at Ingalls. It was known that Mrs. Doolin had made secret visits to her husband at Ingalls. Tilghman went to call upon Mrs. Pierce and she expressed deep appreciation for our treatment of her. She realized that we could have placed a charge against her for harboring bandits at the time of the Ingalls fight, but we had decided not to prosecute her because she induced Arkansas Tom to surrender.

She had just received a letter from Doolin's wife, requesting that she mail a wedding ring that had been left in the hotel on her last visit. The package was to be addressed to Mrs. Will Barry at Burden, Kansas. The letter incidentally referred to her husband's desire to reform.

Many people who knew Doolin had declared he was sincere in his determination to forsake his wild outlaw career. The man's wife was known to be a very sweet character and Doolin had made many sacrifices to protect his little family from contact with his rough companions. The couple had a baby boy who was now past two years old and Doolin idolized the child. I believe when he left his band after the Woodward robbery it was with the firm determination to have nothing more to do with banditry. There is not an indication that he ever made an attempt to communicate with his fellow outlaws after this parting. His mistake lay in not moving much farther away from the scene of his wild escapades. Burden, Kansas, was just a few miles from the line of the Cherokee Strip. Doolin had located here on a farm, assuming the name of Barry. His little home was comfortably furnished and he looked forward to a peaceful life.

Tilghman returned to Guthrie and we discussed his visit with Mrs. Pierce, deciding that he should assume a disguise of some sort and go to Burden, Kansas, to attempt to locate the Doolins. I loaned him a Prince Albert coat and a black derby hat and he procured the other necessary accessories to complete his costume. He was to go to Burden as a preacher. When Tilghman donned this new costume and stood before me for my comments, I was especially impressed with the handsomeness of the man. He always looked well in the rough clothes he wore while on duty in the Territory, but dressed up like this he was as impressive a gentleman as I'd ever seen.

"Why, Bill," I said, "that coat fits you better than it does me. . . . You are a better looking man than its owner."

The big fellow actually blushed at my compliments but I could see that he was very pleased.

"Bill," I said, "if you get a trace of Doolin, wire me at once, and I will come to help you."

Tilghman left at once for Burden, Kansas, armed with credentials that would give him full cooperation and support of the postmasters and other federal officers of any community he might visit. He soon found the farm home of the Doolins and learned directly that the husband and father was away. None of the neighbors seemed to know where he had gone. Tilghman concluded that the man would be communicating with his wife and child, so he arranged with the postmaster at Burden to intercept any mail that

might pass between the couple. Strangely, there
was no mail. Several days passed. Finally, Tilghman learned that Mrs. Doolin had been driving to
Winfield often and he decided at once that she was
mailing letters and getting her own mail there. The
assistance of the Winfield postmaster was enlisted
and within a few days he was able to report that Will
Barry (Bill Doolin) was in Eureka Springs, Arkansas.

The wounds Doolin had received in the Ingalls
fight and the severe pain he suffered from his rheu-
matic trouble had caused him to decide to go to the
Springs for a course of baths.

Tilghman boarded the next train for Eureka
Springs, arriving early in the morning of December
5th, 1895. On account of train connections he had
been obliged to be up all night and he was worn from
the trip. At Eureka Springs he went directly to the
Basin Hotel, where he checked his Winchester and
grip and he decided he would go to the bath-house
and refresh himself with a plunge before eating
breakfast. He stepped across the street and entered the place where he registered for a bath. As
he walked through the reception room that led to the
private dressing booths, he was greatly surprised to
see Bill Doolin resting on a couch, reading a newspaper.

Doolin, with the natural instinctive alertness of a
criminal, glanced over the page of the paper and
watched Tilghman as he crossed the room. The officer was able to turn slightly away before Doolin
caught a glimpse of his face, and he proceeded on
into the booth that had been assigned to him. Once

inside, he drew his forty-five, whirled its cylinder to make sure that it was clicking properly, and stepped out before the astonished Doolin.

"Bill," he said, "consider yourself under arrest."

Doolin acted very much surprised and said: "Why, what do you mean?"

"I am Bill Tilghman," the officer replied calmly. . . . "I have come for you."

Doolin bounded from the couch like a cat and reached for the guns that were strapped beneath his arms, under his vest. Tilghman grasped Doolin by the coat sleeve and the bandit was struggling fiercely.

Tilghman spoke to him in a calm voice. "Listen, Doolin, I remember what you did for me in the dugout on the Dunn place. I don't want to kill you. . . . Be quiet." Doolin continued to struggle and the coat sleeve was tearing in Tilghman's iron grasp.

A bath-house clerk named Allen heard the commotion and came running to see what was the matter. Tilghman ordered him to unbutton Doolin's vest and disarm him. Tilghman's gun was pressing Doolin's stomach but the man refused to surrender and kept trying to reach his guns. Allen's nervous fingers trembled and he fumbled with the vest buttons. He finally opened the garment, but when he saw the wicked forty-fives hanging from scabbards under Doolin's arms, he became so frightened that he turned and ran, leaving Doolin's guns exposed and Tilghman in a very perplexing position. The officer did not want to shoot Doolin, but there seemed no alternative. Tilghman crisply snapped out a final

Offenders against the Laws of the Government
Top row—J. F. Hayler, M. Walker, Chas. Coleman. Second
row—Jess Rule, John P. Rerternik, Gus Mory. Third row—
Harry Cochran, M. Ryan, Chas. Cayler. Fourth Row—
F. Weldon, Pat Hurley, Manly Jackson.

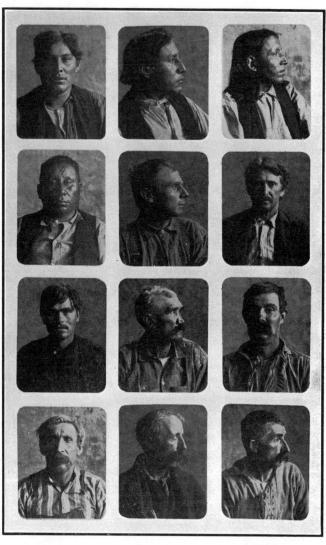

Offenders against the Laws of the Government

Top row—Jack Wildbired, Chas. Daily, Tom West. Second row—John Strait, John Boles, Geo. Wilson. Third row— W. C. Hutchins, James Tohay, Ed. Connell. Fourth row— Neil Grant, Will W. Robert, Thos. Riley.

order to the struggling man: "Doolin, you saved my life once and I don't want to kill you, but make one more move and you are a dead man."

Doolin looked into the eyes of the officer and relaxed, sitting down on the couch while Tilghman stood with his gun at his head. Allen had given the alarm and the city marshal rushed to Tilghman's assistance. He disarmed Doolin and the two officers took him to a nearby hotel.

"Have some breakfast, Doolin?" Tilghman asked.

"No, thanks, Bill," Doolin replied, "I ate an hour ago."

The city marshal guarded the captive while Tilghman ate his breakfast. Within an hour after the deputy marshal had arrived in Eureka Springs, he had his prisoner handcuffed and ready to leave for Oklahoma.

Doolin asked that Tilghman take him to his room to get his baggage. The city marshal guarded the man while Tilghman packed his grip. The officer found a little silver cup and asked Doolin if it belonged to him. There was a mist in the outlaw's eyes as he replied: "Yes, I bought that to take back to my baby boy."

"Well, that's fine," Tilghman answered, "I'll see that he gets it."

Tilghman was exceedingly fond of children and he was impressed with Doolin's love for his baby boy. Such a man could not be all bad. When the two were on the train, Tilghman turned to the surprised prisoner and said. "Doolin, I believe if you make a promise you will keep it. . . If you give me your word of honor that you will not try to escape,

I'll take those handcuffs off and let you travel back to Oklahoma like a free man. Do you promise?"

Doolin looked at Tilghman as if he could hardly believe his ears, then replied: "Tilghman, I don't believe the man lives who could go back on a trade like that. I promise."

It was necessary for the pair to go north to Joplin, Missouri, then across Kansas to the Santa Fe, which would carry them south to Guthrie.

I was much surprised when I received Tilghman's telegram from Arkansas when I thought he was in Kansas and to have him say: "I have Doolin and am on my way. Meet me at Arkansas City," when I expected that he'd be wiring for me to come to help him. The telegram was most gratifying and I felt proud that one of my deputies had been able to accomplish the single-handed capture of so desperate a man.

I met the two at Arkansas City and I was greatly surprised to notice that Doolin was not handcuffed when they stepped off the train. I greeted them pleasantly and we boarded the train again, arriving at Guthrie on the afternoon of December 6th. It was estimated that fully five thousand people were at the train to get a glimpse of the noted Bill Doolin. If the President of the United States had been arriving, he could not have expected a larger crowd in this small community.

As we led our captive through the press of the curious people, a lady stepped out and stood before Doolin. "Why, Mr. Doolin!" she exclaimed, "you don't look bad. . . . I believe I could have captured you."

Doolin looked at her for a moment, his eyes twinkling, then said, "My dear woman, I believe you could."

We proceeded immediately to my office in the federal building where we were joined by my partner, O. D. Halsell, upon whose ranch Doolin had worked for several years before he became an outlaw. The conference in that office was so intensely interesting that we must have stayed there two hours. Halsell, Tilghman, Chief Deputy Hale and myself sat in rapt attention as Doolin related a number of his experiences. I have never known a more interesting story-teller. Bill Doolin had the knack of being able to sketch his stories clearly and of painting in the colorful detail that gave them a literary quality that would have won the approval of the world. Halsell did not condemn the man, nor question him in an embarrassing way, but greeted him as a friend for whom he was extremely sorry.

During the course of our conversation we asked Doolin why the threatened robbery of the Guthrie National Bank did not materialize.

"It would have gone through," Doolin replied, "if I hadn't learned that my friend Halsell kept his account there. I was afraid the robbery might affect him."

It was here that Doolin related other incidents to which I have already referred. Then I remembered Rose of the Cimarron. "Doolin, I have always been curious about that girl," I said; "tell me about her."

Doolin's face softened when he spoke of her. "Why, gentlemen, she was just a sweet little country girl who was unfortunate enough to fall in love with an outlaw. She would have laid down her life for Bitter Creek Newcomb, and he worshiped her . . . . but not enough to go straight. Naturally, folks have suspected, well, you know what, but I'll swear she was as good a girl as ever lived. The entire gang worshiped her. If anybody had ever dared to intimate that she was not all a good woman should be, any one of the crowd would have killed her accuser instantly."

Doolin proceeded to tell us of the incident following the Dover robbery and the killing of the preacher and of Red Buck's ostracism from the gang. "That dog wasn't fit to black the boots of a respectable train-robber," Doolin commented.

Tilghman then spoke up, "I've often wondered why you didn't plug me in the dugout during that snow storm. You could have got away with it."

"I am not so sure about that. If Red Buck had killed you, there would have been a thousand men after us in twenty-four hours. Besides, that wasn't just my idea of how an officer should be killed. Not that I love you damn fellows any too well," he grinned as he finished his reply.

So many romantic stories had been told about Doolin and his reckless band that the publicity had created a very fascinating illusion in the public mind. When our conference ended, more than a thousand people were outside, clamoring to be allowed to shake the hand of Bill Doolin.

After Doolin had been in jail a short time his health began to fail and our government doctor was attending him daily. The night jailer had been fas-

cinated by Doolin's tales of buried treasures. The
prisoner had even drawn a map showing the location
of a cache near the town of Mulhall and the jailer
pored over this map for many hours. The map was
complete except for the key that would reveal the
exact location of the treasure. This Doolin with-
held in spite of the pleading of the jailer.

Doolin had told him that he appreciated his kind
treatment so much that he wanted him to have the
money if he would only promise to take good care
of his wife and baby. The jailer was greatly interested in the possible fortune that awaited him. If
Doolin would only give them the key to the map that
they might decipher its meaning.

On a cold night in the early part of January,
1896, Doolin called to the jailer, affecting a great
weakness, and said that he did not believe he would
live till morning. Clinging to the bars and breathing
heavily, he asked the man to come near that he might
tell him how to find the buried treasure. The watchman came close and Doolin whispered: "Come closer,
I can hardly speak." The man placed his ear near
Doolin's mouth and leaned against the bars. Doolin
quickly thrust his hand through the bars and
grabbed the jailer's six-shooter. He then forced him
to unlock the door.

While the frightened jailer stood watching, Doolin called to the other prisoners, urging them to
make their escape. Running quickly out of the building, he made his way through the darkness and out
upon a country road. As he trudged along he heard
the sound of hoof beats on the frozen earth and he
stepped to the roadside to see who might be coming.

As the horse and vehicle drew near he made out the form of a man and a woman in the dim moonlight. As they came on, Doolin sprang out and caught the bridle rains; drawing the jailer's pistol, he forced the man and woman to get out of the buggy and walk back down the road for a short distance. Quickly unharnessing the horse, Doolin mounted, bare-back, and raced away into the night. Most of the prisoners Doolin had liberated were recaptured, but many weary weeks dragged along before we found a shadow of a clue as to Doolin's whereabouts.

The hunt for Doolin was on again.

CHAPTER XXII

THE END OF THE DOOLIN TRAIL

After the escape of Doolin it was obviously imperative that every possible effort should be made to re-capture Doolin at once. The lines on the situation had to be tightened in every possible way. Not a loophole could be permitted to exist in the effort to cut off from the outlaw all possible avenues of information or assistance that might make it possible for him to evade arrest for a protracted period. This fact compelled the arrest of one of the most unusual characters ever recorded, the Rose of the Cimarron.

The Rose of the Cimarron was an unusually attractive girl born in Texas and reared in the range country. Her folks located on a claim at the opening

of Oklahoma near the Halsell Ranch, where she became acquainted and infatuated with Bitter Creek Newcomb before the Halsell Ranch fully gave way to the settlers. At this time she was a girl of about fourteen.

Newcomb was a fine specimen of young manhood. Knowing him as I did before he turned to the wild life, I could well understand why a country girl would be so attracted to him. Rose of the Cimarron was true to this infatuation to the very last; but after he was killed she withdrew from his associates. This fact, and her youth and apparent sincere effort to disassociate herself from her past had caused us to be lenient in her case. The danger that she might be tempted to aid Doolin in some way, denied us of the further privilege of chivalry in the matter.

To remove her, at least for a short time, from the scene, a warrant for the aiding and abetting of outlaws was turned over to Bill Tilghman. He located her in Payne County, Oklahoma. Tilghman had no trouble in arresting her, and when he had returned to Guthrie and placed the girl in the Federal Jail he came to my office.

"Marshal," he said, "I am almost ashamed of arresting that girl. She don't belong in our jail, I believe everything Doolin and others have said about her is true."

The girl was still under eighteen years of age and on account of her youth, courage and general good character she was admired by both officers and outlaws. She pleaded guilty and Judge Dale gave her a short sentence in the reformatory school at Framingham, Massachusetts, with recommendation of

Group of outlaws. Top—Rose Cimarron, Roy Daughtery, alias Arkansas Tom. Center—Cattle Annie and Little Breeches. Lower—Ben Cravens and Henry Starr.

Group taken at Perry, Oklahoma, 1894. Top—Third from left, Morris Zuckerman. Seated, reading left—Deputies Grant, Owen, and George Starmer together with posse and prisoners.

leniency. Within a few months her perfect conduct had earned her release and she returned to Oklahoma. She married a substantial farmer and lives today surrounded by a happy family that knows nothing of her experience with the bandit ring. Her alias is used by us to protect her and her family. Not more than half a dozen men know the girl's real name and where she lives with her family, and wild horses could not drag the information from these few men.

* * *

Immediately after Doolin's incarceration in the Guthrie jail, his wife broke up their little home near Burden and took the boy to the home of her father near Lawton, Oklahoma. Three or four months after his escape we learned where she had gone, and we assigned a scout to watch her father's habitation for the appearance of Doolin. We were sure that his devotion to his wife and baby would lead him to them.

Then the word came that Doolin had arrived at the father-in-law's home. Deputy United States Marshal Heck Thomas was ordered to proceed to the place. He took a small posse and arrived in the neighborhood where a little inquiry developed that Doolin had planned to leave the country at once, hoping to be fortunate enough to get away from the Oklahoma officers and to reach a haven of safety in some far-off part of the country where he could make a new start in life.

Thomas and his men reconnoitered about the little woods cabin where the Doolins had been staying and saw that he had been outfitted and loaded for the trip. As the officers watched, they saw Doolin bring his wife and baby to the wagon, his wife taking the driver's seat and the reins. Night had fallen and they were ready to make their attempt to get out of the country between suns.

Doolin took his Winchester from the front of the wagon and, holding it across his arm, he grasped the reins of his saddle horse and walked down the moonlit trail, peering furtively about as if to be sure that the road would be safe for his wife and baby. Then he stopped and turned about, motioning for his wife to come ahead.

By this time Heck Thomas, who had concealed himself in the tall weeds beside the trail, stepped out, shotgun in hand.

"Throw up your hands, Doolin!" he called.

Doolin jerked his own Winchester to his shoulder but before he could fire he fell, fatally wounded by buckshot from Thomas' gun. The frenzied wife jumped from the wagon and ran to the body of her dying husband, crying out hysterically. After the usual official formalities, the body of Doolin was turned over to his wife and family. The funeral was attended by hundreds of people.

Thus passed the leader of one of the most notorious outlaw gangs of Southwestern history. With three exceptions, the man's followers had preceded him into the great beyond. Little Bill Raidler was in the Ohio penitentiary. Arkansas Tom was in the Federal prison at Leavenworth, Kansas. Little Bill West had fled from the country and he was not heard of again until the Jennings gang played its brief part in Oklahoma's outlaw drama.

CHAPTER XXIII

THE RAIROAD AND TECUMSEH TOWNSITE FIGHT

This controversy between the railroad and the people of Tecumseh and the government was different from the uprising of the people of Enid and Pond Creek, Oklahoma, against the Rock Island Railroad, in that the Rock Island ran through the towns of Enid and Pond Creek and refused to stop trains or to recognize the government townsites, having established towns of its own. My experience with the Enid and Pond Creek people had taught me a valuable lesson and the importance of diplomacy in such cases, suggesting the imminence of trouble and possible bloodshed. The Choctaw, Oklahoma and Gulf Railroad Company in surveying its line leading east from Oklahoma City and passing through the Kickapoo Indian reservation, left Tecumseh, the county seat of Pottawatomie County, about six miles south of the survey, at which point, directly north of Tecumseh, they established a town under the name of Shawnee. The people of Tecumseh immediately

appealed to the Secretary of the Interior for relief. The secretary refused to approve the survey and ordered a new one. After the profile of the new survey had been placed in his hands he decided in favor of the Tecumseh survey. This decision allayed the disturbance for the time being, as it appeared to the Tecumseh people that they had won their cause and the railroad would be obliged to build through or near their town.

The railroad, however, had different plans. Frances I. Gowen, president of the road, himself an eminent member of the Philadelphia bar, came personally to Oklahoma to handle the legal part of the controversy. Taking advantage of the lull in the controversy, the railroad authorities quietly organized a large force of men consisting of graders, track-layers, tie-haulers and shovelers to rush the work and finish the line across the Kickapoo Indian reservation and from Oklahoma City on to Shawnee before any legal proceedings could be instituted to prevent it. My dream of peace suddenly vanished. Trouble was in the air. I had a force of experienced deputies on the ground, to keep me fully advised of threatened danger. The railroad had completed grading and had its rails laid and was running work and material trains from Oklahoma City to within

a few miles of Dale. Before they had made great headway on the secret plan the people of Tecumseh were up in arms. At this time a term of court was about due to open in Tecumseh, Pottawatomie County, and an injunction proceeding against the railroad company was filed. Arrangements had been made for the court, the official force, together with

U. S. Attorney, Thos. F. McMechan, to take advantage of passage on a work train that was able to
run on the completed line to the end of the track
near Dale, more than half way from Oklahoma City.
On account of heavy rains the roads were nearly impassable and arrangements had been made to have
transportation sent out from Tecumseh to meet
Judge Scott and the court officials at Dale to convey
them to Tecumseh. In the meantime I had advice
from my deputies that serious trouble was brewing
and the railroad, as well as the train, was likely to
be dynamited. I decided immediately that it was
necessary for me to take the first train to Oklahoma
City, which I did and reached there the evening of
March 17. I immediately got in touch with Judge
Scott and advised him of the confidential information I had regarding the situation and the danger to
the court officials in taking advantage of the transportation extended by the railroad company. Judge
Scott said he would take the chance on account of
the road conditions, so I immediately got in touch
with Sam Bartell and a number of my most trusted
deputies to safeguard the court officials, and railroad
crew, including president Gowen, who was going on
the same train to be present at the opening of court
at Tecumseh on the morning of March 19. On account of the serious threats that had come to me
I decided to take charge in person. Thus, all was
set. The entire party was on hand early on the
morning of the eighteenth and boarded the freight
caboose that had been provided. With the court and
railroad officials we had over twenty-five in our
party. A large number of Oklahoma City citizens

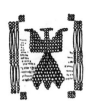

were at the train, as this was the first train to take any passengers. Oklahoma City being one of the very progressive young cities, was greatly interested in this eastern outlet and what it meant in maintaining supremacy in a lead of population at this time. I placed Sam Bartell and another trusted deputy on the cowcatcher and two deputies in the engine cab to keep a close lookout for intruders and any signs of dynamiting or other obstructions. As the road bed was new the train was unable to go over ten miles per hour with safety. When we reached Choctaw City, about twelve miles east of Oklahoma City, we found a very enthusiastic crowd at the train. At this point I got off the train to see if everything was moving satisfactorily. Our next stop was at Harrah, now the seat of the great Oklahoma Gas and Electric Company plant, one of the largest in the Southwest. The next station was McCloud, now a thriving little city, and a stop was made there long enough to give time for investigation as to the safety of the train crew and its passengers. We were drawing near the Kickapoo reservation and the Pottawatomie line. The train crawled slowly. A few miles of Dale the train came to a sudden stop. I ordered everybody to remain seated. I was soon out to find the trouble. I found Sam Bartell making his way toward the passenger caboose to inform me of the seeming danger just ahead of us. I joined him and the deputies were soon around us. It was easy to see the obstruction with the naked eye but with my field glasses in hand I could see the obstruction was a small hut built of timber and boards directly over and on the track. I could also see an object which

gave the appearance of a woman with a Winchester in hand, sitting in front of the hut. I decided it was best for Bartell and myself to take the lead, one on each side of the track and the other deputies divided up likewise covering quite a distance from the railroad to see if it was possible to find any trace of dynamite or anyone hiding in the underbrush. On approaching the obstruction on the track there was no one else visible to the eye but the Indian squaw sitting in front of the hut with her Winchester across her lap. Knowing a good deal about Indians and the uncertainty of their action in such cases, I said to Bartell that we would pass on by the hut in an indifferent way, increasing our distance from the track, and when beyond the hut, we would return, approaching the Indian squaw from each side at the same time. Our appearance at the hut seemed to surprise her and she made an effort to draw her Winchester, but Sam soon had charge of both the squaw and the Winchester. There were other Indians nearby but were taking no hand in the matter, being interested more in the outcome of the Indian squaw's efforts to protect her supposed land rights. My deputies took charge of all the Indians and arranged to take them to Tecumseh.

I immediately returned to the train and on my way I met Judge Scott coming toward me. After explaining to him the conditions as I had found them he turned to me and said, "Marshal, if you were alone here it would be your duty to remove the obstruction but in this case the court officials together with the U. S. Attorney are with you and we will prepare the proper papers at once authorizing your

action in the matter." We returned to the caboose where the railroad and other court officials were anxious to know the conditions. U. S. Attorney Mc-Mechan prepared a complaint for mandatory injunction, which was sworn to by president Frances I. Gowen and duly attested by the clerk of the court. Judge Scott signed a mandatory writ of injunction directed to E. D. Nix, U. S. Marshal for the Territory of Oklahoma, commanding him to forthwith remove the obstruction from the right-of-way of the railroad. The court proceedings were regular in every way barring the fact that the papers were prepared in the freight caboose, which was used by the court as temporary "chambers." We soon had the obstruction removed and the train pulled on safely to the end of the track near Dale without harm to anyone. The railroad and the court officials were soon on their way to Tecumseh, the county seat.

In order to justify the action of Judge Scott in issuing this injunction it is proper to refer to a case in the Supreme Court of Oklahoma Territory in which Chief Justice Frank Dale wrote a very able opinion covering the law of mandatory injunction. In the early days land contests were numerous and the losing party would often refuse to vacate the premises until a patent from the government had been granted and delivered as evidence that title had been vested in the winner. This was a perplexing situation with the early day judges of Oklahoma. Judge Dale reasoned, if a settler had lost his right to claim the title to a track of land on any given date to which he had had the right to assert title prior to that date, he could be enjoined from continuing to

Officers and guards on duty opening Cherokee Outlet, Sept. 16, 1889.

The run for a homestead, Cherokee Outlet, Sept. 16, 1893. The greatest contest for a home known to man.

remain on the land under claim of title that he had lost. In this case Judge Dale's opinion upheld the mandatory writ of injunction commanding the defendant to vacate the said land or to in any manner assert any right, title or interest therein and all the other justices of the Supreme Court concurred, and later the opinion was sustained by the Supreme Court of the United States. Judge Scott having been one of the concurring justices knew exactly what he was doing when he advised the remedy of the mandatory injunction above referred to and in case of serious trouble or bloodshed, I would have been protected under proper legal process.

Judge Scott opened court at Tecumseh the next morning, March 19, 1895, according to schedule. After investigation it was found the Indian squaw, surrounded by a contingent of Kickapoo Indians equally inoffensive, had been put up to this act by irresponsible white folks. Therefore, Judge Scott ordered them released, with a lecture, and had no further trouble from that source.

The case of the injunction was taken up in which the United States had intervened through the attorney general, the attorney for the people of Tecumseh joining with the Government in the action against the Choctaw, Oklahoma and Gulf Railroad Company to restrain the railroad company from further construction of its line through the Kickapoo Country without the approval of its survey by the Secretary of Interior. This action of course was very satisfactory to the people of Tecumseh and had a quieting effect.

Judge Scott set the morning of the 20th to hear

points at issue which gave the attorney for the government, the people of Tecumseh and the railroad time to prepare for the presentation of the law in the case. After the morning adjournment I had lunch with Judge Scott and in the strictest confidence he told me of his plan for a speedy decision of this case, meaning a decision immediately appealable to the higher courts.

In the afternoon following I put in my time mixing with the leading citizens, a good many of them with whom I was personally acquainted, impressing upon them the importance of maintaining order, whatever the outcome might be, allowing the law to take its course in settlement of the issue. An application made by the Government for a temporary injunction was set for March 20. Distinguished lawyers representing the people of Tecumseh, U. S. Attorney McMechan was present to represent the government, and president Gowen with his assistant counsel was present to represent the railroad company. As a result of the hearing Judge Scott granted a temporary injunction, but notified counsel that he would hear a motion to dissolve it at the court house in Oklahoma City on the 23rd day of April, 1895, at 9 A. M., that he was not granting this temporary order on the merits of the case, but largely for the reason that the railroad was prosecuting its work in defiance of government orders, and should suspend until a full hearing could be had. He made the further statement: "When I announce my decision I will promulgate a written opinion setting forth findings of facts and conclusions of law. During the interim, I wish one and all concerned directly or indirectly with the result of the case to show patience and respect for the law."

After the hearing at Oklahoma City on April 23, Judge Scott adjourned the case until May 1. Later in the evening I had an interview with him in his private chambers where he informed me in the strictest confidence that he had adjourned court for the purpose of the promulgation of his decision for two reasons. First—In order to give me time to put the region affected in a condition essential to preserve order as against the possible violence of the disappointed litigants and others in sympathetic accord with them. Second—He desired to place in writing his views in justice to all concerned for the double purpose of respect for the United States authorities who would naturally desire that a decision adverse to their contentions be based upon clear reasoning, and next that the people of Tecumseh were entitled to be advised in plain and unmistakable terms as to the law of the case. From this I understood that the government and the people of Tecumseh had lost and I was not in the least surprised. I have never mentioned the interview with Judge Scott from that moment to this. I was the only person possessing the knowledge of what the judge's decision in this sensational case was to be.

May 1, 1895, soon rolled around. Over thirty-four years have passed since that eventful day but it is as fixed in my memory as if yesterday. I had several of my trusted deputies present as it was my duty to maintain vigilance about the court and to meet any contingency that might arise in connection with the case.

Judge Scott was prompt—the court house being crowded to its fullest capacity to hear the noted opinion soon to be announced. Judge Scott entered the court room from his chambers with a bundle of papers, among them one which I knew to be his typewritten opinion. After calling order, and the usual opening of court, he announced he would read the opinion in full which took more than an hour, ending with the order dissolving the temporary injunction to which he allowed counsel for the government and Tecumseh exceptions. Then he declared court adjourned.

The case was appealed to the Territorial Supreme Court and Judge Scott's decision was affirmed on every point. I am pleased to say that my office was successful in handling the turbulent situation inspired by the adverse decision without further violence, thus placing law and order a grade higher as an accomplished fact and a triumphant realization, which had been my intention as a justification for entering into my plan for preserving the peace without violence or bloodshed.

Another word in conclusion, and I am done with this recital of the clash of this railroad and the people of Tecumseh. The difference between the Choctaw and the Rock Island case was that the Rock Island gave in to the government and the people and the Choctaw railroad did not. The result of my management of both situations was the same—the triumph and vindication of law and order.

CHAPTER XXIV

THE JENNINGS BOYS GO WILD

Temple Houston was one of the most picturesque characters I have ever met. He was a son of General Sam Houston, the only man who ever served as governor of two separate states, as United States Senator from two different states, as commander-in-chief of an army and president of a republic.

With the impressive background of his father's career, and with an inheritance of his father's mental brilliance, Temple Houston became one of early Oklahoma's best known characters. Oklahoma has produced no other orator who could approach the beauty and eloquence of Temple Houston's speeches.

The man allowed his hair to grow so long that it fell about his shoulders and he dressed most eccentrically. He was an admirable horseman and few men ever equaled his marksmanship with a pistol or rifle. I don't believe a more fearless man ever lived. Perhaps Houston's principal fault was in his bull-dog stubbornness. When he had considered any given proposition or circumstance and had formed his opinion, no power on earth could induce him to change. His manner was quiet and unassuming.

I remember an incident that occurred in Judge Burford's court that amused me a great deal. Judge Burford, who was trying special cases for Judge Dale at Guthrie, seemed to share my own aversion to snakes. There are good many things in this world that I am not afraid of, but I wouldn't touch a snake alive for five hundred dollars! I was sitting near the judge's bench one morning when Temple Houston walked into the court room, sporting a very conspicuous necktie made of rattlesnake skin. The idea of that snake skin being tied around a man's neck worried me, as the thought was very repulsive. I didn't notice Judge Burford's nervousness until about an hour later, when I observed that the judge was not able to keep his eyes off that rattlesnake tie.

I watched Judge Burford and became convinced that he was very much worried about that snakeskin tie. Just as the court was adjourning for the noon-hour, the judge turned to Temple Houston and said: "Colonel Houston, I wish you would change that tie at noon. I have been deathly afraid of snakes since I was a kid and that thing gives me the willies." Houston laughed, and when he returned to the court-room that afternoon he wore a more conservative necktie.

I remember that day particularly because of the eloquent speech Houston made on behalf of a prostitute who was brought before the court. Houston had been sitting, unoccupied, in the court-room listening to the procedure. When the judge learned that the woman had no counsel, he appointed Temple Houston to defend her. Houston's extemporaneous speech in her defense was so powerful and appealing that he won an acquittal. The court's stenographer was besieged for copies of the oration and later many thousands of copies of it were circulated. It had a true classic quality.

Houston often resorted to very unique methods of impressing the jury. I remember an occasion when he was defending a man on a murder charge. The accused man had killed a cowpuncher and his plea was self-defense. Witnesses testified the cowpuncher had not drawn his gun. Houston attempted to show that his client had been impressed by the cow man's reputation as a quick-drawing gunman, and that his fear had caused him to shoot before the other man had time to draw. The prosecution had attempted to blast this defense. Houston was making his argument before the jury and stressing that the dead cowpuncher might have drawn his guns and killed his client if he had been given the slightest advantage.

"Gentlemen of the jury," Houston was saying, "this cow man had a reputation as a gunman. My client is a peaceful citizen with little experience in such matters. There are gunmen in Oklahoma so

adept at drawing and shooting that they can place a gun in the hands of an inexperienced man, then draw and shoot their own weapons before he can pull a trigger. Like this—!" he shouted and, with a lightning movement, Houston drew his forty-five, pointed it at the jury box and shot six times so quickly that the men had barely time to dodge. The jury scattered like frightened quail. Houston turned toward Judge McAtee, whipped out his other gun and emptied it at the judge's rostrum. Judge Mc-Atee jumped off his chair and crouched behind the bench.

When the shooting had ended and Houston stood grinning with the smoking guns in his hands, Judge McAtee peeped out to see if all was clear.

"Your Honor," Houston chuckled, "you need not be afraid . . . my cartridges were all blanks."

Judge McAtee was very much peeved when he mounted his seat but without discussing the matter he ordered the bailiff to call the jury back to the court-room. He then turned to Houston and said: "Sir, you seem to have very little respect for the dignity and person of this court."

Houston bowed low and said: "Your Honor, I apologize. I only wanted to impress the jury with the speed with which guns may be drawn and fired by an accomplished two-gun man."

The gesture was perhaps an unwise one, for the jury decided against Houston's client. However, he was able to obtain a new trial because the jury had been allowed to separate and leave the court-room during the hearing of the case.

Chief Bacon Rind. Outstanding chief, statesman and orator
of the Osage tribe. A picturesque American Indian.

Group taken at Pawnee, Oklahoma, 1894. Top—fourth from left Big Elk (Osage Indian), fifth, Deputy Marshal Roebecker, sixth, Chief Bacon Rind of Osage. Lower—left, U. S. Attorney Roy Hoffman, U. S. Clerk Will Glenn, Judge Bierer, Deputy Marshals Lake and Colcord.

Temple Houston had attained a great deal of notoriety because of such eccentric acts as this, although he had also attained a wide reputation as a successful criminal lawyer. His reputation as a fighter had made it easy for him to intimidate opposing counsel with well-directed sarcastic remarks, and Houston often took advantage of this fact, precipitating many bitter clashes in the Territory's court-rooms.

Al and Frank Jennings had been practicing law in the Territory for a few years, making their home in El Reno. Al had been Prosecuting Attorney of Canadian County. Their father was county judge at Woodward, and their brother Ed lived with him. Ed Jennnings and Temple Houston opposed each other in court at Woodward in a case between two cow men, involving pasture rent. The two attorneys clashed over a number of minor points during the course of the trial, each getting angrier as it went on. Then Houston asked a question of a witness. Jennings objected and an argument followed. "You are a liar!" one shouted, and a dozen men rushed to the pair to separate them. The court rebuked the two attorneys and they apologized to the judge, but their own hatred was seething.

That night Temple Houston strode into a saloon where Ed and Frank Jennings were playing poker. Ed saw him coming and arose from his chair, reaching for his gun. Houston fired and Jennings slumped to the floor. Frank leaped up and made a movement toward his own gun, but before he could reach it Houston dropped him in his tracks, seriously wounded. Ed Jennings died almost immediately, but Frank recovered. Houston pleaded self-defense, and was acquitted on a charge of murder.

Al Jennings grew so bitter about the acquittal that he left the court-room, cursing the courts and threatening vengeance. I think it fortunate that fate kept Al Jennings and Temple Houston from meeting after that. I know that Temple Houston was not afraid of a man on earth and that he would not have taken a step out of his way to avoid a fight with Jennings and I am confident that Al Jennings would have shot it out without the least hesitation.

Bill Tilghman used to ridicule the idea that the Jennings boys were outlaws to be mentioned in the same breath with the Daltons and the Doolins. Perhaps a little personal feeling might have entered into that opinion. However, none of us ever felt that Al Jennings and his brother Frank were real outlaw material. Their father was a fine old southern gentleman and had done his best to raise his boys to be good men. The wild environment of the Oklahoma Territory presented temptations that gave the old father many serious problems in handling his boys. Regardless of the notoriety the brothers received, they were not and could not have been dangerous outlaws. They had too much of the South's genteel blood in their veins.

For some time Al and Frank rode about the Territory, making threats against Temple Houston. Houston's friends had persuaded him to give his word that he would not go out looking for the Jennings boys and that he would make no effort to start trouble with them, unless it should be unavoidable.

One morning as I was riding in the country near

Guthrie I met Al and Frank Jennings who were
headed toward Guthrie. We stopped our horses and
chatted there in the road for some time and I could
see that Al was tremendously wrought up about
something. Finally he blurted out: "Marshal, I hear
Temple Houston is in Guthrie. We're lookin' for
him." His face twitched with rage as he mentioned
Houston's name.

I hadn't seen him since the trouble had occurred
at Woodward and I could not help but be astonished
at the radical change in the man. Frank was more
placid, although it was plain that he too had been
affected by the unfortunate incident and that he was
very little like the man he had been before.

I placed my hand on Al's saddle-horn. "Al," I
said, "I am afraid you and Frank are going to run
into serious trouble if you persist in hunting Temple
Houston. That is not like you, Al. I've known you,
Al—."

Our horses stood close together and Al Jennings
placed his hand on my shoulder and looked into my
eyes. I could see tears in his own.

"Marshal," he said, "when I rushed into that saloon at Woodward and looked into the face of my
dying brother, Ed, and at Frank who at that moment seemed to be dying, something happened to me.
I haven't been the same man since. I know that
your advice is good, but I also know that for some
peculiar reason I don't feel I can take it. I am a
changed man and don't know what will be the outcome.

And he put the spurs to his horse, Frank riding
by his side. A few hours later I met Al on the

streets of Guthrie. I too had heard that Temple Houston was in town and I wanted to do all in my power to keep these bitter enemies from meeting. I had always liked Al Jennings and as my wife was gone for the day I took Al to my home for luncheon, trying as tactfully as I could during our visit to persuade him to go to his father's home for I believed that the influence of the old gentleman would keep the boys out of trouble.

An hour or so later I learned that Temple Houston had been in Guthrie before noon but that he had left on a Santa Fe train for Woodward via Wichita, Kansas. The Jennings boys heard this and in their wrought-up state they declared that Houston had fled when he heard they were in town. I am convinced that they were wrong about this for I don't think Temple Houston would have made the least effort to avoid them, or any set of men that ever lived.

The old father of the Jennings boys had been so broken up by the death of his son, Ed, that he had left Woodward, the scene of the tragedy, and moved to Tecumseh where, because of his fitness and ability, he was soon made a county judge.

In the early part of 1896 an attempt was made to rob a Santa Fe passenger train at Edmond, Oklahoma. The robbers hid behind the water tank. When the train drew up to the station and took on water, the bandits boarded the blind-baggage. As the train pulled away, they climbed over the coal in the tender and covered the engineer and fireman, compelling them to run the train down the track about a mile and stop. In the shadow, near this stopping place, an extra man held the bandits' horses while they attempted to rob the train.

The door of the express car was battered in during a fusillade of shots intended to terrify the passengers and crew.   Much to the disappointment of the robbers, who had expected a large shipment of currency, they found but a few hundred dollars.   On this occasion the outlaws overlooked robbing the passengers and the train was allowed to proceed.

The officers later learned that Al and Frank Jennings, Pat and Morris O'Malley and Little Dick West, who had come back to the territory, had done the job.   All but Al fled to a camp on Laury Whipple's place near the Pottawatomie county line.   Al spurred his horse in the direction of his father's home at Tecumseh.

Arriving three or four hours later, he quickly stabled his horse and crept to his room where he went to bed.   He arose early in the morning and told his father he was leaving for a few days.   He then rode back to the Whipple place and joined the other members of the gang.   Together they headed for the southeastern part of the Territory near the Texas line.

As they rode along late in the afternoon they met Deputy Marshal Sam Bartell of Oklahoma City, who had moved to that locality to assist for a short time in special work.   Bartell knew nothing about the Edmond robbery, as news traveled slowly in those days.   As the deputy rode toward the outlaws he recognized Al Jennings, whom he knew quite well, and as he drew near he pulled his six-shooter and shouted, "Throw up your hands!"

In a flash Al Jennings had drawn his gun. Then he recognized Bartell and exclaimed: "That was a fool trick, Sam. If I hadn't recognized you, one of us would be a dead man by now."

Bartell laughed and invited the party to have supper at the little farm house where he and his wife were making their temporary home. The Deputy was glad to see someone he knew and the evening was spent congenially. Mrs. Bartell prepared a good meal for them and their horses were fed. After a few hours rest Al Jennings handed Mrs. Bartell twenty dollars for her trouble, bade the couple goodbye and he and his men rode on their way.

About two weeks later they attempted to hold up an M. K. & T. passenger train at Bond Switch, about twenty-five miles south of Muskogee. A pile of ties was placed on the track, but the engineer opened his throttle and dashed through the obstruction at full speed, scattering the ties, without wrecking the train. A short time thereafter the officers received word that the Jennings band planned to hold up a passenger train at Purcell. Close watch was kept, and a few evenings later a night watchman observed five men hiding behind a box car in the Purcell railroad yards and reported the matter to the agent. A posse was soon on the ground, but the would-be robbers had slipped away as silently as they had come.

A few days later Bill Tilghman received a report that the Jennings gang was preparing to rob a bank at Minco. The deputy immediately sent a telegram to President Campbell of the Minco Bank and Camp-

bell quickly organized a group of cattlemen who surrounded the bank, guarding it in day and night
shifts.

When Pat O'Malley rode into the little town to
reconnoiter for the gang, he saw that a robbery attempt would not be practical and he turned his horse
about as unobtrusively as possible and rode away.
By that time members of the gang were getting desperate; their money had run out and they were eating only occasionally. Each one of the gang was
irritable and disagreeable. The usual happy cama-
raderie of carefree men was absent and the little
band fought and wrangled among themselves.

About this time Al Jennings secured a grubstake
in some mysterious manner and left the country.
I was never able to learn just what particular depredation supplied the money that took him away
but concluded that it must have been something that
also convinced him that he was being closely pursued. On the other hand, it is possible that his adventurous spirit craved new scenery for a while.
He was in Honduras for some months, finally making his way back through Mexico and into the United
States. He had not been in this country long when
he gravitated toward his old gang and brought them
together once more.

They had such poor luck with night robberies
that it was decided to hold up a train in daylight and
about eleven o'clock in the forenoon of October 6th,
five masked men charged down upon a gang of labor-
ers working on the Rock Island tracks between
Minco and Chickasha. A passenger train was due
to pass that point within a few minutes and, cover-

ing the workmen with their guns, they compelled the foreman to station himself where he could flag the train while the bandits hid in the brush nearby.

The train whistled about a half mile down the track, then thundered down upon the waiting robbers and stopped. Conductor Dan Dacy ran forward to investigate and he was quickly covered by a forty-five. One of the O'Malleys leaped into the engineer's cab, where he held the engineer and fireman while the others went back to complete the robbery.

Al Jennings and Little Dick West climbed into the express car while Frank and the other O'Malley drove the passengers out of the coaches and lined them up outside, forcing the terrorized people to give up their money and valuables. Al and Little Dick tried to force the express messenger to open his large safe, but he convinced them that he did not have the combination. Al Jennings backed the messenger into a corner and stood pointing his gun at him as he called to Little Dick to blow the damn thing open.

The other bandit took three sticks of dynamite from inside his shirt, intending to use but one and replace the other two. The two sticks were carelessly laid beside the safe while Little Dick was making preparations for the blasting. Placing the third stick of dynamite on top of the large safe, he called to Al Jennings to give him a hand and the two placed a smaller safe on top of the charge.

Lighting a short fuse, they grabbed the messenger by the arm and jumped to the ground to await the explosion. The express car was splintered. The small safe was shattered, but the larger one stood in the midst of the smoking wreckage unharmed.

Al turned to Little Dick and ordered him to set off another charge. The man hesitated, evidently much confused, "Damn the luck, I left them other two sticks of dynamite lying on a box next to the safes. . . . I'll bet they are all blowed up."

Investigation proved that the charge between the safes had set off the outlaws reserve supply of explosives and they had none left to make another attempt on the large safe.

The robbery netted but a few hundred dollars in cash and a quantity of jewelry and watches. The passengers were driven back into the coaches while Al and Dick West took a look at the mail car, but there seemed to be nothing there they wanted to take.

Conductor Dacy had recognized Al Jennings, whose mask had slipped off. All members of the train crew declared that Al Jennings was the leader of the robbery and they gave an accurate description of the horse he was riding.

When the train reached Chickasha, a posse was quickly organized and another sent from El Reno, but the bandits managed to elude the officers.

A few hours later they made camp and refreshed themselves. After a short rest Al and Frank Jennings left the party and took a circuitous route, landing in El Reno during the night. Here they stayed in hiding for two days at the home of a friend. When they left to join the other members of the band who had concealed themselves in a dugout on

the Cottonwood River, fifteen miles southwest of Guthrie, Deputies Tilghman and Thomas had loaded their horses into a special car and disembarked at Shawnee, where they scattered their posse to watch all trails leading in the direction of the Spike S Ranch, north of Pawnee. While they were resting in the dugout on the Cottonwood, the bandits divided the loot from the Rock Island robbery.

Realizing that the officers would probably be watching all trails leading to the Spike S, the gang wandered into the Indian Territory, riding at night and lying in secluded camps during the day time. Occasionally one would slip into a small town for recreation. Before many nights had passed, they had all spent their supply of money. As they were in an unfriendly country where they needed money to live, they set out in the direction of the Spike S, hoping that the officers' vigilance had relaxed.

Little Dick West could not help but compare this band of battered wanderers with his former companions of the dashing Doolin-Dalton gang, and the situation became intolerable to him. On one chilly evening when the others were saddling their horses for a night's ride, Little Dick West bade them good-bye and rode off to the south without an excuse or a word of comment.

As the Jennings gang rode through the little town of Cushing in the middle of the night, they dismounted before a small general merchandise store owned by Lee Nutter, and Al Jennings went to the home of the proprietor next door and awakened him, telling him they wanted burial clothes for a man who had died. When the store-keeper opened his place, the outlaws proceeded to discard their tattered rags and to outfit themselves from the limited stock of the little store. They then tapped the till for forty or fifty dollars and rode away.

Deputy Marshal Ledbetter of the eastern district had learned that the Jennings band was wandering through the Indian Territory and, with a posse, he had taken their trail. Stopping one evening at the home of Sam Baker, at whose place the Jennings gang had stopped for food on one or two occasions, Ledbetter induced Baker to communicate with the gang and to meet one of their members in a grave-yard at Tecumseh. He was to give them a tale of a big Indian payment that was to be transported across the country, in the hope that the outlaws would be lured into the heart of Ledbetter's district. The ruse succeeded and on November 29th Ledbetter and his posse of six, Payton Talbott, Lon Lewis, John McClanahan, Jake Elliott, Joe Thompson and Thompson's sixteen year old son traced the bandits to the vicinity of Red Hereford's ranch. Thompson's boy was sent to the house to borrow a wood maul and iron wedge and he returned with the information that the gang was there. Nearly a mile of prairie lay between the officers and the ranch house and it was necessary to make a detour of nearly three miles to approach near enough for a surprise attack.

The officers left their horses concealed in a clump of timber and approached the house on foot. Ledbetter mounted a small knoll and was chagrined to see the bandits escaping in the direction of the offi-cers' concealed horses. The outlaws' own tired

horses had been left behind and they had commandeered a team and wagon, in the bed of which all
rode concealed from view, with the exception of Al
Jennings who rode a horse and followed the wagon.
Fortunately for the officers, the wagon turned away
from the trail before it drew near the hidden mounts
of the posse.

Ledbetter and his men hurried back to the woods,
mounted their horses and followed the trail of the
bandits which lay in the direction of the Spike S.
Ranch.

The bandits arrived at the Harkless home on the
Spike S around midnight and Mrs. Harkless soon
had a roaring fire and a hot meal for the half-frozen
men.

Shortly after four o'clock in the morning Ledbetter and his posse had surrounded the ranch house
and were waiting for daylight. Dawn came and
Clarence Inscoe, a brother of Mrs. Harkless, went to
the barn to feed the stock. A cutting north wind
was howling about the ranch buildings and Inscoe
shivered as he ran through the gale to the stable.
When he entered the building he was captured and
securely tied.

Within a few minutes the hired girl stepped to
the back door of the porch and called, "Breakfast!"
then bustled back into the house to finish preparing
the meal.

A short time elapsed and Mrs. Harkless came to
the door to call her brother. When he did not an-
swer, she threw a shawl about her shoulders and
ran to the barn. Ledbetter called to the woman,

then stepped out before her to keep her from running back to the house.

"Don't be frightened," he spoke softly. "We know the Jennings boys are in that house. Tell them the place is surrounded and that there is no chance for them to get away. If they want to surrender, tell them to come out with their hands in the air. If they would rather fight it out, you get the hired girl and hike over the hill to that graveyard till the scrap is over."

The frightened woman ran back to the house and loud voices were heard arguing within. About five minutes elapsed when the woman and the hired girl, wrapped in heavy blankets, came out of the house and hurried toward the graveyard. The officers waited for a few minutes to give the women time to get out of range. Ledbetter and Payton Talbot had taken a position behind an old log cabin that stood a short distance north of the house. Thompson and his boy were placed in a thicket to the northwest. Jake Elliott was put behind a stone wall near the barn and Lon Lewis hid inside the barn.

The officers opened fire and for five minutes bullets flew thick in both directions. A well directed shot from the house silenced Thompson's fire and made the other officers believe that either Thompson or the boy had been hurt. The Thompsons had fired but twice from their hiding place. Not another shot came from their direction.

Lewis, at the barn, was unable to get a good range on either the door or windows. Ledbetter and Talbott, both crack shots, poured such a hail of lead into the ranch house that in five minutes the bandits

fled out of the back door and through an orchard. Al Jennings fired one shot from behind the house as he ran. Lon Lewis fired a charge of buckshot that riddled Frank Jennings' clothing, but did him no serious harm.

Jake Elliott, who hid behind the stone wall, was the only one to see the outlaws leave the house. A shell had jammed in Elliott's gun when his first shot was fired, and he was still vainly trying to extricate it when he saw the bandits running away. Why he did not call to Ledbetter and Talbott remains a mystery. These two officers continued to pour lead into the house for ten minutes.

When they noticed that no more shots came from the building, Ledbetter called out to the others, "Come on, I guess they are all dead in there."

"They are gone," Elliott yelled from behind the stone wall. "Four of them ran through the orchard ten minutes ago!"

Bud Ledbetter filled the air with vitriolic curses. Leaving the posse, he trailed the outlaws a short distance but lost them in the brush thickets of Snake Creek.

A four-day chase followed and the Jennings gang was finally captured without bloodshed and taken to the federal jail at Muskogee.

Following the battle at the Spike S Ranch, Mrs. Harkless, her brother and the hired girl were held until the outlaws were captured. Pending the trial, they were kept under surveillance as material witnesses, but they were not prosecuted for harboring criminals.

Everybody was greatly impressed by the grief of old Judge Jennings while his boys were on trial. Al attempted to establish an alibi regarding the Edmond hold-up, claiming that he was at the home of his father during that night. When the innocent old father testified so definitely about the date of this incident, the prosecuting attorney became a little harsh in his questioning.

"Judge Jennings, your memory has been quite hazy about a number of things that have been asked you today. How can you be so certain as to the incidents of the night of August 18th?"

The old man straightened himself, tears clouding his sight, and replied: "Sir, on the morning following the hold-up of the Santa Fe train, I walked into my court-room, took my seat on the rostrum and requested my bailiff to open the court. A friend of mine handed me an Oklahoman. There on its front page, the glaring headlines stated that my son, Al Jennings, had been accused of the hold-up of the Santa Fe passenger train. I had just left him a few moments before and I knew that he had spent the night in my home. Sir, that vile accusation made an impression on this old heart of mine that time can never erase," and the old fellow's head was bowed with grief.

United States Attorney Roy Hoffman, who had charge of the prosecution, was so affected by the man's emotion that he relaxed in his strenuous cross-examination out of sheer pity for the old fellow.

Al Jennings was sentenced to five years in the penitentiary at Leavenworth on a charge of assault with intent to kill, and was given a life term in the

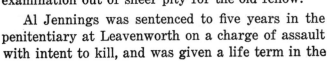

federal penitentiary at Columbus, Ohio, for robbing the United States mails.

Frank Jennings and the O'Malleys drew five-year sentences to Leavenworth.

Through the influence of friends, Al Jennings' life sentence was commuted after he had served five years and he was released from the Ohio prison. He was immediately taken in charge and placed in the Leavenworth prison to serve the five-year term on the assault charge. His friends renewed their activities in his behalf and he soon walked out, a free man.

His brother, Frank, and the O'Malleys served their terms and returned to Oklahoma where they have been very successful and have earned the respect of the communities in which they have lived.

Al Jennings has earned distinction as a writer, lecturer and evangelist. Considering the inherent ability of this man, I am caused to wonder about the heights he might have attained had he not wasted so many of his best years.

With the Jennings gang in jail awaiting trial, the officers turned their efforts to the apprehension of Little Dick West, the only one of Oklahoma's notorious outlaws who remained alive and free. Time had not changed the habits of this peculiar individual. He was still as wild as a March hare, refusing to sleep in any sort of building, regardless of the weather, and making his bed out under the open skies. One could write a book about little Dick West and his escapades.

Three months after the Jennings and O'Malley boys were captured, Marshals Tilghman and Thomas

Late photograph of Major Gordon W. Lillie (Pawnee Bill).
Known throughout the world. Retired after most vigorous
life to his great buffalo ranch at Pawnee, Oklahoma.

No motion picture cowboy is more popular than Tom Mix.

located Little Dick on Turkey Creek in Kingfisher County.   At about the time they learned his where-abouts, he received word that the officers were after him and he dodged, making his way to the home of an old time cow man named Fitzgerald, who lived southwest of Guthrie.

While the fugitive was here he visited a number of times at the home of Herman Arnett, who lived about a half mile away.   Mrs. Arnett remarked to a stranger one day that a strange man had been visiting her husband and she was afraid he would get Herman into trouble, as the officers were looking for him.

Tell a woman!   Mrs. Arnett told Mrs. Hart, the wife of the district clerk, and Mr. Hart informed my office and within six hours Bill Tilghman had learned that Little Dick was hiding within a half hour's ride of Guthrie.   Deputy Marshals Tilghman, Thomas, Rinehart and Fossett were soon on their way to Ar-nett's place.

As they approached through the orchard, they saw Little Dick currying a horse back of the barn. The officers dismounted and managed to conceal themselves among the trees until they could get fairly close to the outlaw.   Drawing nearer, Tilgh-man called for him to surrender.   In a flash he had dropped the curry comb and had a six-shooter in each hand.   The officer's shot struck him, however, before he had time to fire and he fell, fatally wounded.   Thus, Oklahoma's last notorious outlaw went down fighting.

CHAPTER XXV
AN OUTLAW WITH A CODE OF HIS OWN

Henry Starr had served five years of his twenty-five year sentence for the killing of Floyd Wilson, when he was pardoned by the President. He returned to the Territory and after a short time a prominent cattle man, who had a business office in St. Louis, placed Starr in his office. The ex-convict was given good clothes, a good job, an assumed name and every encouragement to go straight. He was a man of magnetic personality and he made friends everywhere. He lived at the Planters Hotel and moved in the best element of society.

One morning he walked into the office beaming and his employer greeted him pleasantly:

"How was the Webster Groves party, Henry?"

Starr had attended a large function at the home of a prominent family the night before, but his mind did not seem to be on this as he answered—"Fine, but do you know I saw a bank right out there on the corner—."

"Hold on there, son," the other man warned, "I hope you're not getting any fool ideas."

Starr flushed, embarrassed,—"Why,—er—er—no, but I couldn't help thinking what easy money that would be."

Starr went about his work, and the conversation was forgotten within a few hours, his friendly employer attaching no significance to the remark.

Two weeks later that particular bank was held up and Starr was gone. No one was ever able to definitely connect him with the affair but his employer always suspected him. He drifted to Colorado and was soon connected with a bank robbery there, receiving a sentence of twenty-five years in the Canyon City penitentiary. After five years, his perfect conduct and the peculiar influence he was always able to exert over prominent people on the outside effected his second pardon and he returned to Oklahoma where he conducted himself so respectably that he won a host of friends.

On March 27th, 1915, he rode into the little town of Stroud and held up two banks. The alarm was given and an army of citizens was soon after him. As he was about to make his get-away, Paul Curry, a sixteen year old lad, rushed into the excited crowd and asked what was the matter. A trembling merchant stood near by with a rifle in his hand. The brave boy jerked the gun from the man's hand, saying: "If you aren't going to use that gun, give it to someone who will."

Running down the street a short distance, he was able to get a shot at the fleeing bandit and he dropped him, painfully wounded in the hip. It is not likely that this incident would have occurred if Starr had not been so determined to hold his promise that he would never commit a murder just to accomplish a robbery. The Floyd Wilson shooting had occurred while Starr was very young and he claimed to have shot in self-defense. This was different. The outlaw's peculiar code of honor would not allow him to shoot into the crowd of townspeople.

Starr was confined in the county jail at Chandler, Oklahoma. I happened to be in the state on business during this time and having had contact with him during my time, I visited him with my friend Tilghman. Starr had used his years in prison to complete the education that had begun in his childhood and I was surprised to hear him quoting great literary classics. He talked like an intellectual. I do not wonder that he was always able to interest influential people and number them among his host of friends.

"Starr, you are a man of most unusual talents," I said. "Just what is the peculiar streak in your nature that is always leading you into trouble?"

"Colonel Nix," he replied, "I wish I could find out. You have known men who craved drugs or liquor or tobacco. I must have excitement. I crave it and it preys upon me until I just step out and get into devilment of some sort."

Once more Starr was given a twenty-five year sentence in prison, and once more his own strange knack for getting out through the influence of prominent citizens gave him freedom. Within less than a year he attempted to rob the People's National Bank at Harrison, Arkansas, and was killed by William J. Myers, a former president of the bank.

In this last escapade, Starr had every chance to shoot his way to freedom, but he preferred to give his own life rather than murder any man. A strange code. Well, Henry Starr was a strange man.

CHAPTER XXVI
THE OLD DAYS ARE NO MORE

"Tempus" has done a pretty consistent job of *"fugit"*ing since the old days of which I have written. And I am old-fashioned enough to be a little frightened at the trend of affairs, except in calmer moments when I reassure myself with the thought that the world will manage, somehow, to wag along. It always has.

Today's Oklahoma stands in radical contrast to the old Territory I knew, with its free ranges, its blanketed Indians and its swashbuckling bandits. The free ranges have been divided with mathematical precision into many 640-acre sections, and around every section is a wire fence and a highway of some sort. There are no more log and sod dugouts or straw and brush stables. Oklahomans luxuriate today in farm and city homes that are equipped to bring the wide world to their very thresholds.

Oklahoma's Indians, with their spouting oil wells and their college degrees, dash about the terrain in high-powered cars. They are already liberal patrons of air transportation. They seem to have assimilated the customs of the paleface and to have been assimilated by the peculiar civilization the paleface brought and thrust upon them. They read books, good and bad, they enjoy music, jazz and classic, and they drink considerable quantities of liquor— also good and bad—all very closely in the footsteps of the paler brother whose superior civilization promised them so much. I sometimes wonder if the

267

intelligent Indian feels honestly compensated for the so-called savagery he gave up for all this. I'm not so sure he got the best of the deal.

There are still a few evidences of the Indian's determination to remain Indian—particularly among the smaller tribes not so richly blessed or cursed by wealth that the others know not how to use. I remember an incident that occurred a year or two ago. A few members of one of the poorer tribes went to Washington to ask the Great White Father for a special settlement under an old and almost forgotten treaty. Several bucks took their squaws and papooses to the capital city and they managed to get the concession they asked.

One big fellow returned to his home town with five thousand dollars in cash in his buckskin pants and a determination to emulate his Osage cousins by purchasing a five thousand dollar car. Followed by his gaily blanketed brood, he made his way to a salesroom and within fifteen minutes a dealer had the five thousand and the buck owned a car. The salesman volunteered to drive the Indians home and to attempt to teach the buck to drive. No manner of persuasion, however, could induce the big fellow to get under the wheel and the salesman finally landed the family at their home in the Indian country. A friend had followed the automobile man with a small car, intending to take him back to town, but, as the big Indian alighted, he waved a disdainful hand toward the new machine, grunting:

"Um-m-ugh. You takum damn thing. Me likum hoss."

Temple Houston, noted lawyer, orator and plainsman. Son
of the renowned Sam Houston. Taken from faded
photograph.

Al Jennings, lawyer, outlaw, writer and evangelist of note.

The wily salesman soon had the Indian's cross-mark, duly witnessed, on the bill of sale and was on his way back home with a car his own earnings could never have bought.

I have come upon a number of instances of reversion to type. During my time in Oklahoma an incident occurred that not only had its humorous aspect but that provided an interesting psychological study. A young Indian was brought before Judge Bierer upon a charge of whiskey peddling. The handsome fellow was a Carlisle honor man and his brilliance had attracted considerable attention among white friends. Something turned him against the ways of the white man and he returned to his people and their customs.

When he was brought into court he wore moccasins, buckskin pants and leggings and a blanket. His hair had grown long and it was braided, with strips of red flannel interwined in the strands. When he was questioned he refused to respond to anything that was said in English. An interpreter was called and the case proceeded. The Indian's stubbornness probably gave weight to the evidence against him and he was convicted. Judge Bierer sentenced him to Leavenworth for two years and proceeded to give the young buck a fatherly lecture. As the talk continued, the redskin fidgeted and, after a few minutes, he began to jabber in Otoe. Judge Bierer turned to the interpreter.

"What is he saying?" he inquired.

The interpreter was plainly embarrassed and he hesitated, then stammered, "He's jest jabberin', Your Honor. Don't pay any attention to him."

"What did he say?" the judge demanded.

The interpreter colored blood-red, gulped and finally mustered enough courage to reply, "Your Honor, he says, 'Wish you damn judge would stop talkin' and let my sentence begin.' "

But in spite of isolated instances of the red man's resistance to white civilization, we now find him losing his racial identity. Some of his people have so perfectly adapted themselves that they have become capable and efficient business and professional men, artists, writers and farmers. Many of the women have succeeded in establishing cultural and domestic standards that are not excelled by those of their white sisters.

There are still others—members of the generation now in its prime—who are throwbacks to all that was savage in their fathers. Now, they must express their barbaric instincts in the white man's way, dressing flashily, driving fine cars madly, drinking bad liquor and slowly decaying in idleness.

As for the old time Oklahoma outlaw, I am reluctant to compare him with the hijacker and gunman of today. As one who fought him to extinction, I must admit that I admire his sportsmanship when I think of the vicious and cowardly tin-horn holdup man of today. I don't believe Bill Doolin ever shot a victim in the back and I know very well he didn't make a practice of robbing needy individuals of their petty all. He and his gang went after organized capital—the railroads, banks and express companies. If he took a horse or forced a lonely rancher to feed his men, it was because of dire necessity and he always tried to compensate the person who was called upon for help.

These men regarded the banks and railroads as being mostly responsible for the breaking up of their ranges. They felt that they had been robbed of their own little world and that they had a right to fight back. And when they fought they stood up to it and took defeat like the cast-iron breed they were.

Banditry did not pay in those days. And the bandits learned it, to their sorrow. For some peculiar reason or set of reasons, they don't seem to be learning it so well today and a lot of them seem to thrive, but they will find as the bandits did of the past that in the end the penalty is greater than the reward. Some day the American people are going to get impatient enough to put an end to the general defiance of law and demand that justice and the rule of humanity and right triumph.

What a transition!

Bill Tilghman lived long enough to see much of the change but it was hard for him to adjust himself, as an officer, to the new conditions. And when he died, with his gun in his hand, it was from the bullet of a drunken fellow officer—*of the new generation.*

Bill had been sent to a wild Oklahoma oil town as a special representative of the governor, to attempt to bring order out of chaos. The town, apparently governed by a lawless majority, resented his coming. A tightly organized booze and dope ring, knowing Bill's reputation as a fearless and fast-shooting officer, determined to kill him and to wipe out the law and order crowd. They chose a young federal prohibition officer to do the job, and playing upon

his gullibility and his jealousy, they planted the thoughts in his mind that led to the murder.

Subtle rumors were set afloat. The young officer was told that Tilghman resented his cockiness and that he was going to mow him down. Tilghman got wind of wild rumors, too, but his experienced judgment discounted them and he went about his business. But the young federal man was not keen enough to see through the scheme and his hand fidgeted nervously near his holster whenever Tilghman was in sight.

The situation grew warmer. Then one afternoon the young officer was taken on a party in the country by one of the schemers and two women and they succeeded in inflaming his thought to a point of action. Heated to a state of unreasonableness by bad whiskey and incendiary conversation, he bundled his pseudo-friends into his car and started for the town of Cromwell.

"I'm tired of these threats!" he shouted hysterically. I'm going after that . . . right now!"

Tilghman had just finished his supper in a restaurant next door to Pa and Ma Murphy's notorious dance hall and had stepped out onto the board sidewalk with his friend, W. E. Sirmans, who was president of the Chamber of Commerce of Cromwell and in full sympathy with Tilghman's work. As they stood there talking a car drove up and parked just across the street. A man jumped out with six-shooter in hand and shot in the ground as he started toward Tilghman. Sensing danger, Tilghman started toward the gunman and as they met Tilghman grabbed his right arm, at the same time

placing his forty-five in his stomach, forcing him to
surrender his gun. Tilghman released his hold on
him and in an instant the federal agent had drawn
another concealed forty-five and shot Tilghman
twice killing him instantly. Sirmans saw the federal
agent make the draw and made an effort to save
Tilghman's life, but was only in time to catch him
as he fell into his arms dead.

Bill Tilghman deserved a better fate than that,
although he always told his friends that he would
never die in bed.

The pioneer officer's body lay in state in the ro-
tunda of the Capitol of Oklahoma City for two days
and he was honored and mourned by hundreds of
people. Perhaps no other peace officer ever received
so signal an honor.

In looking back over my story I find that it has
been impossible to cover the almost infinite number
of incidents that contributed to the establishing of
law and order in Oklahoma. I regret that all these
things cannot be related for not only would they be
extremely interesting, but they would acquaint the
reader with dozens of other fine Oklahomans who
have not been mentioned here. No one understands
better than I the sacrifices these early citizens made
that were solely inspired by their altruistic desires
to contribute to the building of a great commonwealth.

Those distinguished justices who braved all sorts
of hazards and threats and stood firmly for the rigid
enforcement of the federal laws during the territorial days were men whose brilliant minds and sub-

stantial characters would grace the highest and most honorable position within the gift of the people.

Chief Justice Frank Dale, A. G. C. Bierer, Henry W. Scott, John H. Burford, John L. McAtee, all Associate Justices of the Territorial Supreme Court, dealt so closely with the blood-red realities of this raw period that their influence is still felt in Oklahoma's government of today. United States Attorneys Caleb R. Brooks, Brig. General Roy Hoffman and Thomas F. McMechan worked so closely with the Justices and with the United States Marshal that their part in establishing law and order in this new country must be fully acknowledged.

The old-time frontiersmen are nearly all gone. Chris Madsen and Charles Colcord are two of the oldest living members of my original force of deputies. Time is thinning the ranks. I visit the surviving few of my old companions occasionally and each visit finds the hand of Time resting a little more heavily upon their aging shoulders.

I must not close my story without a word of praise for some of the outstanding Indians of the old days—men whose keen foresight procured treaties from the United States Government that have showered wealth upon their progeny. Our own dealings with such men as Chief Bacon Rine of the Osages, Chief Keokuk of the Sac and Fox, and Chief Rhone of the Pawnees gave us ample proof of the splendid characters and brilliant minds of these leaders. They were invaluable friends to those conscientiously striving for a decent, equitable handling of the national problems. If the Indian often had cause to feel distrust in the white man, it is also true that

these leaders frequently found leaders among the
better element of the white settlers who repaid their
friendship at full value.

I am particularly happy to recall the real service
returned to the Indians by a character endeared to
all who know him as "Pawnee Bill." In his contact
with the Indians Major Gordon W. Lillie offers one
of the finest expressions of the better side of our
national political policy in Indian affairs. In him
the Pawnees found an honest counsellor well deserv-
ing of the highest honor they could pay him in his
adoption by their tribe. As the directing hand of
the destiny of the Pawnee Indians for over a quarter
of a century, Major Lillie's business sagacity, integrity, and earnest effort represent one of the outstanding things that do much to offset some of the
less happy experiences of our Indian citizens in their
contacts with the white man. If I have tended to
disparage some of the modern tendencies of the
younger Indians I must remind the reader of the
splendid record of our Indian boys in the late war.
They shared their obligation of citizenship with our
own sons willingly and courageously.

Very few of the old time cowpunchers are left.
The cattle business has progressed in a manner that
has outgrown the methods of the old range days.
But two, at least, who were schooled in the old range
methods have won national acclaim. Perhaps no motion picture cowboy ever brought more actual experience to the screen than Tom Mix, and for this reason
his pictures have always reflected a greater element
of realism than most of the wild West productions
of the day. Will Rogers' background as a range

rider provided an ideal environment and experience for the development of his exceedingly keen, yet homely philosophy. Here is a man who is able to place an analytical finger on the very heart of modern events and dissect and describe them in his cowboy vernacular much more vividly than would be possible in more formal but less graphic language.

Looking back is pleasant. Some of us old-timers get a little cynical sometimes when we recall the hardships and sacrifices that were necessary to produce the environment and conditions of today.

I sometimes wonder in our rush and great progress if we are not loosing sight of the human touch and personal interest in our fellow. Let us not forget, the happiness and contentment of our people as a whole is an important factor in the life of an enduring nation.

After all, it is a privilege to live in an age of such fast changing conditions and great development. With it all I feel sometimes that I would be willing to live over the grand old days of the past again.

I met Sam Bartell, an old deputy of mine, in Oklahoma City a while back. After we had chatted a while, he slapped me on the shoulder.

"Marshal," he said, "them was the good old days." Oklahombres! . . . . . . They were!

F I N I S

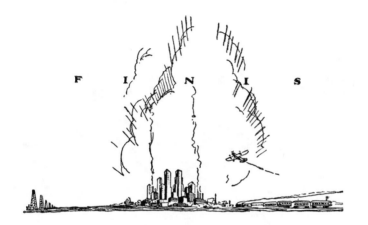

CHRONOLOGY OF OKLAHOMA

1762 - November 3.—Region claimed as part of Louisiana, conveyed by France to Spain.

1800 - October 1.—Louisiana retroceded to France.

1803 - April 30.—Ceded to United States by Louisiana Purchase Treaty.

1804 - March 26.—Included in District of Louisiana, which becomes Louisiana Territory (March 3, 1805), and Missouri Territory (June 4, 1812).

1819 - February 22.—Treaty with Spain settles boundary between Mexico (Texas) and Louisiana Purchase. March 1819, included in Arkansas Territory.

1820 - March 3.—Slavery permitted by Missouri Compromise.

1820 - 1840.—Indian Territory (unorganized) set apart by various Indian Treaties as home of Five Civilized Tribes (Cherokees, Creeks, Seminoles, Chickasaws and Choctaws), with local self-government. Other Indians (Friendly Tribes) also located in western part of Territory.

1824 - May 26.—Arkansas Territory reduced in size. Again reduced May 6, 1828. Territorrial Government over region ends.

1845 - March 1.—Western Panhandle acquired by United States with annexation of Texas into the Union.

1850 - September 9.—Texas cedes her claim to the Panhandle.

1862 - June 9.—Territorial slavery abolished.

1889 - April 22.—"Oklahoma Territory." First opening of land to homestead settlement by white people.

1890 - May 2.—Oklahoma Territory organized under Territorial Government, provided that all future Indian reservations opened for settlement should become a part of Oklahoma Territory, and subject to its laws, Territorial and National.

1891 - September 22.—Iowa, Sac and Fox, Pottawatomie and Shawnee Indian Reservations opened to Homestead Settlement.

1892 - April 19.—Cheyenne and Arapahoe Indian Reservations Opened to Homestead Settlement.

1893 - September 16.—Cherokee Outlet opened to Homestead Settlement.

1895 - May.—Kickapoo Indian Reservation opened to white settlement.

1896 - March 16.—Greer County, having been won from Texas in a case decided by the United States Supreme Court, was added to Oklahoma Territory.

1901 - July.—Kiowa, Comanche and Apache Indian Reservations were opened to white settlement.

1890 - May 2.—Under the Organic Act of May 2, 1890, the Panhandle or "No Man's Land" became subject to Oklahoma Territorial jurisdiction.

1905 - Completion of the work of Dawes Commission; tribal government of the Five Civilized Tribes dissolved. Lands allotted in severalty to Indians and they become American citizens.

1906 - November 20.—First Constitutional (Statehood) Convention met, pursuant to an Enabling Act passed by Congress.　Convention finishes labors and adjourns July 16, 1907.　Election follows, Constitution adopted, state, county and municipal officers elected, county boundaries fixed, counties named, or approved, also covering and including the area of the Five Civilized Tribes, meaning old Indian Territory, both territories being joined into one State under the name of the State of Oklahoma.

1907 - November 16.—Proclamation signed by President Theodore Roosevelt admitting Oklahoma into the Union as the forty-sixth state, under the Joint or Double Statehood Bill providing for the admission of Oklahoma and Indian Territory as one state.